the THIRD edition

New Headway

Elementary
Teacher's Book

Liz and John Soars
Amanda Maris

OXFORD
UNIVERSITY PRESS

OXFORD
UNIVERSITY PRESS

Great Clarendon Street, Oxford OX2 6DP

Oxford University Press is a department of the University of Oxford.
It furthers the University's objective of excellence in research, scholarship,
and education by publishing worldwide in

Oxford New York

Auckland Cape Town Dar es Salaam Hong Kong Karachi
Kuala Lumpur Madrid Melbourne Mexico City Nairobi
New Delhi Shanghai Taipei Toronto

With offices in

Argentina Austria Brazil Chile Czech Republic France Greece
Guatemala Hungary Italy Japan Poland Portugal Singapore
South Korea Switzerland Thailand Turkey Ukraine Vietnam

OXFORD and OXFORD ENGLISH are registered trade marks of
Oxford University Press in the UK and in certain other countries

Printed in Spain by Just Colour Graphic S. L.

ACKNOWLEDGEMENTS

*The authors and publisher are grateful to those who have given permission to reproduce
the following extracts and adaptations of copyright material:* p139 *Colours* Words and
Music by Donovan Leitch. © Copyright 1965 Donavan (Music) Ltd. Reproduced
by permission. p144 *I Just Called to Say I Love You* Words and Music by Stevie
Wonder. © 1984 Black Bull Music Inc, USA Jobete Music (UK) Ltd, London
WC2H 0QY. Reproduced by permission of International Music Publications
Ltd. All Rights Reserved. p149 *Wonderful Tonight* Words and Music by Eric
Clapton © 1976 Throat Music Ltd Warner/Chappell Music Ltd, London W6
8BS. Reproduced by permission of International Music Publications Ltd. All
Rights Reserved. p153 *Summertime* (from *Porgy and Bess*) by George Gershwin,
Du Bose and Dorothy Heyward and Ira Gershwin © 1935 (Renewed 1962)
George Gershwin Music, Ira Gershwin Music and Du Bose and Dorothy
Heyward Memorial Fund. *Porgy and Bess* is a registered trademark of Porgy
And Bess Enterprises. Gershwin, George Gershwin and Ira Gershwin are
trademarks of Gershwin Enterprises. All Rights Reserved. Used by
Permission.

*We would like to thank the following for permission to reproduce the following
photographs:* Getty Images p138 (portrait of woman/Denis Felix/Taxi); Kobal
Collection p152 (Johnny Depp/Touchstone); OUP pp140 (woman in
scarf/Imagesource, young family, businessman/Photodisc), 146
(Manhattan/Digital Vision, tropical beach/Corbis/Digital Stock); Pictures
Colour Library Ltd p146 (Colosseum/Brian Lawrence Images Ltd,
paella/Dennis Jackson); Punchstock pp140 (kids on roundabout/Imagesource,
walking the dog/imageshop).

Illustrations by: Mark Duffin pp136, 137

Photocopiable pages designed by: Keith Shaw.

Contents

New Headway Elementary – the THIRD edition

Introduction

Unit 1	*am/is/are* – *my/your/his/her* – Countries – Everyday objects – Numbers – Hello and goodbye	6
Unit 2	*am/is/are* – questions and negatives – Possessive *'s* – Family – Opposites – In a café	11
Unit 3	Present Simple 1 – *he/she/it* – Questions and negatives – Jobs – What time is it?	19
Unit 4	Present Simple 2 – *I/you/we/they* – Leisure activities – Social expressions	28

Stop and check 1 154

| **Unit 5** | *There is/are* – Prepositions – *some/any* – *this/that/these/those* – Furniture – Directions 1 | 37 |

Progress test 1 162

Unit 6	*can/can't/could/couldn't* – *was/were* – Words that sound the same – On the phone	46
Unit 7	Past Simple 1: regular verbs – Irregular verbs – Words that go together – What's the date?	56
Unit 8	Past Simple 2: negatives – *ago* – Spelling and silent letters – Special occasions	66

Stop and check 2 156

| **Unit 9** | Count and uncount nouns – *I like/I'd like* – *some/any* – *much/many* – Food – Polite requests | 75 |
| **Unit 10** | Comparatives and superlatives – *have got* – City and country – Directions 2 | 85 |

Progress test 2 165

| **Unit 11** | Present Continuous – *Whose?* – Clothes – Words that rhyme – In a clothes shop | 96 |
| **Unit 12** | *going to* future – Infinitive of purpose – The weather – Making suggestions | 106 |

Stop and check 3 158

| **Unit 13** | Question forms – Adjectives and adverbs – Describing feelings – At the chemist's | 116 |
| **Unit 14** | Present Perfect + *ever, never, yet,* and *just* – At the airport | 125 |

Stop and check 4 160

Progress test 3 168

PHOTOCOPIABLE MATERIALS

Units 1–4	135	Stop and checks	154
Units 5–8	140	Progress tests	162
Units 9–12	145	Answer keys	171
Units 13–14	150		

Introduction

New Headway Elementary – the THIRD edition

What remains the same?

The basic *Headway* methodology is the same. Proven traditional approaches are used alongside those which have been developed and researched more recently.

Starter

Each unit begins with a *Starter* section, which is designed to be a warmer to the lesson. It is a short activity and always has direct relevance to the language to be introduced in the unit.

Grammar

The grammatical syllabus is largely unchanged because the requirements of lower-level students are usually more predictable than at later levels.

Grammar spot

Each grammar presentation contains a *Grammar spot*. This is a mix of explanation, questions, self-check, and pronunciation tasks to reinforce the grammar being taught. Each *Grammar spot* has a link to the fuller *Grammar Reference* section at the back of the book.

Practice

There is a wide variety of practice activities covering all the skills. There is great emphasis on personalized speaking.

Vocabulary

Vocabulary is not only integrated throughout, but also developed in its own section.

Skills work

Skills work is both integrated and balanced. All the texts for listening and reading come from authentic sources, and are simplified and adapted to suit the level.

Everyday English

This section focuses primarily on aspects of spoken English.

Tapescripts

There is a full bank of unseen tapescripts in a section at the end of the Student's Book.

What are the differences?

Reading and listening texts

The vast majority of the texts are new. Teachers can get fed up with using the same texts year after year, so we took this opportunity to freshen up the topics. Sometimes we have found a parallel text on the same topic, and sometimes we have selected a new topic and a new text.

Speaking

We acknowledge that speech prosody (the patterns of sounds and rhythms in speech) varies depending on accent, register, the message, sentence length, etc. Nevertheless, we have made the conscious decision in this third edition of *New Headway Elementary* to offer more guidance to students in this area of their English pronunciation. We have done this in two ways:

- **stress highlighting:** When beneficial to spoken tasks, we have indicated through highlighting where main stress falls to help students sound more natural. On many occasions a recorded model can be used for listen and repeat. At times, we have chosen one stress pattern over another/ others in an attempt to offer a sensible model for students to follow.

- **Music of English** focuses on word and sentence stress, word-linking, and intonation patterns in high-frequency everyday expressions. It reminds teachers and students to listen for and practise all the elements of spoken English. The accompanying recordings exaggerate intonation, stress, and word-linking to help students hear and follow the patterns. Students, in turn, should also aim to exaggerate the patterns in practice exercises.

Some students will struggle more than others with pronunciation and Music of English. However, with plenty of encouragement, and the higher incidence of practice given to these elements of spoken English in *New Headway Elementary – the THIRD edition*, students' awareness and subsequent delivery of spoken English should gradually improve.

For further practice of all aspects of pronunciation see *New Headway Pronunciation Course – Elementary*.

Student A and Student B pairwork exercises

These information gap and speaking activities are now in a section at the end of the Student's Book for ease of access for both students and teacher. They are cued from the relevant units.

Writing

The *Writing* section now appears separately at the back of the Student's Book. This section provides models for students to complete, adapt, and follow in order to produce a satisfying piece of writing. The syllabus begins at Unit 3 and comprises twelve complete writing lessons cued from the unit, which can be used at the teacher's discretion.

Grammar Reference practice exercises

The *Grammar Reference* has been extended to include short practice exercises which test students' understanding of the language areas being studied. These can be used at the teacher's discretion – for homework, or as an adjunct to the *Practice* section in the unit.

Design

The design is completely new. It is cleaner, fresher, and more modern and lively. Photographs and illustrations have been carefully chosen not only to enhance and clarify activities, but also to inform and stimulate students.

What's in the Teacher's Book?

- **Full teaching notes**, answers, and suggestions about how to deal with possible problems; additional guidance on stress, intonation and connected speech.

- *Don't forget!* **section** which refers to relevant exercises in the Workbook, the Pronunciation book, the Video/DVD, and to the Word list in the Student's Book.

- **Tapescripts** in the main body of the teaching notes. Students also have tapescripts at the end of the Student's Book. These can be used in a variety of ways:

  - **consolidation and support:** Students often enjoy reading and listening to a script after a task to confirm their ideas about the speakers, contexts, or other details, or to clarify any misunderstandings. Students may enjoy listening and reading aloud with the recording.

  - **language work:** Students highlight specific examples of recently presented language (structural or lexical). Teachers can supply gapped or cut up scripts for students to complete or put in order. This would need to be prepared in advance of class and photocopied. In a gap fill task, care should be taken not to focus on too random a set of vocabulary. Lexical sets or key structural items (auxiliaries, question words, past tenses, past participles, prepositions etc.) are useful items to gap.

  - **pronunciation and fluency work:** Students listen and analyse a particular section or line of a tapescript, listen, repeat, and role-play dialogues.

- **Photocopiable material:** There is a range of new materials to further practise and consolidate grammar, vocabulary, and skills from the Student's Book. The activities include roleplays, controlled speaking/writing, freer speaking, language games, etc.

- **Extra ideas and songs section:** notes on how to use them. For use during and after Units 1–4, 5–8, 9–12, and 13–14.

- **Stop and check tests**
  There are four *Stop and check* revision tests which cover Units 1–4, 5–8, 9–12, and 13–14. These can either be set in class, or given for homework (preferably over a weekend) and then discussed in the next lesson. Students can work in small groups to try to agree on the correct answer, then

you can go over it with the whole class, reminding students of the language items covered. It is important that, in the translation sentences which come at the end of each *Stop and check* test, students translate the ideas and concepts, and not word for word.

- **Progress tests**
  There are three *Progress tests* which cover Units 1–5, 6–10, and 11–14.

What's in the Workbook?

The Workbook is an important component of the course as it revises the grammatical input of the Student's Book. Many of the exercises are on the Student's Workbook CD/cassette for valuable extra listening practice. The tapescripts at the end of the Workbook can also be used to complete tasks.

What are the other materials?

Tests

In addition to two versions (A and B) of each Unit Test, there are six new Review Tests and two separate Exit Tests. There is also a bank of optional Listening Tests.

DVD/Video

There is a New Headway Elementary DVD/video with Student's Book, and Teacher's Book. The video is fresh and modern, and comprises six short, comic episodes. Each episode consolidates and extends key language presented in the Student's Book. The accompanying Student's Book and Teacher's Book help to fully exploit video material.

Interactive Practice CD-ROM

This contains a variety of interactive tasks for revision and practice, and exploits materials from the video.

Headway online

There is a teacher's website with a comprehensive range of additional materials for teachers at www.oup.com/elt/teacher /headway. These materials further supplement and extend the Student's Book.

There is also a student's site with interactive practice exercises and games at www.oup.com/elt/headway.

Finally!

We try to guide students to an *understanding* of new language, rather than just have examples of it on the page. We attach great importance to practice activities, both controlled and free, personalized and impersonal. The skills work comes from a wide range of material – newspapers, magazines, biographies, short stories, radio programmes, songs – and features both British and American English.

We hope you and your students enjoy using the books, and have success with them, whether using *New Headway* for the first time, or having learned to trust its approach from previous use.

am/is/are • my/your/his/her
Countries • Everyday objects • Numbers
Hello and goodbye

Hello everybody!

Introduction to the unit

As you begin *New Headway Elementary – the THIRD edition*, you are probably starting a new course with a new group of students. The title of Unit 1 is 'Hello everybody!', and one important aim is that students get to know each other and you, and you get to know them. Obviously students will have relatively little English to use at this stage, but nevertheless a convivial classroom atmosphere can be established through quite basic interchanges.

Language aims

Grammar – *am/is/are* The verb *to be* is introduced in all persons, singular and plural. The focus is on the positive, and questions with question words (*where*, *what*, and *how*). The negative and *Yes/No* questions are dealt with in Unit 2.

Possessive adjectives *My, your, his*, and *her* are introduced in the unit. The other possessive adjectives are given in Grammar Reference 1.2 on p137.

Vocabulary Names of countries are introduced as part of the work on introductions. In the *Vocabulary and pronunciation* section, the alphabet is introduced and practised. Students look at the organization of a bilingual dictionary entry, and everyday objects such as a bag and a ticket. If possible, bring enough bilingual dictionaries for students to share at least one between two. Students are asked to work out the rules for using *a/an* and the formation of regular plurals with *-s*.

Everyday English Numbers 1–20 are revised and practised. The situational focus includes practice on exchanging telephone numbers and work on saying hello and goodbye. Students are introduced to *Music of English* boxes.

Workbook Nationality adjectives (*Italian, German, French, etc.*); the numbers 1–20 are practised.

The writing syllabus begins in Unit 3.

Notes on the unit

STARTER (SB p6)

1   Say your own name – *I'm (Liz)* – and point to yourself to make the meaning clear. Then invite students to say their names – *I'm Jean, I'm Keiko*, etc. Encourage students to listen to each other's names and to memorize as many as they can. If appropriate, play a memory game by pointing to individual students and yourself and getting the group to say just the name, e.g. *John! Keiko!* Encourage students in a multilingual group to pronounce each other's names (and your name!) as accurately as possible.

2   Check students understand 'alphabetical order' by putting letters a–g on the board in random order and asking students to reorder them alphabetically. With stronger classes you may wish to briefly introduce the whole alphabet. (Don't worry too much if students pronounce the letters wrongly as the alphabet is covered later in the unit.) Check by writing the names from *Starter* 1 and 2 on the board and getting students to say them in order.

Then ask students to stand up in alphabetical order and say their name. If appropriate, repeat this, getting progressively faster each time.

If there are not too many students in the class, put their names on the board so that everyone can begin to learn them.

INTRODUCTIONS (SB p6)

NOTE
From the very beginning of *New Headway Elementary the THIRD edition* Student's Book, the students are alerted to the rhythms in spoken English through highlighting of stressed words/parts of words. You can use international words such as com**put**er, **In**ternet, **tel**ephone to show students how there are both stressed and unstressed syllables. It may also show students how English stress patterns vary from their own.

am/is/are, my/your

1 **T 1.1** [CD1: Track 2] Ask students to read and listen once, and then ask them to point to Marco and Emma in the photo. Ask *Where are Emma and Marco?* and elicit the answer (in an Internet café). Play the recording a second time, focusing on the highlighted stress patterns. Students repeat as a class, closely following the stress pattern and the intonation. Play the recording again then practise it in both open (i.e. students ask and answer the question across the room with the rest of the class listening) and closed pairs (i.e. the whole class working in pairs). Make sure students can accurately produce the contracted forms *name's, what's,* and *I'm* and the contrastive stress in: *My name's* Marco. *What's* your *name?*

GRAMMAR SPOT

Focus attention on the contractions. Ask students to circle the contracted forms in exercise 1.

2 Elicit the word that goes in the first gap (*name's*) and then ask students to complete the conversation. Remind them to use contracted forms. Ask students to point to Mike and Lisa in the photo.

T 1.2 [CD1: Track 3] Play the recording and let students check their answers. Ask students to say the dialogue in open and closed pairs.

Answers and tapescript
A Hello. My **name's** Lisa. What's **your** name?
B Mike.
A **Where** are you from, Mike?
B **I'm** from Boston. Where **are** you from?
A **I'm from** Boston, too!

3 This is a mingle activity. Demonstrate the dialogue first in open pairs, and then get students to move around the class and talk to as many people as possible. Monitor and check for accurate pronunciation. Don't let this activity go on too long. If you have a large class, it will be impossible for all the students to talk to everyone.

4 Students look at the photos and write the countries.

NOTE
Students may query the use of *is* (third person singular of *to be*) to introduce two people – Lisa and Mike: *This is Lisa and Mike.* Do not go into detail at this stage, just explain that we use *This is* to introduce one or more people.

T 1.3 [CD1: Track 4] Play the recording and let students check their answers. Play the recording again. Students listen and repeat.

Answers and tapescript
1 This is Marco. He's from **Italy**.
2 This is Emma. She's from **England**.
3 This is Lisa and Mike. They're from **the USA**.

GRAMMAR SPOT

Check comprehension of *he/she/they* by referring students to the photos and then pointing to male/female and pairs/groups of students to elicit the correct pronoun. Focus attention on the contractions. Ask students to circle contracted forms in exercise 2.

ADDITIONAL MATERIAL

Workbook Unit 1
Exercises 1 and 2 These practise *What's your name?*, *Where are you from? I'm from …* , and *I'm (a) …* .

Countries, *his/her*

SUGGESTION
A world map/globe is useful for presenting country names.

5 Focus attention on the table with the names of the countries. Draw students' attention to the bullets and stress highlighting. Explain that these show the pattern of stressed syllables for each column by using L1 if possible, or by playing the recording.

T 1.4 [CD1: Track 5] Ask students to read the list of countries as you play the recording. Play the recording a second time and ask students to listen and repeat. Practise the countries as a class, then in closed pairs.

6 Focus students' attention on the example. Ask them *Where is Danka from?* (*She's from Poland.*) Ask them what *Cześć!* means (*Hello* in Polish). Ask students in pairs or groups to continue to write where the people are from, using the countries in the table. Students are not expected to know how to say *Hello!* in all the different languages! This is merely a fun way to introduce countries and the third person singular and plural. Encourage students to pool their knowledge.

7 Introduce the questions *What's her/his name?* and *Where's she/he from?* Point to some of the photos in exercise 6. Ask the questions yourself, and let the students reply. Drill the questions and correct any mistakes in the use of *she/he* and *her/his* carefully. Practise the questions and answers in open pairs. Encourage students to follow the stress pattern highlighted in the speech bubbles.

Ask the students to continue the activity in closed pairs. Monitor and check for correct use of *she/he* and *her/his*, and if necessary, drill the language again using the photos in the book. Finally, consolidate the forms by eliciting examples of *His/Her name's …*, *He's/She's/They're from ….*

GRAMMAR SPOT

Ask students to complete the table with *am*, *is*, and *are*. Check the answers.

Answers
I	**am**	
He / She / It	**is**	from England.
We / You / They	**are**	

Briefly check comprehension of the subject pronouns which are not covered in exercise 6 (*we, it,* and *you* plural) by using the photos and the students themselves. *It* can be checked using international food and drinks, e.g. *champagne – It's from France.*

Read Grammar Reference 1.1 and 1.2 on p137 together in class, and/or ask students to read it at home. Encourage them to ask you questions if appropriate.

PRACTICE (SB p9)

Talking about you

1 Focus attention on the examples. Demonstrate the activity by getting students to ask and answer the same questions in open and/or closed pairs about the other people in the class. In a monolingual class, you could make role cards giving students a new country of origin, or the identity of a famous person whose country of origin the class would know. This practises the vocabulary of the exercise, too.

2 Ask the students to introduce their partner to the rest of the class. Check for the correct use of *he/she* and for the correct stress on the names of countries.

Listening and pronunciation

3 **T 1.5** [CD 1: Track 6] Play the recording. Ask students to tick the sentence they hear. This is an exercise that tests discrimination, but you can make it productive afterwards by asking students in pairs to practise the pairs of sentences. Pay particular attention to the sounds /ɪ/, /iː/, and /s/.

Answers and tapescript
1	He's from Spain.	4	Where's she from?
2	What's her name?	5	He's a teacher in Italy.
3	They're from Japan.		

Check it

4 Ask students to work in pairs to put *am, is, are, his, her,* or *your* into the gaps. Afterwards, you can ask them to make the contractions in numbers 1 (*name's*), 3 (*I'm*), and 7 (*Where's*).

Answers
2 Where **are** you from?
3 I **am** from Italy.
4 'What's **your** name?' 'My name's Daniella.'
5 Lisa and Mike **are** from Boston.
6 This **is** my teacher. **His** name's Richard.
7 Where **is** he from?
8 This is my sister. **Her** name's Miho.

Reading and writing

> **NOTE**
> The aim of this section is to allow students to see how much English they already know through a short writing task. The verbs *have, live,* and *want* appear in their Present Simple form, but you don't need to review this tense at this stage.

5 **T 1.6** [CD 1: Track 7] Focus attention on the photo and ask *What's her name?* to check if students recognize Svetlana from p8. Ask them to read and listen to the text. Make sure students understand *married, children,* and *flat* by doing simple board drawings and referring to the photo. You could ask one or two students to read the text aloud, or in closed pairs, and the students can help each other with pronunciation.

6 Focus attention on the photo and ask *What's his name?* to check if students recognize Tiago from p8. Ask students to complete the text about Tiago. Make sure they understand *international language* by eliciting the countries where English is spoken.

T 1.7 [CD 1: Track 8] Play the recording to check. Again, you could practise the text around the class and/or in closed pairs.

7   After quite a lot of oral class work, the silent, individual work in this exercise provides variety and balance. Ask students to write about themselves, following the models in exercises 5 and 6. Students read their writing to the class. Don't worry if there are a lot of pronunciation mistakes: the aim is for students to show what they can do, and to say a little about themselves and their families. You can't do everything at once!

> **NOTE/SUGGESTION**
> The next section of this unit deals with everyday objects and introduces dictionary work. Check which students have their own bilingual dictionary and, if possible, bring extra copies to the lesson.

ADDITIONAL MATERIAL

Workbook Unit 1
Exercises 3–5 Third person *is* and *are*, short and long forms.
Exercises 6 and 7 Possessive adjectives
Exercises 8 and 9 Countries and nationalities with stress practice.

VOCABULARY AND PRONUNCIATION (SB p10)

Everyday objects

> **SUGGESTION**
> Whatever your students' knowledge of the alphabet at this stage of the course, remember that they will all need regular practice in the alphabet and spelling. This can easily be integrated into any lesson when teaching new vocabulary (*How do you think you spell … ?*), or when reviewing vocabulary (*How do you spell … ?*), and by the use of spelling games or cards.
>
> At this early stage you may want to write the alphabet on the board and drill the letters in groups of five before moving on to the alphabet song.

1   **T 1.8** [CD 1: Track 9] Focus attention on the letters in exercise 1 and tell the students that they are going to listen to the alphabet in the form of a song. Ask them to join in where they can. Play the recording and note down the letters students get wrong or don't know, paying particular attention to *a, e, g, i, j, r, u, w,* and *y* which cause problems for many students. Drill the letters which students found difficult.

Practise the letters as a class and in closed pairs. Listen to the song again and let the students sing it if they want to.

Pre-teach the question *How do you spell … ?* and the use of *double* for spelling (e.g. *apple = a, double p, l, e*). Get students to practise asking the question and spelling in pairs, using their own names or the names of famous people. Do not focus on the use of *do* to form questions in the Present Simple as in *How do you spell … ?* This will be covered in full in Units 3 and 4.

2   Check who has a bilingual dictionary and, if possible, hand out a copy to pairs of students who don't. Ask students to find *apple* in the dictionary. If appropriate, you could have a conversation in L1 to compare the dictionary entries, but don't let this go on too long. Explain *part of speech* as 'the type of word'. Explain pronunciation by referring to the phonetic symbols on SB p159 and explain they are sounds, not letters. This will be practised further in Unit 3.

3   Students match the words and pictures. Encourage them to work in pairs and match the words that they recognize first. Then they can use a dictionary to complete the activity. Monitor and check for pronunciation.

> **Answers**
>
> | | | |
> |---|---|---|
> | a an apple | f a newspaper | k a postcard |
> | b a stamp | g a magazine | l an orange |
> | c a dictionary | h a watch | m a camera |
> | d a mobile | i a bag | |
> | e a key | j a ticket | |

T 1.9 [CD 1: Track 10] Play the recording and get students to repeat the words as a class and individually. If they have problems with incorrect stress, refer them to the highlighted stress patterns in the table. If necessary, drill the words, stopping the recording after each word.

4   Demonstrate the activity by saying the letter of some of the photographs and asking a student what the object is and how you spell it. Students continue in closed pairs.

5   Ask students to look at the words. If necessary, point out that *a, e, i, o,* and *u* are vowels. Students work out the rule if they don't already know it.

> **Answers**
> *a* goes before a word starting with a consonant, *an* goes before a vowel.

Point out the following sound rules:
• when we pronounce *u* /ju:/, we use *a*, e.g. *a university*
• when *h* is silent, we use *an*, e.g. *an hour.*

6   Ask students to look at the words and work out the rules for the formation of plurals. Get students to say the plurals of the other words in exercise 3. Refer students to Grammar Reference 1.4 and 1.5 on p137.

> **Answers**
> Most nouns add -*s*. Nouns ending in a consonant + *y* take away the -*y* and add -*ies*.

Workbook Unit 1
Exercises 10 and 11 *a/an*
Exercise 12 Check it
Exercise 15 The alphabet

EVERYDAY ENGLISH (SB p11)

Hello and goodbye

1 Focus attention on the numbers 1–20 in green and get students to say them around the class. If necessary, drill them and check for correct stress on 13–19, e.g. *thirteen*.

2 **T 1.10** [CD 1: Track 11] Ask students to read and listen to the telephone numbers. Focus attention on the use of 'oh' for 0, rather than *zero* and the use of *double* for repeated numbers. Make sure students realize that each number is read individually in English, unlike some languages where *94* would be read as *ninety-four*. Get students to read the telephone numbers aloud, either as a class or in pairs.

3 **T 1.11** [CD 1: Track 12] Tell students they are going to hear six sentences, each with a number. Play the first sentence as an example and elicit the answer. Play the rest of the recording and ask students to write down the numbers they hear. If necessary, pause the recording after each sentence, or play the recording a second time. Check the answers. Ask students to practise the numbers.

Answers and tapescript
1 My brother has **four** children. 4 I live at number **19**.
2 I have **10** stamps in my bag. 5 Goodbye. See you at **five**.
3 Hello, extension **4177**. 6 Hello. **01913 786 499**?

4 Drill the question with each answer. Then get students to ask other people what their home and/or mobile phone number is and to write a list. If you have a big group, check a few of the numbers across the class. If you have a small group, you could check the numbers by writing up the list on the board.

5 **T 1.12** [CD 1: Track 13] Play the first two lines of conversation 1 as an example and ask students to write *2* in the appropriate box. Then play the rest of the recording and get students to write the conversations in the correct order. Play the recording again to check.

Answers and tapescript
1 A Hello, Lisa Jefferson.
  B Hello, Lisa. It's Mike.
  A Mike! How are you?
  B I'm fine, thank you. And you?
  A I'm OK, thanks.
2 A Bye, Marco! Have a nice day!
  B Thanks, and you. See you later!
  A Yes, at 7.00 at the cinema.
  B Great! Bye, Emma!

3 A Hello, 270899.
  B Hi, Alice! It's me, Charles. How are you?
  A Not bad, thanks. And you?
  B Very well, thanks. How are the children?
  A They're fine.

MUSIC OF ENGLISH

T 1.13 [CD 1: Track 14] Read through the *Music of English* box as a class. Refer students back to stress highlighting in Exercise 1 on SB p6. Ask students *What words are important?* (*Hello, Marco, your, Emma* etc. i.e. the shaded words). Look at the expressions in the box. Again, ask students to identify the important words – i.e. the words carrying the most meaning (*you, OK, thanks, not bad*, etc.). Play the recording. Students listen and repeat, exaggerating the stress and intonation in the same way as the recording.

6 Students practise the conversations in open and then closed pairs. Then ask students to practise again, using their own names and telephone numbers. Encourage students to attempt the intonation and stress patterns they encountered in the *Music of English* box while role-playing the conversations. Be content with a good effort.

SUGGESTION
You can consolidate the language of saying *hello* and *goodbye* with the photocopiable activity on TB p135. Photocopy enough pages for students to work in pairs and cut up the lines of conversation, keeping each set together. Hand out a set to each student and get them to order the lines to make two conversations. Check the answers.

Ask where the people are (1 on the phone; 2 in the street). Then get students to practise in pairs, using their own names and phone numbers.

Don't forget!

Workbook Unit 1
Exercise 13 Translation
Exercise 14 Listening: Hello and goodbye
Exercises 16 and 17 These are exercises on numbers 1–20.

Grammar Reference
Look at the exercises on SB p137 as a class, or set for homework. The answers are on TB p176.

Word list
Look at the Word list on SB p152 as a class. Tell students that the most important words from the unit are here. They could translate the words, learn them at home, or transfer some of the words to their vocabulary notebook.

Pronunciation Book Unit 1

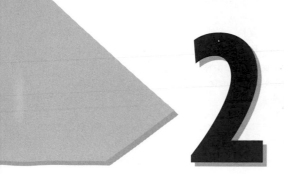

2 Meeting people

am/is/are – questions and negatives
Possessive 's • Family
Opposites • In a café

Introduction to the unit

The title of Unit 2 is 'Meeting people', and various characters are introduced to practise the grammar. The first real fluency activity of *New Headway Elementary – the THIRD edition* is the reading and listening exercise – Danka's email to Jacek. It is important for elementary-level students to be exposed to language in a natural context.

Language aims

Grammar – questions and negatives The verb *to be* is given further practice, with an emphasis on questions, negatives, and short answers. The question words *what*, *where*, *who*, *how old*, and *how much* are revised or introduced.

Note that in the negative, we use the contracted forms of *not*, not the contracted forms of the verb *to be*: i.e. *she isn't, they aren't, you aren't, we aren't*, and not *she's not, they're not, you're not, we're not*. Try to keep to these forms as you speak to the class. The contraction **I amn't* isn't possible, and this is pointed out in the *Grammar Spot* on p13.

Having been introduced to contracted forms, students are tempted to use them in short answers, for example, *Are you married? *Yes, I'm,* but this is not possible. Where other languages will answer an inverted question with simply *yes* or *no*, English prefers to add a short answer. Without the short answer, the speaker can sound rather abrupt.

Possessive 's It can come as quite a surprise to students to learn that not only does *-s* signify a plural noun, but *'s* is both the contracted form of the verb *to be* and an indicator of possession.

Vocabulary Members of the family (*father, aunt,* etc.), other words for personal relationships (*boyfriend/girlfriend*), plus common adjectives and their opposites are introduced. If possible, have a class set of dictionaries for students to use in the matching task on p16 exercise 1.

Everyday English This section practises the language required in a café. *Can I have … ?* is taught idiomatically. Food and drink vocabulary is introduced, and prices are practised. You might feel your students would benefit from doing exercises 16 and 17 in the *Workbook* before doing the *Everyday English* section.

Workbook The spelling of plural nouns is practised.

Notes on the unit

STARTER (SB p12)

> **POSSIBLE PROBLEMS**
> The *Starter* section revises and practises numbers. Numbers 1–20 and phone numbers were introduced in Unit 1, but you might feel that your students need more classroom work on these areas.
> Learners of English often experience difficulty in recognizing and producing the difference between the 'teen' numbers (13–19) and the corresponding 'ten' numbers (30, 40, 50, etc.). Point out the different word stress:
> *thirty*   *thirteen*

1 Get students to count from 1–20 around the class. Repeat so that everyone has a chance to practise, or if students make mistakes.

2 Now ask students to count in tens from 10–100 around the class. Check for correct stress, and repeat until students can say the numbers quickly and accurately.

3 Tell students your age and then briefly revise numbers that reflect the age of your students. Drill the question *How old are you?* Ask students to work in groups of three or four and ask and answer about ages. Ask for a few examples of ages to practise *He's ...* , *She's ...* , *They're ...* , and *We're ...* .

WHO IS SHE? (SB p12)

Questions and negatives

1 Check comprehension of the key vocabulary: *surname*, *first name*, *address*, and *journalist* by referring to your own name and address and defining *journalist*. Ask students to read about Lisa Jefferson.

2 If you think that your students will be familiar with most of the question words in this exercise, you can ask them to work in pairs. Otherwise, complete the questions as a class.

T 2.1 [CD 1: Track 15] Play the recording so students can check their answers. Point out that *isn't* is the negative, and that *n't* is the short form of *not*.

Answers and tapescript
1 A What's **her** surname?
  B Jefferson.
2 A **What's** her first name?
  B Lisa.
3 A **Where's she** from?
  B The USA.
4 A **What's her** job?
  B She's a journalist.
5 A What's **her address**?
  B 89, Franklin Street, Cambridge, Boston.
6 A **What's her** phone number?
  B (616) 326 1204.
7 A How old **is she**?
  B Twenty-six.
8 A Is she **married**?
  B No, she isn't.

Before students practise the questions and answers in pairs, let them practise in open pairs. If your students are confident, also focus on intonation. English has a very wide voice range, and this is apparent in questions. Questions with a question word start high and fall.

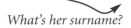

What's her surname?

Listen to the models on the recording and ask students to imitate them. Point out that the question in number 8 is different, as you can answer *Yes/No* and it has a different intonation pattern. *Yes/No* questions usually rise at the end.

Is she married?

Practise the questions as much as possible without boring the class! Have a mixture of open and closed pairs.

3 Students write questions about Lisa's brother, basing their questions on exercise 2. With weaker classes, remind students to use *he/his* in the questions. Check answers as a class.

Answers

Where's he from?	What's his phone number?
What's his job?	How old is he?
What's his address?	Is he married?

T 2.2 [CD 1: Track 16] Play the recording so students can listen and complete the chart. If students need more practice, get them to ask and answer the questions in pairs.

Answers and tapescript
1 A What's his surname?
  B **Jefferson**.
2 A What's his first name?
  B **Rudi**. That's R-U-D-I.
3 A Where's he from?
  B **The USA**.
4 A What's his job?
  B He's an **actor**.
5 A What's his address?
  B **82 Beacon Street, Boston**. That's Beacon, B-E-A-C-O-N Street. Boston.
6 A What's his phone number?
  B **(617) 227 5930**
7 A How old is he?
  B **28**.
8 A Is he married?
  B **No**, he isn't.

Negatives and short answers

4 Tell students they are going to continue asking questions first about Lisa, and then about her brother.

T 2.3 [CD 1: Track 17] Ask students to read and listen to the *Yes/No* questions and short answers. Play the recording. Play the recording again and ask students to repeat, emphasizing the rising intonation on the question and the stress pattern.

If necessary, practise the pronunciation of the contracted form *isn't* and the use of the full form in the positive answer *she is* separately.

Allow students to practise the questions and answers which appear in full in the Student's Book in open and closed pairs. Students then ask questions 1 and 2, following the same pattern.

Answers

1 Is she a student?	No, she isn't.
Is she a teacher?	No, she isn't.
Is she a journalist?	Yes, she is.
2 Is she eighteen?	No, she isn't.
Is she twenty-one?	No, she isn't.
Is she twenty-six?	Yes, she is.

5 Students continue asking about Lisa's brother, following the same pattern and working in closed pairs.

Answers

1 Is his first name Peter?	No, it isn't.
Is his first name Daniel?	No, it isn't.
Is his first name Rudi?	Yes, it is.
2 Is he a journalist?	No, he isn't.
Is he a student?	No, he isn't.
Is he an actor?	Yes, he is.
3 Is he sixteen?	No, he isn't.
Is he thirty?	No, he isn't.
Is he twenty-eight?	Yes, he is.

GRAMMAR SPOT

SUGGESTION

This is the first time that students have seen all the short answers and negative forms of the verb *to be*, so go through the *Grammar Spot* very carefully. You might want to practise the short answers in open pairs and drill the negative sentences.

1 Students complete the short answers, using the contracted form where possible (*No, it **isn't***). Check the answers.

Answers

Is Lisa American?	Yes, she **is**.
Is her surname Smith?	No, it **isn't**.
Are you a journalist?	No, I'm **not**.

Make sure students understand that positive short answers can't be contracted to *Yes, she's.

2 Focus attention on the negative forms and point out especially that we cannot say **I amn't*.

Read Grammar Reference 2.1 on p138 together in class, and/or ask students to read it at home. Encourage them to ask you questions about it if appropriate.

PRACTICE (SB p13)

Who is he?

POSSIBLE PROBLEMS

This is the first information gap activity in *New Headway Elementary – the THIRD edition*, and it may be the first time your students have ever done such an activity. Students may find it strange that Student A has different information from Student B, so explain this activity very carefully, in L1 if you want. Stress that they mustn't show each other the information! Students will need to spell the proper nouns, so review the question *How do you spell that?* and relevant sets of letters that students often confuse, e.g. *a, e, i, o, u; m* and *n; c,* and *k*, etc.

1 Divide the class into pairs, and ask Student B to turn to p150. You could do the first two questions yourself, and/or with the class, as an example. Give students enough time to complete the information exchange.

Answers

SURNAME	Binchey
FIRST NAME	Patrick
COUNTRY	Ireland
JOB	Accountant
ADDRESS	20 Model Farm Road, Cork City
PHONE NUMBER	(21) 434 1075
AGE	48
MARRIED	Yes

POSSIBLE PROBLEMS

Students first saw the short answers *Yes, he/she is, No, he/she isn't*, and *No, I'm not* in *Negatives and short answers*. This speaking exercise and the exercises in *Talking about you* extend and consolidate this focus. It is inadvisable to embark on an explanation of what short answers are and how they operate, as you run the risk of overloading students with too much information. It is better to let students see them in context and use them in controlled exercises.

2 Demonstrate the activity by asking the first question about Patrick's surname and getting students to answer. Students continue to ask and answer in closed pairs. Monitor and check for correct formation of questions and short answers, and for correct pronunciation and intonation.

Talking about you

3   Demonstrate the activity by asking students the example questions. If necessary, remind them of the short answers *Yes, I am* and *No, I'm not*. Focus students' attention on the stress highlighting and remind students these words/parts of words carry the stress. Get students to ask you the questions for each category listed on the form. Correct mistakes carefully.

4   Read the instructions as a class and get two or three pairs of students to model example questions and answers, e.g. *Where are you from? I'm from Milan./I'm from Italy*. The students should complete the information exchange with two other students, either working in pairs or doing the task as a mingling activity.

Ask four or five students to tell the rest of the class about one of the others. They could well have problems with the shift from first and second persons to third person, i.e. *your* to *her*, *are* to *is*, etc., but allow students to feed back without correcting every mistake. You could write corrections on the board later.

ADDITIONAL MATERIAL

Workbook Unit 2
Exercises 1–8 Verb *to be*: questions, negatives, short answers, short forms, and long forms

PATRICK'S FAMILY (SB p14)

Possessive *'s*

> **POSSIBLE PROBLEMS**
> Students may well have problems distinguishing the contracted forms *he's/she's/it's* and the marker for possessive *'s*. The *Grammar Spot* for this section clarifies the usage, but be prepared to review this point as necessary and get students to explain the different uses of *'s* where they appear in the Student's Book.

1   Focus attention on the vocabulary table and on the example. Use the symbols to show students that the words are in male-female pairs.

Students complete the table working with a partner and using a dictionary if necessary. Monitor and check for correct pronunciation, especially of *daughter* /ˈdɔːtə/ and of *grandmother/grandfather* /ˈɡrænmʌðə/, /ˈɡrænfɑːðə/. Check the answers. Drill some of the words to practise the pronunciation.

2   **T 2.4** [CD 1: Track 18] Point to Patrick in the photo and ask *What's his name?* to check if students recognize Patrick Binchey from p13. Ask students to read and listen and put the names next to the right person. Check the answers by calling out the numbers 1–5 and asking students for the correct name.

GRAMMAR SPOT

1   Focus attention on the use of *'s* as the contraction of *is* and as an indicator of possession.

2   Refer students back to the text about Patrick. In pairs students underline examples of possessive *'s* and circle examples of *'s* as the contraction of *is*.

Refer students to Grammar Reference 2.2 on p138.

3   Focus attention on the example. Get two strong students to model the example, stressing important words and parts of words according to the highlighting. Students ask and answer questions about Patrick's family in closed pairs.

PRACTICE (SB p15)

You and your family

1 Students ask you questions about the names of people in your family, i.e. *What's your mother's name?* not *Who's your mother?*

2 Focus attention on the family photos. Students write down the names of some of their relatives on a piece of paper. Focus attention on the example names in the Student's Book and on the big group photo of the family having lunch in the garden. Model the example questions and answers in the Student's Book in open pairs following the highlighted stress pattern in the examples. Students then exchange pieces of paper with a partner and ask and answer questions about each other's families.

3 This exercise consolidates the verb *to be* in a range of persons, and allows students to make true sentences about themselves. Check comprehension of *at home*, *at work*, and *café* by using pictures or simple explanations.

Answers
There can be no set answers for this exercise, but get students to check their answers in pairs. Then check that students haven't made mistakes in the forms of *to be*.

Check it

4 This task reviews the key language from both Units 1 and 2. Students work in pairs or small groups to identify the correct sentence.

Answers
1 I'm a doctor.	5 She's married.
2 I am twenty-nine years old.	6 I'm an uncle.
3 I'm not married.	7 I have two brothers.
4 My sister's name Is Michelle.	8 Peter's my sister's son.

ADDITIONAL MATERIAL

Workbook Unit 2
Exercises 9–12 Possessive *'s*, and family vocabulary

VOCABULARY (SB p16)

Opposites

1 If dictionaries are available, ask students to use them to match the adjectives and their opposites. Alternatively, get students to work in pairs or small groups to pool their knowledge.

Answers
big	small	easy	difficult
old	young	hot	cold
new	old	expensive	cheap
lovely	horrible	fast	slow

Point out that *old* has two opposites (*young* or *new*), depending on the context. Drill the words to practise pronunciation. Ask students to mark the stress on words with two syllables or more.

Answers

● ● ●   ● ● ●   ● ● ●
difficult   expensive   lovely
horrible   easy

2 This exercise practises the vocabulary and revises subject pronouns and the verb *to be*. Students write sentences for each picture.

T 2.5 [CD 1: Track 19] Play the recording so students can check their answers. Students practise saying the sentences in pairs.

Answers and tapescript
1 It's small. It's big.
2 It's easy. It's difficult.
3 He's old. She's young.
4 They're old. They're new.
5 It's lovely. It's horrible.
6 It's fast. It's slow.
7 They're hot. They're cold.
8 It's cheap. It's expensive.

An email from England

> **POSSIBLE PROBLEMS**
>
> This is the first piece of extensive skills work in *New Headway Elementary – the THIRD edition*. Students read and listen to the email at the same time, even though this might be deemed an unnatural activity. Learners of English find reading easier than listening, because they can recognize cognates without the interference of different pronunciation. However, if they read the email silently at their own speed, they could become distracted by unknown and unimportant vocabulary.
>
> The aim of this activity is to show students language that they have already been exposed to in a relatively natural context. If you feel your students would not be able to cope with the activity as it stands, pre-teach the following items of vocabulary, or set them as homework prior to the lesson:
>
> | | | |
> |---|---|---|
> | *funny* | *near* | *software designer* |
> | *computer company* | *friendly* | *nightclub* |
> | *sea* | *happy* | *soon* |
>
> However, if you feel your students don't need so much support, simply encourage them not to worry about the unknown words.

1   Read the introduction as a class.
    T 2.6 [CD 1: Track 20] Students then read and listen to Danka's email.

2   Ask students to match a photograph with a part of the email. Get students to quote from the email to illustrate their answers.

> **Answers**
> Picture 1   I have classes ... I'm in a class with seven students.
> Picture 2   Brighton isn't ... It's lovely to be near the sea.
> Picture 3   I live with an English family ...

Play the recording a second time and ask students to read the email again.

3   If you feel your students would be happy to correct the false sentences in pairs or small groups, ask them to do this. Otherwise, answer the questions as a class.

> **Answers**
> 3   ✗ No, she isn't. She's in Brighton.
> 4   ✗ No, they aren't. They're all from different countries.
> 5   ✗ No, it isn't. It's a small class – eight students (including Danka).
> 6   ✗ No, they aren't. James is a software designer.
> 7   ✓
> 8   ✓

4   Students often have problems with the formation of questions, so this task provides further practice. If you feel students would be happy to work in pairs or small groups for this exercise, let them do so. If necessary, drill the questions for pronunciation practice, encouraging accurate intonation.

> **Answers**
> 2   Where are the (other) students from?
> 3   What's their/the teacher's name?
> 4   Who are James and Becky?
> 5   How old are James and Becky?
> 6   Is Brighton big?

5   **T 2.7** [CD 1: Track 21] Tell students they are going to listen to Danka in three different situations. Play the recording, pausing after each conversation to check the answers to the two questions. Refer students to the tapescript on p126 and play the recording again. Students listen and read.

> **Answers and tapescript**
> 1   She's in class with a student.
> 2   She's in school with the teacher.
> 3   She's at home with Valerie and Becky.
>
> **T 2.7**
> **D=Danka, K=Klaus**
> 1   **D** Hello. My name's Danka.
>   **K** Hello, Danka. I'm Klaus.
>   **D** Where are you from, Klaus?
>   **K** I'm from Germany, from Hamburg. And you? Where are you from?
>   **D** I'm from Poland.
>   **K** From Warsaw?
>   **D** Yes, that's right.
> **S=Simon, C=Class, D=Danka**
> 2   **S** Good morning everybody.
>   **C** Good morning, Simon.
>   **S** How are you all?
>   **C** Fine. Good. OK.
>   **S** How are you Danka?
>   **D** I'm fine, thank you. And you?
>   **S** Very well. Now listen everybody ...
> **B=Becky, D=Danka, V=Valerie**
> 3   **B** Bye, Danka. Have a nice day.
>   **D** Pardon?
>   **B** Have a good day at the language school.
>   **D** Ah, yes. Thank you.
>   **B** What's your teacher called?
>   **D** My teacher called?
>   **V** What's his name?
>   **D** Ah, yes. His name's Simon.
>   **B** And is he good?
>   **D** My teacher good?
>   **V** Yes. Simon, your teacher, is he a good teacher?
>   **D** Oh yes, yes. Very good, very nice.

Writing

6 This is a free writing activity. With weaker classes, you could give students a list of ideas by referring back to Danka's email, e.g. name of the school, number of students, where the students are from, teacher's name, and a short description of the teacher. Set the writing task for homework, and mark it sympathetically. Or you could do this during the lesson and monitor their work, encouraging them to help each other.

EVERYDAY ENGLISH (SB p18)

In a café

> **SUGGESTION**
>
> The activities in exercise 1 allow students to focus just on prices before being exposed to them in a fuller context. If you feel your students need to do more work on prices prior to the lesson, see Workbook Unit 2, exercises 16 and 17.

1   1   **T 2.8** [CD 1: Track 22] Students read and listen to the prices to familiarize themselves with the system and the pronunciation.

Play the recording again and get students to say the prices aloud. Check pronunciation of 'p' (/piː/) and that students follow the highlighted stress pattern on longer prices. Make sure they realize we only use 'p' for prices under a pound.

2   **T 2.9** [CD 1: Track 23] Tell students they are going to hear six prices, each in a context. Get them to write down the prices they hear. (In number 6, ask stronger students to write the correct price.) Check answers.

> **Answers and tapescript**
>
> **T 2.9**
>
> 1 That's **five pounds fifty**, please.
> 2 Look, it's only **twelve pounds**.
> 3 Here you are. **Twenty p** change.
> 4 Pizza is **three pounds seventy-five**.
> 5 **One hundred pounds** for that is very expensive.
> 6 **Nine pounds fif*teen***, not nine pounds fifty.

2 Students read the menu and match the food with the pictures. Drill the pronunciation of the food and drink. Pay particular attention to *hamburger and chips* /ˈhæmbɜːgərən ˈtʃɪps/, *chocolate cake* /ˈtʃɒklət ˌkeɪk/, *orange juice* /ˈɒrɪndʒ ˌdʒuːs/, and *apple pie* /ˌæpl ˈpaɪ/. Students practise the menu items in pairs by pointing to the pictures and saying the names.

> **Answers**
>
> | | | | |
> |---|---|---|---|
> | 1 | Hamburger and chips | 7 | Ice-cream |
> | 2 | Apple pie | 8 | Chocolate cake |
> | 3 | Coffee | 9 | Fish and chips |
> | 4 | Chicken salad | 10 | Orange juice |
> | 5 | Pizza | 11 | Tuna and egg salad |
> | 6 | Mineral water | 12 | Tea |

3   **T 2.10** [CD 1: Track 24] Students listen and repeat, stressing highlighted words and copying the intonation. Do this chorally, pausing the recording, then individually.

Check comprehension of the question *How much … ?* Students ask and answer questions about the prices on the menu. Do this first in open pairs, then in closed pairs. Correct pronunciation and intonation carefully.

4   **T 2.11** [CD 1: Track 25] Get students to read through the gapped conversations first and try to predict possible answers. Students listen and fill in the gaps.

> **Answers and tapescript**
>
> **T 2.11**
>
> 1 A Good morning.
>   B Good **morning**. Can I have a **coffee**, please?
>   A Here you are. Anything else?
>   B No, thanks.
>   A **One pound fifty**, please.
>   B Thanks.
>   A Thank you.
> 2 A Hi. Can I help?
>   B Yes. Can I have a **tuna and egg** salad, please?
>   A Anything to drink?
>   B Yeah. A **mineral water**, please.
>   A OK. Here you are.
>   B **How much** is that?
>   A **Six** pounds **thirty-five**, please.
>   B Thanks.

> **MUSIC OF ENGLISH**
>
> 1 **T 2.12** [CD 1: Track 26] Read through the *Music of English* box as a class. Focus students' attention on the linking lines. Write *Can I help?* on the board. Say the sentence to the class slowly, pronouncing each word separately. Then say the sentence faster, linking *Can* and *I* as in natural speech. Say it again, but this time draw in the linking line on the board as you say the words to demonstrate that a final consonant sound links with an initial vowel sound.
>
> Play the recording. Drill the sentences as connected speech. You may wish to point out to students that sometimes an extra sound is naturally introduced between the two linked words, e.g.: *a tuna* /r/ *and egg salad* and *Here you* /w/ *are.*

5 Students practise the conversations in pairs. Then make the activity a little freer by roleplaying. Take the role of the person working in the café yourself first and choose one of the students to be the customer. You can increase the vocabulary according to the level of your students, asking, for example: *Do you want mayonnaise in your sandwich? Diet Coke?* etc.

Students then practise the conversations in the Student's Book and their own conversations. You could record some for later examination and correction.

SUGGESTION

You can consolidate the language in this unit with the photocopiable activity on TB p136. Stronger students may want to try the Unit 3 part of this activity, but judge if they are ready for this! Photocopy enough pages for students to work in groups of three or four. You will also need dice and counters for each group. Students put their counters on 'Start' and take turns to throw the dice and move around the board. They make a sentence with the cues on the 'square' where they land. If their sentence is correct, they stay on that 'square'; if not, they move back one. The first student to reach 'Finish' is the winner.

Don't forget!

Workbook Unit 2
Exercise 13 Adjectives and nouns that go together
Exercise 14 Spelling of plural nouns
Exercise 15 Translation
Exercises 16 and 17 Numbers and prices

Grammar Reference
Look at the exercises on SB p137 as a class, or set for homework. The answers are on TB p176.

Word list
Remind your students of the Word list for this unit on SB p152. They could translate the words, learn them at home, or transfer some of the words to their vocabulary notebook.

Pronunciation Book Unit 2

DVD/Video
A DVD/Video, Student's Book and Teacher's Book accompany *New Headway Elementary – the THIRD edition.* There are six short, comic episodes which consolidate and extend grammatical, functional, and lexical language presented in the Student's Book. The first episode, 'A new neighbour,' covers language from Units 1 to 4.

Present Simple 1 – *he/she/it*
Questions and negatives
Jobs • What time is it?

The world of work

Introduction to the unit

Work and jobs are the themes of this unit as they lend themselves to the practice of the grammatical aim, which is the introduction of the third person singular of the Present Simple. The skills work includes a reading text about a man who lives on a remote Scottish island and has thirteen jobs! This was chosen to complement both the themes and grammar of the unit. The text also acts as a preview of other forms of the Present Simple in context.

Language aims

Grammar – Present Simple 1 The Present Simple is the most used tense in the English language. It is therefore important to introduce it early in an elementary course. In *New Headway Elementary – the THIRD edition* the introduction is staged over two units. In this unit only the third person singular with its questions and negatives is presented and practised. All the other persons are introduced in Unit 4.

POSSIBLE PROBLEMS

- The English language does not have many inflections. Unfortunately, this means the few that do exist cause a disproportionate amount of difficulty for foreign learners. The *-s* on the third person singular of the Present Simple is a classic example of this. Therefore we introduce it first in the hope that it will be more memorable and students will be less likely to omit it.
- The *s* can be pronounced in three ways:
  /z/ comes   /kʌmz/
  /s/ works   /wɜːks/
  /ɪz/ teaches /ˈtiːtʃɪz/
  The difference between /s/ and /z/ endings is practised in the opening texts on István Kis and Pamela Green.
- The use of *does/doesn't* in the question and negative often seems strange to students, because of the absence of the auxiliary in the positive.

NOTE

For the first nine units, the verb *have* is introduced and practised as a full verb with its *do/does* forms. *Have got* is introduced in Unit 10. This is for several reasons:

- By introducing the *do/does* forms, the verb *have* operates like any other verb in the Present Simple (with the exception of *has* in the third person singular).
- When students have just learnt the Present Simple and have been introduced to the auxiliary verbs *do/does*, it is very difficult and confusing for them when they come across the verb form *have got*, which operates differently.
- Although *have got* is common, especially in the spoken language, the full verb *have* with its *do/does* forms covers all the uses in a way that *have got* doesn't. *Have got* expresses possession, but it cannot express a habitual action. So students can learn *How many children have you got?*, but then it is very confusing when they are introduced to *What time do you have lunch?* We cannot say **What time have you got lunch?*
- Finally, *have* with its *do/does* forms is becoming more common in spoken British English. It is the standard form in American English.

Vocabulary and pronunciation A variety of jobs with related activities are introduced. Dictionary work is encouraged and there is a certain amount of work on the phonetic spelling of some of the words. If possible, bring enough bilingual dictionaries for students to share at least one between two.

Everyday English Students focus on how to tell the time in English. This is practised in short dialogues.

Writing The writing syllabus begins in this unit. Object pronouns (*me, him, them*) are introduced and practised.

Workbook The spelling of the third person singular is practised (*watches, goes*).

Question words such as *Where?* and *How much?*, and *Yes/No* questions are practised.

Verbs of daily routine (*get up, make breakfast*) are introduced, with practice of questions and negatives.

Notes on the unit

STARTER (SB p20)

The *Starter* activity recycles the family vocabulary from Unit 2 and allows students to use some of the jobs vocabulary they already know. Give some examples of jobs of the people in your own family and then get students to continue the activity in pairs. If students ask for the names of individual jobs, give some examples that are common to the whole class, but do not let the *Starter* activity go on too long or reduce the usefulness of the *Vocabulary and pronunciation* section on p26.

THREE JOBS (SB p20)

Present Simple *he/she/it*

> **SUGGESTION**
> Before you start this unit, set the vocabulary homework below in preparation for the presentation texts on István and Pamela. This will save a lot of classroom time where you would have to check vocabulary, and it will give you more time to focus on the grammar.
>
> **Homework prior to lesson**
> Ask students to write the translation of the following words and learn them for the lesson. They can use a bilingual dictionary to look up words they don't know.
>
> **Verbs**   *come fly help like love play speak work*
> **Nouns**   *Canada day hour town week*
> **Adjectives**   *Canadian free time ordinary*
>
> Pre-teach *music professor* and *flying doctor*.

1 Focus attention on the photos of István and Pamela. Students answer the first questions. (*He's a music professor. She's a flying doctor.*)

Ask students *Where's he from?* and *Where's she from?* and then ask them to look quickly at the texts to find the answers (Budapest in Hungary, and Canada).

T 3.1 [CD 1: Track 27] Now play the recording and ask your students to read and listen to the texts at the same time. If you think your class will experience some difficulty, you could deal with the texts one at a time, doing the *Grammar Spot* exercises with them for the first text and then asking them to repeat the process on their own for the second.

GRAMMAR SPOT

1 Tell students that they should only look for verbs in the positive form. Ask them to work on their own to underline the verbs and then check their answers with a partner before you conduct a full class feedback. Point out that *is* and *has* are irregular verbs.

2 Ask the whole class what the last letter is (*-s*) and point out that this is the ending for the third person singular – *he, she, it* – of the Present Simple tense.

Answers
is comes lives works speaks has likes flies loves

Pronunciation

3 **T 3.2** [CD 1: Track 28] Play the recording. Tell students to listen for the pronunciation of the final -*s*, and to decide whether it is pronounced /s/ or /z/. Do verbs *works* /s/ and *is* /z/ as examples with the class. Students listen and write the other verbs in the chart. Check answers as a class. Play the recording again. Students listen and repeat as a class first, then individually.

Answers and tapescript
/s/ works speaks likes
/z/ is comes lives has flies loves

T 3.2 is comes lives works speaks has likes flies loves

2 Working in pairs, students take it in turns to practise reading the texts in pairs. Monitor for correct pronunciation. Round off the activity by asking one or two students to read a text aloud to the whole class.

3 Students write their answers, and then check with a partner. Make it clear that each gap represents a word and that question 8 requires a positive verb in the second sentence because of the negative expressed by *never*.

T 3.3 [CD 1: Track 29] Students listen and check.

Answers and tapescript
1 István's a music professor. Pamela**'s a** doctor.
2 He comes from Hungary. She **comes from** Canada.
3 He lives in a big city, but she **lives** in a **small** town.
4 He **works** four days **a** week. She **works** 16 hours a day **non-stop**.
5 He **speaks** three languages. She **speaks** to sick people on her radio.
6 He loves his job and she **loves her job**, too.
7 He **has a** daughter. She **isn't** married.

8 He **likes** playing* tennis in his free time. She never **has** free time.
*Note that *like + -ing* is dealt with in Unit 4.

Ask students in pairs to read the sentences aloud. Monitor for correct pronunciation of the *-s* ending. If necessary, play the recording again and get students to repeat.

PRACTICE (SB p21)

Talking about people

1 The aim of this activity is to give students the chance not just to produce single sentences, but to speak at some length to describe Fernando. It is both useful and satisfying for low-level students to use language for 'display' purposes in this way and not always engage in the more 'natural' question-and-answer activities.

Ask the whole class to look at the picture of Fernando and the information about him. Check comprehension of *walking his dog*. Start to build a profile of him orally with contributions from different students. Point out any errors in the third person *-s* ending and major problems with pronunciation, but also allow students to self-correct and encourage peer correction from the other students as much as possible.

2 Focus attention on the examples. Then ask one or two students to give a connected description of Fernando.

> **Sample answer**
> Fernando's a tourist guide. He comes from Peru and he lives in Lima. He works in a tourist office. He speaks Spanish, English, and a little German. He isn't married, but he has a dog. In his free time he likes walking his dog and playing football.

3 Now ask your students to write a short paragraph about a friend or relative. With weaker classes, give a short description of a friend or relative, or elicit an example from a confident student. Students work in pairs and talk about their friend/relative to their partner. Go round the class to check and help them. Bring the whole class together again, and ask one or two students to tell the others about their friend or relative.

ADDITIONAL MATERIAL

Workbook Unit 3

Exercises 1 and 2 These provide further practice of the third person positive of the Present Simple.

Exercise 3 This is a vocabulary activity in two parts. It should be done with a dictionary. (It is *not* an opportunity to practise other persons of the Present Simple, only to see the verbs in their infinitive forms!) It would be a good idea to set the first part for homework and then follow it up in class – the pictures of Rupert's day are particularly suitable for a classroom activity, where the story is built orally *before* students write or listen and check.

WHAT DOES HE DO? (SB p22)

Questions and negatives

> **NOTE**
> Be prepared for some students to make mistakes in the use of *does/doesn't* to form the question and negative. Try to review these forms as often as necessary. In the Present and Past Simple tenses, where there is no auxiliary in the positive, the use of the auxiliary verbs can seem very strange. Many students feel that it would be much more logical to say:
> **Lives he in Paris?*
> **Where lives she?*
> **She lives not in London.*
> The short answers *Yes, he does./No, he doesn't.* and common mistakes of form like **he doesn't comes* also cause problems and need to be pointed out to students.

1 You need to signal that you are going to introduce the question form. You can do this by drawing a large question mark on the board and/or repeating the sentences yourself with exaggerated intonation.
   T 3.4 [CD 1: Track 30] Play the recording and ask your students to read and listen, and complete the answers.

> **Answers and tapescript**
> 1 Where does István come from? Budapest, **in** Hungary.
> 2 What does he do? He's **a** music professor.
> 3 Does he speak German? **Yes**, he does.
> 4 Does he speak Spanish? **No**, he doesn't. He doesn't speak French or Spanish.

Play the recording again and get students to repeat both chorally and individually. Then get them to ask and answer in open pairs across the class.

> **NOTE**
> Encourage good pronunciation at all times. Highlight the pronunciation of *does* and *doesn't*, getting students to repeat the weak and strong forms in isolation, and as part of the question and short answers.
>
> Also take care with the intonation, falling at the end in the *wh-* questions and rising in the *Yes/No* questions.
>
> *Where does he come from?* /weə dəz hɪ kʌm frɒm/
>
> *Does he speak German?* /dəz hɪ spiːk ˈdʒɜːmən/

1   Make sure students understand that *What does he/she do?* means the same as *What's his/her job?*, but that *What does he/she do?* is the more common question.

2   Ask students to complete the sentences using the verb *come*.

> **Answers**
> **Positive**: He **comes** from Hungary.
> **Negative**: He **doesn't come** from Poland.
> **Question**: Where **does** he **come** from?

Point out that the -*s* isn't used on the main verb in the negative and question, but appears in *does*.

Pronunciation

3   **T 3.5** [CD 1: Track 31] This exercise serves to further reinforce the weak and strong forms of *does*. Students will see from the stress highlighting that when unstressed, i.e. in positive sentences, the form is weak: /dəz/. However, when stressed, i.e. in a short answer or the negative, it is strong: /dʌz/, /'dʌznt/.

Play the recording. Students listen for the weak and strong forms of *does/doesn't*, then listen again and practise saying them. Drill the forms as necessary.

Read Grammar Reference 3.1 on p138 together in class, and/or ask students to read it at home. Encourage them to ask you questions about it.

2   **T 3.6** [CD 1: Track 32] Students complete the sentences then check with a partner. Play the recording and get them to listen and check. Finally, ask individuals to read their answers to the class paying careful attention to stress and pronunciation.

> **Answers and tapescript**
> 1   Where **does** Pamela **come** from? Canada.
> 2   What **does** she **do**? She's a doctor.
> 3   **Does** she live in Canada? No, she **doesn't**.
> 4   **Does** she **like** her job? Yes, she **does**.

3   Focus attention on the example question and answer. Students write similar questions about Fernando and then ask and answer in pairs.

> **Sample questions and answers**
> What does he do? He's a tourist guide.
> Does he work in a tourist office? Yes, he does.
> Does he speak Italian? No, he doesn't.

Asking about people

1   Divide the class into pairs. Get the students to read about Iman or Giorgio. Check comprehension and drill the pronunciation of *businesswoman* /'bɪznəswʊmən/, *Somalia* /sə'mɑːliə/, *vegetarian* /ˌvedʒə'teəriən/, *chef* /ʃef/, *relaxing* /rɪ'læksɪŋ/.

2   Get students to say a sentence about each person as an example. Students describe Iman/Giorgio to a partner. Go round the class to check and help them. Round off the activity by bringing the whole class together again, and asking one or two students to tell the others about Iman and Giorgio.

3   Ask each pair to choose either Iman or Giorgio. Focus attention on the example. Students work individually and write the questions.

> **Answers**
> Where does she/he come from?
> Where does she/he live?
> Where does she/he work?
> Does she/he speak French?
> How many children does she/he have?
> Does she/he have a dog?
> What does she/he do in her/his free time?
> Does she/he like cooking?

Check the questions quickly round the class, getting students to read them aloud.

4   Ask your students to close their books, as they are going to work from memory. Write the names *Iman* and *Giorgio* on the board, then ask students to work in pairs and take it in turns to ask and answer questions about them. Don't make the activity too laborious by insisting they ask every question about both characters, as this would probably take too long. Let your students choose their questions and which character they talk about.

Round off the activity by asking for a few questions and answers in open pairs. Check for accurate pronunciation.

5   This is a personalized activity. Tell students they can answer questions about any friend or relative. Feed in any necessary vocabulary, e.g. *cousin*, (*sister*)-*in-law*, if students request this. Go round and check as they do the activity, focusing on the formation of questions. Ask one or two students to tell the whole class about their or their partner's relative.

Listening and pronunciation

6 Do this exercise as briskly as possible with the whole class. Demonstrate the activity by going through the examples with the class and practising the responses *Yes, that's right, No, he/she doesn't, No, he isn't*. Encourage students to follow the highlighted stress patterns.

T 3.7 [CD 1: Track 33] Play the recording or read the sentences (3–10 below) yourself and nominate individuals in the class to respond. Allow students to correct each other if a wrong answer is given. It should be quick and fun to do, so don't insist on the full correct answer if it slows down the activity – *No, he/she doesn't*, etc. is enough, especially with weaker classes.

> **Answers and tapescript**
> **Iman**
> 3 She's a tourist guide. **No, she isn't.** (She's a model and a business woman.)
> 4 She speaks five languages. **Yes, that's right.**
> 5 She likes playing tennis in her free time. **No, she doesn't.** (She likes cooking vegetarian food in her free time.)
> 6 She isn't married. **Yes, she is.** (She's married to David Bowie.)
> **Giorgio**
> 7 Giorgio works in an office in London. **No, he doesn't.** (He works in a restaurant.)
> 8 He is Italian. **Yes, he is.**
> 9 He has three sons. **No, he doesn't.** (He has a son and a daughter.)
> 10 He likes relaxing with his family in his free time. **Yes, that's right.**

7 **T 3.8** [CD 1: Track 34] This should follow on immediately from the previous exercise. Play the recording and ask students to tick the sentence they hear. This exercise tests receptive comprehension, but you can make it productive by asking students to say the sentences with a partner. Check for accurate pronunciation.

> **Answers and tapescript**
> 1 She likes her job.
> 2 She loves walking.
> 3 He isn't married.
> 4 Does he have three children?
> 5 What does he do?

Check it

8 Ask students to work in pairs or small groups and tick the correct sentence. Ask them to work quite quickly, then conduct a full class feedback. Get students to correct each other and to explain any mistakes they hear.

> **Answers**
> 1 She comes from Somalia.
> 2 What does he do in his free time?
> 3 Where does she live?
> 4 He isn't married.
> 5 Does she have two sons?
> 6 He doesn't play football.
> 7 She doesn't love Peter.
> 8 What's his address?

ADDITIONAL MATERIAL

Workbook Unit 3
Exercises 4–9 Questions and negatives in Present Simple third person singular

WRITING (SB p114)

Natural writing

Using pronouns

This is the first unit of the writing syllabus. It reviews subject pronouns and possessive adjectives, and also introduces object pronouns. Knowing how to use pronouns is an essential skill in fluent writing and it helps students understand how a text fits together.

1 Write the following sentence on the board and get students to identify the subject pronoun, object pronoun, and possessive adjective:
*I lend **him my** car every week.*

Look at sentence 1 as a class. Elicit from students any other pronouns/possessive adjectives in the sentence (pronouns: he, her). In pairs, students continue to underline the pronouns and possessive adjectives in sentences 2 and 3. Check answers as a class.

> **Answers**
> **Pronouns** they, us
> **Possessive adjectives** our, her our

2 Get students to complete the table in exercise 2 working individually before checking with the whole class.

> **Answers**
>
> | Subject pronouns | Object pronouns | Possessive adjectives |
> | --- | --- | --- |
> | I | me | my |
> | **you** | you | **your** |
> | he | him | his |
> | **she** | her | **her** |
> | it | it | its |
> | we | us | **our** |
> | **they** | them | their |

3 With weaker classes, focus attention on the *Caution Box* and ask students to read this before starting the exercise. More able classes can do exercise 3 straight away and focus on the *Caution Box* as consolidation.

Focus attention on the example and get students to say what *she* and *it* refer back to (*sister* and *car*). Get students to complete the sentences working individually and then check the answers with the whole class.

Answers		
2 He; them	5 We; us	8 He; it
3 it	6 us	9 me
4 She; him/He; her	7 her/them	10 She; them

Focus attention on the *Caution Box* if students didn't read it before doing exercise 3.

4 Ask the gist questions to remind students who István is. (He's the music professor from p20.) Ask students to guess who is in the photo and elicit *his wife* and *his daughter*.

5 Read the first sentence of the text aloud and get students to say what is wrong with it (the repetition of *István* makes it sound unnatural). Get students to read the first sentence of the text and elicit the nouns that can be replaced (see *Answers*). Students read to the end of the text and underline the relevant nouns. Check the answers with the class.

Answers
István Kis is Hungarian, but <u>István</u> lives in the USA because <u>István</u> is married to an American. <u>István</u> is a music professor. <u>István</u> likes his job because <u>his job</u> is interesting, and <u>István</u> loves playing in concerts. <u>István</u> travels around the world to play, but <u>István's</u> wife, Stacey, doesn't go with <u>István</u> because <u>Stacey</u> doesn't like travelling. <u>István and Stacey</u> have a nine-year-old daughter. <u>István and Stacey's</u> daughter's name is Mary-Jane. <u>Mary-Jane</u> goes to school, and <u>Mary-Jane</u> also plays the piano every day. <u>Mary-Jane</u> wants to be a pianist, too, and travel with <u>Mary-Jane's</u> father. Stacey doesn't want to go with <u>István and Mary-Jane</u>. When <u>István and Mary-Jane</u> travel around the world, <u>Stacey</u> says she wants a dog!

6 Focus attention on the example rewriting of the text and then get students to continue the task. With weaker classes, elicit a longer section of the text as a whole-class activity and write the answers on the board before students complete the task individually.

Check the answers either orally or by collecting in the students' written task.

Answers
István Kis is Hungarian, but **he** lives in the USA because **he** is married to an American. **He** is a music professor. **He** likes his job because **it** is interesting, and **he** loves playing in concerts. **He** travels around the world to play, but **his** wife, Stacey, doesn't go with **him** because **she** doesn't like travelling. **They** have a nine-year-old daughter. **Their** daughter's name is Mary-Jane. **She** goes to school, and **she** also plays the piano every day. **She** wants to be a pianist, too, and travel with **her** father. Stacey doesn't want to go with **them**. When **they** travel around the world, **she** says she wants a dog!

READING AND LISTENING (SB p24)

Seumas McSporran – the man with thirteen jobs!

NOTE
This is an important activity because it brings together, in one text, much of the grammar your students have been studying so far. It should give them great satisfaction to feel that they can already master a piece of continuous prose of this length.
It also acts as a preview of the daily routine in Unit 4. Seumas McSporran is a real person (and a real name), and the text is based on a newspaper article. It has been carefully simplified and graded for students of this level.

SUGGESTION
You could begin the lesson by asking students: *How many jobs do you/most people have? What time do you/most people start and finish work?*

1 Ask students to look quickly at the photographs on the page and tell you a little about what and who they can see. Do not insist on accuracy at this stage – use this as an opportunity for students to get into the topic and predict what they might read in the text.

2 Ask students to work in pairs and match the sentences with the photographs. Tell them not to worry about new vocabulary, but to use the words that they recognize and the information in the photographs to help them.
Check the answers.

Answers
1 h   2 a   3 e   4 g   5 c   6 b   7 d   8 i   9 f

Check the key vocabulary by giving short definitions accompanied by mime and getting students to tell you the word, e.g. *You eat this in the morning – breakfast*; *the people who stay in a hotel – guests*; *you need this in your car to drive it – petrol*, etc.

3 Pre-teach/check some of the key vocabulary before the students start to read, so that they do not stop at every new word and ask for an explanation.

You can teach/check the following through mime or short definitions, or by referring to the photographs: jobs – *postman, policeman, fireman, school-bus driver, boatman* (a man you pay to take you out in a boat or for the use of a boat), *ambulance man, accountant, petrol attendant, undertaker*; verbs – *get up, make breakfast, collect, deliver, watch TV, make supper, go to bed*.

Ask students to work in pairs or small groups to find the answers. Tell them not to worry about words they do not recognize and just to focus on the key information. They can consult the text whenever necessary.

Check the answers. Decide according to the speed and ability of your students whether you want quick, short answers or fuller answers (see brackets).

Answers

1 On the Island of Gigha (pronounced /ˈɡiːjə/). (He lives on the Island of Gigha in the north of Scotland.)
2 60. (He's 60 years old.)
3 Thirteen. (He has thirteen jobs.)
4 Margaret. (His wife's name is Margaret.)
5 She works in the shop.
6 120. (120 people live on Gigha.)
7 150 every day. (150 tourists visit Gigha every day in summer.)
8 He makes breakfast, drives the children to school, collects the post from the boat, and delivers the post to the houses.
9 Margaret makes supper, and Seumas does the accounts. They have a glass of wine and then go to bed.

If appropriate, ask students for their reaction to the text. Ask if they know anyone who has a lot of jobs.

4 Ask students to look at the photos. Briefly review the times that go with each photograph, by introducing *o'clock*. Do not spend too long on this as students will revise telling the time more fully in the *Everyday English* section at the end of this unit. Demonstrate the activity by getting two students to ask and answer using the example in the Student's Book. Students continue to ask and answer questions. Encourage them to stress the questions and answers according to the highlighted stress pattern in the example. Go round the class to check. Feed back on any common errors.

5 **T 3.9** [CD 1: Track 35] Ask students to cover the conversations in exercise 6. Focus attention on the three questions and demonstrate the activity by playing conversation 1 and checking the answers (see below).

Play the remaining three conversations, stopping after each one to allow students to complete their answers. Check the answers with the whole class.

Answers and tapescript
Conversation 1
1 Afternoon
2 Seumas and a customer in Seumas's shop
3 Shop assistant

Conversation 2
1 Morning
2 Seumas and a woman who lives on the island
3 Postman

Conversation 3
1 Evening
2 Seumas and Margaret
3 No job – Seumas isn't working

Conversation 4
1 Morning
2 Seumas and schoolchildren
3 School-bus driver

T 3.9
1 A Good afternoon. Can I have two ice-creams, please?
  B Chocolate or vanilla?
  A One chocolate, one vanilla, please.
  B That's one pound eighty. Anything else?
  A No, thank you.
2 A Only two letters for you this morning, Mrs Craig.
  B Thank you very much, Mr McSporran. And how's Mrs McSporran this morning?
  A Oh, she's very well, thank you. She's busy in the shop.
3 A A glass of wine before bed, my dear?
  B Oh, yes please.
  A Here you are.
  B Thank you, my dear. I'm very tired this evening.
4 A Hello, Mr McSporran.
  B Good morning, boys and girls. Hurry up, we're late.
  A Can I sit here, Mr McSporran?
  C No, no. I want to sit there.
  B Be quiet all of you, and SIT DOWN!

6 Students complete the conversations as far as they can, using what they remember from the reading, and the information from exercises 3 and 4. Students can then exchange and pool information with a partner.

T 3.9 [CD 1: Track 35] Play the conversations again to allow students to complete their answers. Check the answers.

Answers

1 afternoon   have   £1.80   else
2 two   morning   how   morning   busy
3 wine   Here   tired   evening
4 morning   want   all

Put students into pairs to practise the conversations.

VOCABULARY AND PRONUNCIATION (SB p26)

Jobs

1 Focus attention on the photos and elicit the names of the
jobs that students already know. In pairs, students match
a photograph with a job in column A, checking any
words that are still unknown in their dictionaries. You
could also ask them to mark the stress.

Conduct a class feedback on the correct answers and
drill the words both chorally and individually as you go,
taking care with the stress (see below). Keep revising by
asking *Tell me again! What's '1'? What's '4'?* etc.

Answers

1 e An actor	4 f A journalist	7 c A nurse
2 i A shop assistant	5 a A pilot	8 b A chef
3 g A model	6 d A lawyer	9 h An architect

2 Ask students to work in pairs or small groups and match
a job in column A with a line in column B. They will
probably need to continue to use their dictionaries, or if
you have a monolingual class, you could give quick
translations of any words they ask about.

T 3.10 [CD 1: Track 36] Listen and check.

Answers and tapescript

a   A pilot flies planes.
b   A chef cooks in a restaurant.
c   A nurse looks after people in hospital.
d   A lawyer helps people in court.
e   An actor makes films.
f   A journalist writes for a newspaper.
g   A model wears beautiful clothes.
h   An architect designs buildings.
i   A shop assistant sells things.

3

NOTE
The idea of this activity is to give a very short
introduction to and practice of the phonetic script. It
is also an opportunity to start getting your students
familiar with the phonetic symbols chart on SB p159.
You need to make clear what exactly phonetic script
is, i.e. that it is only the sounds of the words that are
transcribed, and that it is important to know this in
English, because the spellings and the sounds often
do not relate exactly.

Ask the class to look at the phonetic transcriptions and
say if they can recognize any of the words. Ask them to
turn to SB p159, not to study it, but so that they get the
idea of what phonetic script is.

Now ask them to write the spellings of the words and
then check them with a partner and practise saying them
together. Let them use the phonetic chart for help.

T 3.11 [CD 1: Track 37] Play the recording and get
students to listen and repeat.

Answers and tapescript

1 nurse	3 actor	5 architect
2 model	4 shop assistant	6 chef

If you have time, you could put a few additional words in
phonetic script on the board for students to work out, e.g.

/'bɪldɪŋz/	(buildings)	/'hɒspɪtəl/	(hospital)
/weə(r)s/	(wears)	/'restrɒnt/	(restaurant)
/lʊks/	(looks)	/selz/	(sells)
/'piːpl/	(people)	/pleɪnz/	(planes)

4 Make this exercise fun, like a game, and do it as quickly
as possible. Ask students to learn the sentences by heart,
then to close their books. Call out the name of a job and
tell your students to call out the complete sentences.

Teacher	**Student(s)**
A journalist ...	*writes for a newspaper!*
A pilot ...	*flies planes!* etc.

Focus attention on the question and example in the
Student's Book. Elicit another question and answer
exchange, e.g. *What does an architect do? He/She designs
buildings.* Finally, ask students to work in pairs for a few
minutes with their books still closed, and ask and answer
questions about the jobs.

ADDITIONAL MATERIAL

Workbook Unit 3
Exercise 11 Verbs and nouns that go together, e.g. *have a
shower*
Exercise 12 This revises vocabulary from Units 1–3.

What time is it?

Introduce the subject of telling the time by asking *What time is it now?* and *What time does the lesson end?* Initially you can accept answers in the hour + minutes form, e.g. *five thirty*, but explain that the system used in *New Headway Elementary – the THIRD edition* uses *past* and *to*.

> **NOTE**
> To help students learn the time in English the clocks in exercise 1 are arranged in four groups of four: o'clock/half past; quarter past/to; minutes past; minutes to. Each example has a similar time alongside to help students write the correct answers.

1 Ask students to work in pairs, look carefully at the clocks and the examples provided, and write in the times.

T 3.12 [CD 1: Track 38] Play the recording for students to check their answers.

> **Answers and tapescript**
> It's five o'clock. **It's eight o'clock.**
> It's half past five. **It's half past eleven.**
>
> It's quarter past five. **It's quarter past two.**
> It's quarter to six. **It's quarter to nine.**
>
> It's five past five. **It's ten past five.**
> It's twenty past five. **It's twenty-five past five.**
>
> It's twenty-five to six. **It's twenty to six.**
> It's ten to six. **It's five to six.**

Focus attention on the stress highlighting. Play the recording again. Encourage students to follow closely the stress pattern as they practise saying the times.

If possible, bring a toy clock with moveable hands to the lesson as an easy way of giving further practice. First, you can change the times on the clock, and then your students can also have turns, coming to the front of the class, moving the hands, and asking *What time is it?* Continue to encourage students to use accurate stress patterns.

2 This exercise introduces useful expressions for times just before or after an exact division of the clock.

Read through the examples with the class and practise with the toy clock (if you have one!) or by drawing further examples on the board.

T 3.13 [CD 1: Track 39] Read the *Music of English* box as a class. Play the recording. Focus students' attention on the stress and intonation arrows. Play the recording again. Students follow the highlighted stress pattern and intonation. Really encourage a good imitation of the recording – this should help them sound very polite. Practise the dialogues across the class. Keep the activity light-hearted and fun.

Ask students to draw three or more clocks on a piece of paper and practise the conversation again in pairs. Ask one or two pairs to act out the conversations in front of the class. Tell them (in L1 if possible) to imagine that they are stopping a stranger in the street and that they must use the correct intonation if they want to sound polite.

> **SUGGESTION**
> You can consolidate the language in this unit, and also review Unit 2, with the photocopiable activity on TB p136. Photocopy enough pages for students to work in groups of three or four. You will need dice and counters for each group. Students put their counters on 'Start' and take turns to throw the dice and move around the board. They make a sentence with the cues on the 'square' where they land. If their sentence is correct, they stay on that 'square', if not they move back one. The first student to reach 'Finish' is the winner.

ADDITIONAL MATERIAL

Workbook Unit 3
Exercise 13 This gives more practice of telling the time.
Exercise 10 Translation

Don't forget!

Grammar Reference
Look at the exercises on SB p139 of the Student's Book as a class, or set for homework. The answers are on TB p176.

Word List
Remind your students of the Word list for this unit on SB p153. They could translate the words, learn them at home, or transfer some of the words to their vocabulary notebook.

Pronunciation Book Unit 3

Video/DVD Episode 1 A new neighbour

Present Simple 2 – *I/you/we/they*
Leisure activities
Social expressions

Take it easy!

Introduction to the unit

The theme of this unit is free time and leisure activities. This lends itself to much practice, personalized and otherwise, of the main grammatical aim, which is the introduction of all other persons (those without the -*s*!) of the Present Simple tense. The skills work includes reading and listening tasks where people from three different countries talk about their favourite season and what they do. This provides the opportunity to bring together and revise all persons of the Present Simple.

Language aims

Grammar – Present Simple 2 This unit follows on from the introduction of the third person in Unit 3 and introduces all other persons of the Present Simple, *I*, *you*, *we*, *they*, and the question and negative. The verb forms with these are all the same, without the inflection -*s*, and tend to cause less difficulty as a result. The third person is constantly revised alongside the other persons so that students can perceive the differences in form.

Vocabulary A variety of leisure activities (sports and hobbies) are introduced and these are practised in a personalized activity with the verb *to like*.

Everyday English Some common and useful social expressions are introduced and practised in short dialogues.

Writing Informal letter-writing is introduced via a letter to a penfriend.

Workbook Adverbs of frequency, e.g. *always*, *sometimes*, *never* are practised.

Notes on the unit

> **SUGGESTION**
> Setting some vocabulary for homework before you start this unit will give you more time to focus on the grammar. It is worthwhile to get students used to taking some responsibility for the learning of vocabulary. Encourage them to enter the new words in their vocabulary notebooks.
>
> **Homework prior to the lesson**
>
> 1 Ask students to learn the days of the week in English. You could give them a handout with phonetic script such as this:
>
> Monday /'mʌndei/   Thursday /'θɜːzdei/   Sunday /'sʌndei/
> Tuesday /'tʃuːzdei/   Friday /'fraɪdei/
> Wednesday /'wenzdei/   Saturday /'sætədei/
>
> 2 Give students these new verbs to look up in a bilingual dictionary. Ask them to learn them and write down the translations.
>
> *train   go running   relax   cook   win   visit*

STARTER (SB p28)

1 Use a calendar that shows the year, months, and days as a visual aid. (Alternatively, write the day, month, and year on the board in abbreviated form, e.g. Tues., Sept., 2005). Focus attention on the year and elicit how we say this in English. Do the same for the month. (Do not spend too long on this, as students will focus on months more fully before the *Reading and listening* section.)

2　Use the calendar and get students to go through the days of the week. Say the days yourself and ask them to repeat each one both chorally and individually. This will take less time if you have set the above for homework.

Ask *What day is it today?* Chorus through the days of the week with the whole class and then make the individual practice fun by getting one student after another to give consecutive days very quickly round the class until they are firmly fixed. (If time allows, you could then ask one or two students to go through the whole week and perhaps also ask them to spell some of the days, to revise the alphabet.)

Ask *Which days are the weekend?* Check that students understand the word *weekend*.

Ask students to ask and answer the *Starter* questions in pairs. Go round and check students' pronunciation and feed back on any common errors.

EXTRA SUGGESTIONS

If you feel your students need more practice on days, months, and years, try the following activities:

- rearranging the jumbled spelling of days and months
- matching phonetic script to days and months
- conducting a favourite day or birthday survey
- a word association activity for different days/months
- doing an 'important year' quiz with simple headline-style sentences (to avoid the use of the Past Simple), e.g. *the Olympics in Athens*, and students supply the correct year, e.g. *2004*.
- linking days and months to horoscope signs. This can be done as an information gap activity where students have some of the names of the signs and some of the dates missing.

WEEKDAYS AND WEEKENDS (SB p28)

Present Simple *I/you/we/they*

As homework prior to the lesson students could check the meanings of the following verbs from the presentation texts in their dictionaries. This will help maintain a lively pace: *train, work, play, relax, love, get up, go out, visit, cook, watch, want*.

1　**T 4.1** [CD 1: Track 40] The text reminds students of the third person of the Present Simple before they are introduced to the other persons. Focus attention on the photograph and on the headline, and elicit basic information: *What's her name?* (Ceri) *Where is she in the photos?* (on the rugby field and in the changing room). Play the recording and get students to answer the gist questions.

Answers
1　She's a lawyer.
2　She plays rugby.

2　Students complete the text with the verbs.

Answers and tapescript
Ceri **is** 28 years old and **lives** in Cardiff, Wales. She **works** hard as a lawyer from Monday to Friday, but she **doesn't relax** at weekends. She **plays** rugby for the Women's Welsh Rugby team. On Saturdays she **trains** with her team at the Rugby Club, and on Sundays she **plays** in a match. She **has** no free time, but she **loves** her job and playing rugby.

Ask a few questions to revise the third person:
Where does Ceri live?　(*In Cardiff.*)
How old is she?　(*Twenty-eight.*)
What does she do?　(*She's a lawyer.*)

3　**T 4.2** [CD 1: Track 41] Tell students that Ceri is now talking about her life. Ask *Where is Ceri now?* (in the office/at work). Check or pre-teach the following vocabulary from the text: *busy, lunchtime, swimming pool, gym, tired*. Ask students to close their books and listen to the text. Ask *Does she have a busy life?* Students answer, giving examples.

Possible answers
Yes, she does. She's a lawyer, she plays rugby, she goes running, she goes swimming, she trains, she plays matches ... etc.

4　Students read and complete the text with the verbs from the box in the correct form.

T 4.2 [CD 1: Track 41] Play the recording again so that students can check their answers.

Answers and tapescript
I love my job as a family lawyer, because I like helping people. But I **love** playing rugby, too, so my life is very busy! Every lunchtime I go **running** in the park near my office. On Monday and Thursday evenings I **go** to the swimming pool with my boyfriend Alex. On Tuesday and Friday mornings I **get up** at 5.30 and **go** to the gym before work. And on Wednesday evenings I **train** with my team at the club. On Friday evenings I just **relax** because I'm usually very tired! I sometimes **visit** my sister. She **lives** in the centre of Cardiff, too. Or I **cook** a nice dinner at home with Alex. We **love** cooking. After dinner we often **watch** a DVD. We never **go out** on Saturday evenings, because I always **play** in a match on Sundays. I **want** our team to win the next World Cup!

Questions and negatives

5 **T 4.3** [CD 1: Track 42] Elicit the answer to the first question as an example. Ask students to complete Ceri's answers and play the recording to check their answers.

Answers and tapescript
A Where do you work?   B **In** Cardiff.
A Do you like your work?   B Yes, I **do**.
A Do you relax at weekends?   B No, I **don't**.
A Why don't you relax at weekends?
B **Because** I play rugby.

Play the recording again or model the questions and answers yourself. Practise the questions and answers in open pairs across the class to correct any mistakes. Take particular care with these aspects of pronunciation:

Sounds
The weak vowel sound /də/ in the question, and the strong vowel sound /duː/ in the short answer.
Do you like your work?   *Yes, I do.*
/djə laɪk jə wɜːk/   /jes aɪ duː/

Stress and intonation
The intonation rises at the end of *Yes/No* questions and falls at the end of short answers and *wh-* questions.

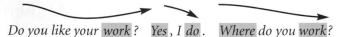

Do you like your work? *Yes, I* do. *Where do you* work?

Roleplay

6 Tell students to read the texts on pp28–9 again first, but then to cover them and try to remember the information about Ceri's life. Ask students to work in pairs and take it in turns to be Ceri Bevan. Demonstrate the activity by getting two students to ask and answer the first two questions across the class. Ask students to continue the activity in pairs. Go round and check for the correct use of the auxiliary *do/does* and for the correct use of strong and weak forms in the pronunciation of *do*.

1 Ask students to complete the table with the positive and negative forms. Check the answers.

Answers

	Positive	Negative
I	work	don't work
You	**work**	**don't work**
He/She/It	**works**	**doesn't work**
We	**work**	**don't work**
They	**work**	**don't work**

Ask students to focus on the positive forms in the table. Ask them which have a different form (*he/she/it*) and how they are different (they end in *-s*).
Ask students to focus on the negative forms in the table. Ask them how the *I/you/we/they* forms are different from the positive forms (they use the auxiliary *don't*). Ask students to focus on the *he/she/it* forms and ask them how they are different from the other negative forms (they use the auxiliary *doesn't*).

2 Ask students to complete the questions and answers. Check the answers.

Answers
Where **do** you work?
Where **does** she work?
Do you work in Cardiff? Yes, I **do**.
Does he work in Cardiff? No, he **doesn't**.

Ask students which auxiliary verb is used in questions with *I/you/we/they* (do) and which with *he/she/it* (does). Remind students that questions can begin with a question word, or have no question word and the answer *Yes/No*. Ask students to give you examples of each type of question from the table.

SUGGESTION
Do exercises 6 and 7 in the Workbook to introduce adverbs of frequency before this activity.

3 Students find the adverbs of frequency in the text about Ceri Bevan.

Read Grammar Reference 4.1 and 4.2 on p139 together in class, and/or ask students to read it at home. Encourage them to ask you questions about it.

Answers
. . . because I **always** play in a match on Sundays.
. . . because I'm **usually** very tired!
After dinner we **often** watch a DVD
I **sometimes** visit my sister.
We **never** go out on Saturday evenings . . . .

PRACTICE (SB p30)

Talking about you

1 Focus attention on the example and then ask students to work on their own. Students who finish early can then check their answers with a partner.

> **Answers and tapescript**
> 1e What time do you go to bed? At 11 o'clock.
> 2b Where do you go on holiday? To Spain or Portugal.
> 3d What do you do on Sundays? I always relax.
> 4c When do you do your homework? After dinner.
> 5a Who do you live with? My mother and sisters.
> 6f Why do you like your job? Because it's interesting.
> 7g How do you travel to school? By bus.
> 8h Do you go out on Friday evenings? Yes, I do sometimes.

T 4.4 [CD 1: Track 43] Play the recording and let students check their answers. As preparation for the next activity, ask students to listen and repeat the questions and answers chorally and individually. Take particular care with intonation.

2 This activity gives practice of the first and second persons only. Ask students to work in pairs to ask and answer the questions in exercise 1. Demonstrate the activity by getting a pair of students to ask and answer the first question across the class. Remind students to have the whole question ready before they speak. Go round and check as students do the activity, listening for correct intonation. Students who finish early can be encouraged to ask similar questions but with different days or question words, e.g. *Do you go out on Saturday evenings? Where do you do your homework?*

3 This activity practises the third person singular alongside the other persons. It also pulls the class together after the pairwork. Focus attention on the examples in the Student's Book. Then ask a few individuals to tell the rest of the class about themselves and their partner. If necessary, remind students they need to use the third person *-s* when talking about their partner. (Unless you have a small class, it would take too long to give everyone a turn.)

Listening and pronunciation

4 **T 4.5** [CD 1: Track 44] Play the recording. Ask students to listen carefully and tick the sentence they hear. Play the recording again. Stop after each sentence and ask students to discuss the answer with a partner before you establish the correct one. You can make this exercise productive by asking students to read the pairs of sentences aloud.

> **Answers and tapescript**
> 1 What does she do on Sundays?
> 2 Do you stay at home on Thursday evenings?
> 3 He lives here.
> 4 What do you do on Saturday evenings?
> 5 I read a lot.
> 6 Why don't you like your job?

Positives and negatives

5 This exercise revises the verb *to be* alongside other verbs in the Present Simple. The exercise could be set for homework, but it can be quite fun if done orally and at a brisk pace with the whole class. Focus attention on the examples and then get students to complete the exercise orally. They could then write their answers afterwards.

> **Answers**
> 3 She speaks Spanish.
> 4 They don't want to learn English.
> 5 We aren't tired and don't want to go to bed.
> 6 Roberto doesn't like watching football on TV, but he likes playing it.
> 7 I don't work at home because I don't have a computer.
> 8 Amelia is happy because she has a new car.
> 9 I don't smoke, I don't drink, and I go to bed early.
> 10 He smokes, he drinks, and he doesn't go to bed early.

VOCABULARY AND SPEAKING (SB p30)

Leisure activities

1 In pairs or small groups, students look at the photos and match as many as they can with the names of the activities. Ask them to check the others in their bilingual dictionary. Encourage them to enter any new words in their vocabulary notebooks.

> **Answers**
>
> | | | | |
> |---|---|---|---|
> | i | playing football | l | sailing |
> | p | dancing | j | listening to music |
> | b | skiing | h | swimming |
> | o | watching TV | k | reading |
> | f | going to the gym | n | eating in restaurants |
> | g | taking photographs | e | going to the cinema |
> | c | cooking | a | going running |
> | d | playing computer games | m | sunbathing |

2 Focus attention on the form *like* + *-ing* using the examples in the Student's Book. Drill the sentences getting students to follow the highlighted stress patterns. Choose a student and give examples of what you think he/she likes doing. Then ask students what they think you like doing. Ask them to continue in groups, choosing five activities from the Student's Book.

Students ask you questions to find out if they were correct about what you like, using the examples in the Student's Book. (Students are often interested to find out about their teacher, but keep this fairly short to allow time for the personalized stage.) Encourage students to follow the stress pattern and use rising intonation for the *Yes/No* questions.

3 First build a dialogue with two students, using the example in the Student's Book and the possible follow-up questions. Then tell the students some true things about yourself, encouraging them to respond to your likes and dislikes as in the example.

Now ask students to continue in pairs and go round the class to check and help them. Make sure they use the *-ing* form.

4 Ask students to think about other activities which are not in the Student's Book. They can look them up in their bilingual dictionary, or ask you for help. Encourage students to mime or describe the activities rather than ask in L1. Finally, ask a few students in the class to report back on themselves and their partners (thereby practising different persons of the Present Simple).

SUGGESTION
You can consolidate the Present Simple and leisure activities from this unit, and also review frequency adverbs from the Workbook, with the photocopiable activity on TB p137. Photocopy enough pages for each student. Briefly review the expressions of frequency from Workbook p21. Put students into pairs. Hand out the questionnaires and get students to complete the questions, using their own ideas for questions 9 and 10. Divide the class into pairs and get students to interview each other, recording their partner's answers. Then put two pairs of students together and get them to compare answers, and report back to the class.

ADDITIONAL MATERIAL

Workbook Unit 4
Exercise 1 This practises all persons of the Present Simple and question formation.
Exercise 2 This practises *do* and *does*, and the verb *to be*.
Exercises 3–5 Present Simple: questions, short answers, and negatives
Exercises 6 and 7 Adverbs of frequency

READING AND LISTENING (SB p32)

My favourite season

SUGGESTION
It would save time in the lesson if you could ask your students to learn the names of seasons and months in English for homework before the lesson. You could give them this list to learn and test them in class.

Seasons

spring /sprɪŋ/	*autumn* /'ɔ:təm/
summer /'sʌmə/	*winter* /'wɪntə/

Months

January /'dʒænjəri/	*July* /dʒu:'laɪ/
February /'februəri/	*August* /'ɔ:gəst/
March /mɑ:tʃ/	*September* /sep'tembə/
April /'eɪprɪl/	*October* /ɒk'təʊbə/
May /meɪ/	*November* /nəʊ'vembə/
June /dʒu:n/	*December* /dɪ'sembə/

With weaker classes, you could ask students to check some of the key words before the lesson: *water sports, surfing, cousin, rainy, cool, flowers, festival, sing, joke.*

1 Ask students to work in pairs and answer the questions in exercise 1. They will obviously find this easier if you set the seasons and months for homework. Monitor, noting any problems with pronunciation and confusion with the months of the year.

POSSIBLE PROBLEMS
Students often confuse the months *March* and *May*, and *June* and *July*. They may also need particular help with the pronunciation of *February* /'februəri/ and *autumn* /'ɔ:təm/.

If your students had difficulties with the questions in exercise 1, now is a good time to present the key language again. Use a calendar as a visual aid, and go through the seasons and months. Say them first yourself and ask students to repeat each one in order both chorally and individually. Repeat the months and seasons a few times, making it fast and fun if you can. If necessary, check further by asking:

What's before/after September? etc.
When's your birthday? (Make sure that students give only the month in their answers *not* the actual date.)

Then ask students the questions in exercise 1 again, checking for accurate pronunciation.

If your students had few difficulties with the questions in exercise 1, briefly go through the answers as class feedback, highlighting any specific problems you noted earlier. If necessary, do further spot checks by asking similar questions to those above.

---

2 Ask students to look at the photos and see if they can identify the seasons. Don't confirm the answers at this stage. Ask students which colours they can see (blue, green, red, pink, yellow, white).

3 **T 4.6** [CD 1: Track 45] Ask students to read the texts and listen to the recording at the same time. Ask them which seasons are mentioned and the speaker's favourite season.

Pause the recording after each speaker to check. You can also ask for the nationality of the speaker. (Check the stress patterns of the nationalities.)

Answers
Daniella is Australian. Her favourite season is summer.
Sumalee is Thai. Her favourite season is 'winter'.
Axel is Norwegian. His favourite season is spring.

4 Ask students to do this exercise in groups of three if possible. Ask each one in the group to read about a different person. Then they can share the information to answer the questions, which will generate more speaking. Ask someone in each group to write down their answers. Give them 5–10 minutes and then bring the whole class together to conduct the feedback. Encourage them to expand answers where applicable (see suggestions in brackets in the answer key).

Answers
1 Daniella likes water sports (surfing, waterskiing, and sailing); Sumalee doesn't play sport; Axel goes skiing.
2 Daniella likes waterskiing and Axel likes skiing down mountains.
3 In the garden.
4 In Chiang Mai (in the north of Thailand).
5 The cool season (their 'winter').
6 They have a flower festival. They sing and dance.
7 No, she doesn't.
8 Because it's the best time to go skiing.
9 In England.
10 Daniella from Australia: July and August
   Sumalee from Thailand: November to February
   Axel from Norway: December to February

5 Ask students to remain in their groups to find the six mistakes in the summary. Point out that students will need to change the use of *and* and *but* in some of the sentences. Get one or two students to read aloud the corrected version to the rest of the class.

Answers
Daniella comes from (1) **Australia**. In summer she goes surfing and sailing. She loves the beach (2) **but she doesn't like** sunbathing.
Sumalee comes from the (3) **north** of Thailand. Her favourite season is (4) '**winter**'. She loves dancing.
Axel comes from Norway. He likes (5) **spring** best. He likes skiing, (6) **and he skis** very fast.

6 **T 4.7** [CD 1: Track 46] Ask students to listen and decide which one is Daniella, Sumalee, and Axel. Play the recording and stop it after each conversation. Ask *Who is it? Where are they? How do you know?* and let students discuss their answers in pairs before checking with the whole class.

Answers
Conversation 1: Axel. (He is with a friend called Mick. They are on a skiing holiday. We know this because they are talking about skiing, the mountains, and the blue sky.)
Conversation 2: Daniella. (She is with her family. They are in their garden having lunch. We know this because they are talking about the weather, and food and drinks.)
Conversation 3: Sumalee. (She is with an American tourist/visitor. They are at the February Flower Festival. We know this because they are talking about the flowers, colours, and dancing.)

T 4.7
A=Axel, M=Mick
1 A So, do you like Norway, Mick?
  M Yes, it's beautiful. Look at the mountains and blue sky! I love skiing here.
  A Yes, I love it too. I ski here every winter and spring.
  M You are lucky.
  A I know! Do you want a coffee now?
  M Yes, please. Good idea.
D=Daniella, M=Mum, B=Bob (Dad)
2 D Phew! It's hot today.
  M It is. Daniella, here are the drinks.
  D OK, Mum!
  M Bob, how are the hamburgers?
  B They're ready!
  M Lovely. And here's the salad. Daniella, can you tell your brother that lunch is ready?
  D Sure, Mum.
  M Thanks. Bob, come and have a drink!
  B Great!
T=Tourist, S=Sumalee
3 T Hello! Can you help me? Can you speak English?
  S Yes. A little.
  T Can you tell me – what festival is this?
  S It's our Flower Festival. We have it every February.
  T It's so beautiful! I love the small pink and white flowers.
  S They are orchids.
  T Wow! There are hundreds!
  S Do you like dancing? We have Thai dancing here this evening.
  T Oh yes. I want to see that!

You could round off the activity by playing the recording again referring students to the tapescripts on SB p128.

What do you think?

This is an attempt to generate some personalized discussion and give further freer practice of the Present Simple. Don't worry if at this level it turns out to be quite a short activity. Just a little free speaking is still worthwhile.

It can be helpful to ask students to discuss the topic in small groups, before you conduct feedback with the whole class.

It would also be a nice idea to encourage students to ask *you* questions about *your* favourite season.

SUGGESTIONS

- Students interview each other to find out when the best month/season is for a certain activity in their country: *When's the best month for (skiing, walking, sunbathing, shopping, visiting your city,* etc.*)?*
- Students write a description of how their home area changes from season to season. Get them to include information on the weather, the colours they can see, the activities people do, and the number of visitors.

Song

The song *Colours* appears in photocopiable format on TB p139. You will find the song after **T 4.7** on the Class Cassette/on CD1 Track 47. Students listen and choose the correct words in the song and then do two comprehension exercises. The answers are on p171.

WRITING (SB p115)

Informal letters

To a penfriend

This writing syllabus continues with the first genre-based section – an informal letter. Writing a letter to a penfriend is a useful task in that it is something that many students may want to do in real life. The unit introduces the conventions in writing informal letters and consolidates basic letter layout. The content of the letter also recycles key language from Units 1–4.

1   Introduce the topic of penfriends by talking about a friend you have from another country – say who the person is, where he or she is from, and whether you write, phone or email each other in English or in another language to stay in touch. Elicit examples from one or two students. Students continue to talk about their foreign friends in pairs. Get brief class feedback.

2   Focus attention on the photo of Becky and elicit basic information about her age and possible nationality. Get

students to read the questions in exercise 1 and then find the answers in Becky's letter.

Answers

- Becky is in Brighton.
- Tiago is in Brazil.
- Becky writes about her name, age, job and family, the languages she speaks, and her leisure activities.

---

3   Ask students to read the letter again and answer the questions. Allow students to check their answers in pairs before checking with the whole class. For the last question, elicit how students write addresses in their country, especially if you have a multilingual class.

Answers

- The letter begins *Dear Tiago* and ends *Best wishes.*
- The date is 5 April.
- 20 Holland Street
  Brighton
- BN2 2WB
- Students' own answers

Focus attention on the two guidance notes on the letter. Remind students that you cannot use *Dear penfriend/ friend* in an informal letter in English. If appropriate, ask students if they can use similar expressions to end an informal letter in their language and elicit any other similarities/differences.

4   Draw up a paragraph plan with the class for the students to follow when they write their own letter:

Greeting
Paragraph 1 thanks; personal information, job, family
Paragraph 2 languages
Paragraph 3 leisure activities/free time
Paragraph 4 questions to penfriend
Ending

Give students time to write their letter in class or set it for homework. If possible, allow students to read and check each other's letters, both for interest and for peer correction. When you check the letters, point out errors but allow students to correct them themselves and try to limit correction to major problems to avoid demoralizing.

Do you have a healthy lifestyle?

1 Focus attention on the title of the questionnaire and on the photo. Check comprehension of the verbs in the questionnaire to explain the idea of healthy lifestyle: *smoke, drink alcohol, drink mineral water, like fast food, walk to school/work.* Students answer the questions and complete the *Me* column about themselves. Then get them to calculate their score and read the answer key.

2 Focus attention on the examples in the Student's Book. Get students to practise the questions and answers following the highlighted stress pattern. Encourage rising intonation for inverted questions. Ask individual students to ask you the questions so that you help and correct them before they continue working with partners.

Ask all the class to stand up and 'mingle' to do the next part of the activity (if there is enough space to do so!). Tell them to take it in turns with two other students to ask and answer the questions.

3 Elicit a range of scores from the class to establish which students are healthy. With larger classes, divide the students into groups, and get them to compare their scores before reporting back to the class.

Writing

4 This part of the activity is designed to revise the third person singular again alongside the other persons. (It could be set for homework or done orally.)

Focus attention on the examples in the Student's Book and highlight the use of the auxiliary *does* to avoid repeating the main verb. Point out that we don't say
* *I don't go to bed early on weekdays, but Sofia goes,* or …
* *Sofia yes.* Ask students to use the information they have collected to write and compare themselves with another student. Then ask one or two students to read what they have written aloud for the others to comment on.

Sample answer
I smoke, but Ana doesn't. She drinks alcohol. We both like fast food, but we don't have breakfast every morning. Ana plays tennis, but I don't. We both get up early on weekdays.

SUGGESTIONS
- You can 'test' how much students can remember about each other's lives by using the ideas in the 'Do you have a healthy lifestyle?' questionnaire and getting the others to guess who is being referred to.
- Students imagine they have a very extravagant and luxurious lifestyle and interview each other, practising *wh-* and *Yes/No* questions.
  Where do you work?   I don't work!
  What time do you get up?   About 11 o'clock.
  Where do you live?   In a very big house in Paris.
  Do you have children?   Yes, but they don't live with me.
  Do you like cooking?   No, I never cook. I have a chef.
  Do you have a busy life?   Of course! I go shopping every day and I go to parties every night!

Social expressions

These conversations introduce and practise expressions for day-to-day conversational exchanges.

1 **T 4.8** **[CD 1: Track 48]** Ask students to work in pairs and complete the conversations with the expressions given. Then play the recording for them to listen and check their answers. Ask students where each conversation takes place and who the speakers are.

Answers and tapescript
1 A **I'm sorry I'm late.** The traffic is bad today.
  B **Don't worry.** Come and sit down. We're on page 25.
2 A **Excuse me.**
  B Yes?
  A Do you have a dictionary?
  B **I'm sorry,** I don't. It's at home.
  A **It doesn't matter.**
3 A It's very hot in here. Can I open the window?
  B **Pardon?**
  A The window, can I open it?
  B **Yes, of course.**
4 A **Excuse me!**
  B Oh, good morning Marco. Can I help you?
  A Yes, please. Can I have a ticket for the trip to York?
  B Yes, of course. It's £80. Do you want to pay £20 deposit now?
  A Sorry. **What does 'deposit' mean?**
  B It means you can pay £20 now and £60 later.
  A Ah! **I see.** Yes, please.

MUSIC OF ENGLISH

T 4.9 [CD 1: Track 49] Read through the *Music of English* box as a class. Play the recording. Students listen and repeat paying special attention to stress patterns and intonation, following the model as closely as possible.

Tapescript

I'm sorry I'm late.	Pardon?
Don't worry.	Yes, of course.
Excuse me.	I see.
I'm sorry.	Excuse me.
It doesn't matter.	What does deposit mean?

2   Students practise the conversations with a partner then, in pairs, learn one of the dialogues by heart to act out for the rest of the class. Remind students to attempt to use the appropriate stress and intonation on an expressions from the *Music of English* box. Acting out dialogues can improve their pronunciation considerably.

SUGGESTIONS

- Students can think of other situations when these expressions would be useful and write or act out parallel conversations.
- Encourage students to use these expressions in class whenever appropriate, e.g. apologizing for being late, asking to borrow something, checking what a new word means, etc. You could put key phrases on a classroom poster.

Don't forget!

Workbook Unit 4
Exercise 8 Listening comprehension practice
Exercise 9 Prepositions of time
Exercise 10 Verbs with opposite meaning, e.g. *love/hate*
Exercise 11 Translation
Exercise 12 A listening exercise on social situations

Grammar Reference
Look at the exercises on SB p140 as a class, or set for homework. The answers are on TB p176.

Word list
Remind students of the Word list on SB p153. They could translate the words, learn them at home, or transfer some of the words to their vocabulary notebook.

Pronunciation Book Unit 4

DVD/Video Episode 1 A new neighbour

PHOTOCOPIABLE MATERIAL: EXTRA IDEAS UNITS 1–4

Reading TB p138
The reading exercise is about a businesswoman and revises Units 1–4. Exercises 1 and 2. Exercise 3 could be used as follow-up in class. could be done for homework. An activity to exploit the reading is provided, and the answers are on TB p171.

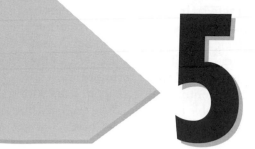

5

There is/are • Prepositions
some/any • *this/that/these/those*
Furniture • Directions 1

Where do you live?

Introduction to the unit

The theme of this unit is places. Students describe a living room, a kitchen, their classroom, and where they live themselves. There is a reading text about a man who has an unusual home – a house that is round like a bubble! This text consolidates the language of the unit and hopefully students will be interested to find out about the home. There are also four very short listenings about homes around the world, as far apart as the USA and Samoa.

Language aims

Grammar – *There is/are*

> **POSSIBLE PROBLEMS**
>
> Students often confuse *It's a …* with *There's a …* . The difference is that *It's a …* defines something and gives it a name. *There's a …* expresses what exists. This is quite a subtle area, and we don't suggest that you explore it with students unless absolutely necessary, using translation as a support.
>
> Learners confuse *there* and *their*. For such a short structural item, there are also a lot of pronunciation problems. Many nationalities have difficulty with the sound /ð/. In *There's*, the *r* is often silent. In *There are* and the question when the following word begins with a vowel, the *r* is pronounced as a linking sound. Again, students need to be encouraged to start questions 'high' and fall, ending with a rise in inverted questions. It is worth working on these pronunciation areas, but not to the point of exhaustion!

Prepositions Simple prepositions of place, such as *on*, *under*, and *next to*, are introduced and practised.

some/any In this unit, *some* and *any* are presented only with count nouns. In Unit 9, they are presented with both count and uncount nouns.

> **POSSIBLE PROBLEMS**
>
> *Some* also presents problems of pronunciation with its weak form /səm/.
>
> *Some* as a concept has a tangible meaning, i.e. a certain, unspecified number of (something). The same cannot be said of *any*. It is a determiner used often (but not exclusively) in questions and negatives. We suggest you do not go into the deeper areas of *any* expressing fundamentally negative ideas. This is unnecessary, and difficult for elementary-level students.

Vocabulary There is quite a high vocabulary load in this unit, including furniture and electrical appliances, classroom and business items, and local amenities. The vocabulary is taught and recycled alongside the main target structures and, for this reason, there is no self-contained *Vocabulary* section.

It is worth checking from time to time how students are progressing with their vocabulary notebooks. Are they still adding to them? Have they started a new one? Do they try to revise regularly? Have they thought of new ways of organizing their notebooks?

Everyday English This is the first activity on directions. The topic is picked up again in Unit 10, where prepositions of movement are introduced.

Writing The syllabus continues with the first focus on linking words: *and*, *so*, *but*, and *because*. Students write a description of their home.

Workbook There is further practice on *there is/are*, *some/any*, prepositions, and *this/that/these/those*. There are also exercises to help students distinguish *There's a …/It's a …* and *this/that/these/those*.

In the *Vocabulary* section, rooms and objects/appliances are revised through a labelling activity and there is also an exercise on verb and noun collocations.

There is a translation exercise to consolidate language from the unit. Further listening practice is provided for directions.

Notes on the unit

> **SUGGESTION**
>
> **Homework prior to the lesson**
>
> Ask students to look up the following words in their dictionary, and put them in their vocabulary notebook.
>
> | | | | |
> |---|---|---|---|
> | *sofa* | *shelf* | *fireplace* | *bedroom* |
> | *armchair* | *cupboard* | *rug* | *bathroom* |
> | *plant* | *curtains* | *flowers* | *living room* |
> | *DVD player* | *lamp* | *mirror* | *kitchen* |

STARTER (SB p36)

> **POSSIBLE PROBLEMS**
>
> Students may need help with pronunciation of some of the key words in this section: *cupboard* /ˈkʌbəd/, *kitchen* /ˈkɪtʃɪn/, *fridge* /frɪdʒ/, *DVD* /diːviːˈdiː/.
>
> You will also need to highlight the stress on the compound words:
> *washing machine*
> Students often confuse *cook* and *cooker*, believing that *cooker* should be a person and not a thing. Be prepared to explain the difference here.

1 Focus attention on the vocabulary and ask students to give two or three examples of correct words to go in the *living room* column. Students continue categorizing the vocabulary in pairs. Check the answers with the whole class. (Note that these are the most usual answers and that students may highlight different places for some items, e.g. a television/telephone in the kitchen.)

> **Answers**
>
> | living room | kitchen | both |
> |---|---|---|
> | an armchair | a fridge | a table |
> | a television | a cooker | a shelf |
> | a CD player | a washing machine | a plant |
> | a lamp | a dishwasher | a cupboard |
> | a telephone | a sink | |
> | a sofa | | |

Drill the pronunciation of the words chorally and individually, focusing on the words in *Possible problems* above in particular.

2 Demonstrate the activity by saying what's in your own living room. You can do this in a natural way starting the sentence *In my living room, there's a/an …* but do not give too much extra detail like size, colour, etc., as the main focus here is the core lexis of furniture and appliances. Students continue the activity in pairs. More able students may be able to include *There is/are …*, but do not insist on this and keep the activity brief.

WHAT'S IN THE LIVING ROOM? (SB p36)

There is/are, prepositions

1 Focus attention on the photos. Read the instruction as a class. Check comprehension by asking who the woman in the photo is (*It's Suzie.*), and where she is (*in the living room of her new flat*). If necessary, you could briefly revise/check the names of the other main rooms in a house or flat: *kitchen*, *bedroom*, *bathroom*, and *toilet*.

Call out the following words and get students to point to the objects in the photo of the living room: *sofa*, *plants*, *shelf*, *television*, *DVD player*, *lamp*, *rug*, *fireplace*, *mirror*, *magazines*, *photos*. (If students have looked up the words for homework, this shouldn't take too long.)

Model the words yourself, and drill them around the class. Correct pronunciation carefully.

Read the example sentences as a class. In a monolingual class, you might want to ask for a translation of *There's* and *There are*. You could ask *Why 'is' and why 'are'?* to establish singular and plural.

Again, model the sentences yourself and do some individual drilling. Insist on accurate linking between *There's a/an …* and *There are … .* Point out that with plural nouns students need to state the exact number. Do not ask them to produce *some* at this stage. Also point out the irregular plural form of *shelf*, *shelves*.

Students then work in pairs to produce more sentences. Allow them enough time to give three or four examples each, but do not let the activity go on too long. Monitor and check for correct use of *there is/are*.

Bring the whole class together again to check the answers. Correct mistakes carefully.

> **Possible answers**
>
> | | |
> |---|---|
> | There's a sofa. | There's a fireplace. |
> | There's a mirror. | There's a DVD player. |
> | There's a television. | There are three plants. |
> | There's a rug. | There are six shelves. |
> | There's a lamp. | |

2 **T 5.1** [CD 1: Track 50] Students read and listen to the questions and complete the answers.

Play the recording again and get students to repeat. Students then practise the questions and answers in open pairs and then closed pairs. Monitor and check for accurate pronunciation (sounds, intonation, stress).

GRAMMAR SPOT

Focus attention on the table. Check students are clear about which words are singular and which words are plural. Get students to complete the table, using contracted forms where they can. Check the answers with the whole class.

Briefly highlight the use of *some* in the positive plural sentence and *any* in the negative plural and question, but do not go into a long grammatical explanation at this stage. (*Some/any* is covered in the next presentation *What's in the kitchen?*)

Read Grammar Reference 5.1 and 5.2 on p140 together in class, and/or ask students to read it at home. Encourage them to ask you questions about it.

3 Focus attention on the words and make sure students realize that the first set is singular and the second set is plural, and that they are going to ask and answer questions about Suzie's living room.

Get a pair of students to ask and answer the example question in open pairs. Elicit an example with a plural word, e.g. *Are there any plants? Yes, there are.* Drill the questions and answers and get students to work in closed pairs to ask and answer questions about the things. Go round the class monitoring, helping as necessary.

Check the answers with the whole class, getting students to repeat their questions and answers in open pairs.

4 This exercise practises/revises prepositions. If you think they will be new to your class, you will need to present them first. Do this very simply, perhaps using classroom objects, such as a book or chair (*The book is on the desk*), or the students themselves (*Juan is next to Maria*).

Refer students back to the photo of Suzie's living room. Ask students to work in pairs to put a preposition into each gap. Check the answers.

Highlight the difference between *in front of*, *behind*, and *next to* by using gestures. You could practise the prepositions further by using your classroom layout.

PRACTICE (SB p37)

What's in your picture?

1 Read the instructions as a class. Divide the class into pairs. Make sure students understand that Student B has a complete picture and that Student A has to draw in objects in the correct place to complete his/her picture. These objects are set above Student A's picture so that he/she knows what to ask about. (The most important thing is that they don't look at their partner's picture!)

Look at the speech bubbles. Point out the use of *Where exactly?* to get precise information about the position of the different objects and the use of the prepositions to give exact positions. Focus attention on the stress highlighting, and remind students that in English it is the important words (i.e. those giving important information) that are stressed.

Pre-teach/check *floor* and then ask students to work in pairs, asking and answering so that Student A can complete their picture. Allow students enough time to complete the information exchange.

When students have finished, get them to compare their pictures and see how well they transferred and interpreted the key information.

> **Answers**
> The lamp is on the small table. Next to the sofa.
> The magazines are on the coffee table. Next to the radio.
> The photos are on the bookshelves.
> The plants are on the floor, in front of the window.
> The clock is on the television.
> The rug is on the floor. Under the coffee table.

2 **T 5.2** [CD 1: Track 51] Ask students to look at the complete picture together on p150 rather than Student A's completed version, just in case there are some objects wrongly located. Read the instructions as a class. Students listen and shout 'Stop!' when they hear a mistake. Point out that we say *on the sofa*, but *in the armchair*. Focus attention on the example and highlighted contrastive stress used when correcting mistakes.

> **Answers**
> **These are the mistakes:**
> 1 There aren't three people. There are four people.
> 2 The girl isn't in the armchair. She's in front of the television.
> 3 There isn't a cat.
> 4 There are some photographs on the bookshelves.
> 5 There aren't any flowers on the table next to the sofa. They're in front of the mirror.
>
> **T 5.2**
> **What's in your picture?**
> There are three people in the living room. A man and a woman on the sofa and a little girl in the armchair. There's a radio on the coffee table and a rug under it. There's a cat on the rug in front of the fire. There are a lot of pictures on the walls but there aren't any photographs. There are two plants on the floor next to the television and some flowers on the small table next to the sofa.

ADDITIONAL MATERIAL

Workbook Unit 5
Exercises 1–4 *There is/are, some/any*, and prepositions.

WHAT'S IN THE KITCHEN? (SB p38)

some/any, this/that/these/those

1 Use the photos in the Student's Book to pre-teach/check the items in the box. Drill the example questions and answers chorally and individually. Elicit the question and answer for a plural form: *Are there any cupboards? Yes, there are.* Drill again. Students continue asking and answering about the things in the box. Monitor and check for correct use

of *Is there a/Are there any* and for accurate pronunciation. Check the answers, drilling again as necessary.

> **Answers**
> Is there a cooker? Yes, there is.
> Where is it? It's in front of Suzie.
> Is there a fridge? Yes, there is.
> Where is it? It's next to Matt.
> Are there any cupboards? Yes, there are.
> Where are they? They're behind Suzie and Matt.
> Are there any cups? Yes, there are.
> Where are they? They're in Suzie's hands.
> Are there any flowers? Yes, there are.
> Where are they? They're next to the cooker.

2 **T 5.3** [CD 1: Track 52] Use the photos in the Student's Book and board drawings to pre-teach/check: *plate, glass, fork, spoon, knife*. Check the plural of these words, pointing out the irregular form *knives* (refer students back to *shelves* on SB p37) and the pronunciation of *glasses*. Students listen to the conversation and fill in the gaps. Let them check in pairs, then play the recording again if necessary. Check the answers. Notice that students are not expected to produce *some* until they have seen and heard it in context.

> **Answers and tapescript**
> **Suzie's kitchen**
> **S=Suzie, M=Matt**
> **S** And this is the kitchen.
> **M** Mmm, it's very nice.
> **S** Well, it's not very big, but there **are a lot** of cupboards. And **there's** a new fridge, and a cooker. That's new, too.
> **M** But what's in all these cupboards?
> **S** Well, not a lot. There are some cups, but there aren't any plates. And I have **some** knives and forks, but I don't have **any** spoons!
> **M** Do you have any glasses?
> **S** No. Sorry.
> **M** Never mind. We can drink this champagne from those cups! Cheers!

3 Students now need to practise using *there is/are* and *a/some/any* in statements. Drill the following sentences around the class. Make sure *some* is weak /səm/.

There's a cooker.	*There are some cupboards.*
There aren't any glasses.	*There's a new fridge.*
There are some flowers.	*There aren't any spoons.*

Describe what is in your own kitchen and how it differs from Suzie's. Get students to talk about their own kitchen in pairs. Go round checking and helping where necessary, but don't over-correct grammar mistakes, as the emphasis here is on fluency.

Bring the class back together and ask for any interesting examples you heard, e.g. the washing machine being kept in the bathroom, or in a special room on its own, or on a balcony! You could ask follow-up questions like *Where's the fridge? Where do you keep food?*, etc.

1 Look at *Grammar Spot* question 1 as a class. Allow students time to think before checking the answer.

2/3 Get students to work in pairs to answer question 2 and complete the sentences in 3. Check the answers with the whole class.

> **Answers**
> 1 *Two magazines* gives us the exact number. *Some magazines* doesn't give us the exact number.
> 2 We say *some* in positive sentences. We say *any* in negative sentences and questions.
> 3 1 I like **this** champagne.   3 **That** cooker is new.
>   2 **These** flowers are lovely. 4 Give me **those** cups.

SUGGESTION

If students have difficulty with the use of *this/that/these/those*, use the classroom environment to briefly revise this language focus. Choose objects near to you to demonstrate *this/these*, e.g. *This is my desk. I like these posters* and objects that you have to point to demonstrate *that/those*, e.g. *That TV is new. We use those books.* Give students objects to hold, or point to objects and get students to say sentences using *this/that/these/those*.

Refer students to Grammar Reference 5.3 and 5.4 on p140.

PRACTICE (SB p39)

In our classroom

1 Elicit the answer to sentence 1 as an example. Students work in pairs or small groups to fill in the gaps.

> **Answers**
> 1 In our classroom there are **some** books on the floor.
> 2 There aren't **any** plants.
> 3 Are there **any** Spanish students in your class?
> 4 There aren't **any** Chinese students.
> 5 We have **some** dictionaries in the cupboard.
> 6 There aren't **any** pens in my bag.

SUGGESTION

If your students need more practice with *some/any*, you could get them to make the statements in exercise 1 true for their own classroom.

2 Elicit an example about your classroom, e.g. *There are some pictures.* Get students to work in pairs and describe their classroom. If necessary, give word cues to

help generate forms, e.g. *television, video, flowers, photos*, etc.

3 Briefly revise the use of *this/that/these/those* and relevant adjectives, e.g. *big, small, new, old*, etc. Focus attention on the examples in the Student's Book. Drill the sentences focusing on the highlighted stress patterns. Then get students to continue talking about things in the classroom in pairs.

What's in Yoshi's briefcase?

4 **T 5.4** [CD 1: Track 53] Focus attention on the photo of Yoshi and get students to say who they think he is, where he is, and what his job is. Read the instruction as a class to check.

Students listen to Yoshi describing what is in his briefcase, and tick the things that are in it.

> **Answers**
> ☑ a newspaper   ☑ a notebook   ☐ a letter
> ☑ a dictionary   ☑ keys   ☑ a mobile
> ☐ a sandwich   ☐ a bus ticket ☐ stamps
> ☑ pens   ☑ photos   ☐ an address book

> **T 5.4**
> **Yoshi's briefcase**
> What's in my briefcase? Well, there's a newspaper – a Japanese newspaper – and there's a dictionary – my Japanese/English dictionary. I have some pens, three, I think. Also I have a notebook for vocabulary. I write words in that every day. And of course I have my keys – my car keys and my house keys. Oh yes, very important, there are some photos of my family, my wife, and my daughter. And there's my mobile. I phone home to Tokyo every night. That's all, I think. I don't have any stamps and my address book is in my hotel.

5 Get students to practise the questions in open pairs focusing on stress highlighting to ensure good rhythm, then continue working in closed pairs. Ask one or two students to say what is in their or their partner's bag. However, try not to be over-curious, as some students may consider it too personal.

Check it

6 Students work in pairs and tick the correct sentence.

> **Answers**
> 1 There aren't any sandwiches.
> 2 Do you have a good dictionary?
> 3 I have some photos of my dog.
> 4 I have a lot of books.
> 5 How many students are there in this class?
> 6 Next to my house there's a park.
> 7 Look at that house over there!
> 8 Henry, this is my mother. Mum, this is Henry.

Workbook Unit 5
Exercises 5–8 *this/that/these/those* and *it/they*

READING AND SPEAKING (SB p40)

Living in a bubble

You could lead in to the topic of the reading text by asking students: *What type of home do you/most people have? Do you know anyone who lives in an unusual home?* (e.g. on a houseboat, in a windmill).

1   Get students to brainstorm rooms in a house and write a list on the board. Elicit possible actions for each room, e.g. *have a shower – bathroom*. Focus attention on exercise 1 and get students to match the sentence halves. Check the answers.

> **Answers**
> We cook in the kitchen.   We eat in the dining room.
> We watch TV in the living room. We work in the study.
> We sleep in the bedroom.

If appropriate, elicit other true sentences for each of the rooms, e.g. *We listen to music in the living room.*

2   Focus attention on the photos and elicit the rooms shown.

> **Answers**
> living room, dining room, bedroom, kitchen, garden room

3   Tell students they are going to read a text about a man with an unusual home. Pre-teach/check *bubble* and *round* using the photos. Check comprehension of the questions. Ask students to work in pairs. Tell them not to worry about words they do not recognize and just to focus on finding the answers. (You may want to set a time limit for this to discourage students from reading too intensively.)

Check the answers. Decide according to the speed and ability of your students whether to settle for quick short answers or whether you want fuller answers (given in brackets).

> **Answers**
> 1   In the south of France. 40 years old. (It's in the south of France. It's 40 years old.)
> 2   Because it's (completely) round. (Because the house is (completely) round.)
> 3   He's a designer.
> 4   Old records, clocks, and round furniture. (He collects old records, clocks, and round furniture.)
> 5   Six. (The living and dining room is one room. There's also a kitchen, garden room, music room, bedroom and bathroom.)
> 6   Yes, there is.

4   Give students time to read through the questions and check the vocabulary. Get them to answer the questions in pairs. Check the answers with the whole class. Encourage students to correct some of the false answers.

> **Answers**
> 1   False. The house is 40 years old.
> 2   False. There are more bubble houses like this in the south of France.
> 3   True.
> 4   False. The centre of the house is the living room and dining room.
> 5   False. He has a music room and collects old records.
> 6   True.
> 7   False. There are two rooms – a bedroom and bathroom.
> 8   False. Lovag is the architect of the bubble houses.

5   Practise the questions and answers in open and closed pairs. Check students can reproduce highlighted stress patterns in the bubbles, and drill the pronunciation of the list of things students have to ask about.

Students continue to ask and answer about the things in the list. Monitor and check for accurate use of *Is there a/an … ?* and *Are there any … ?* and feed back on any common errors. Check the answers with the whole class.

> **Answers**
> Is there a study?   No, there isn't.
> Are there any pictures?   No, there aren't.
> Are there any curtains?   No, there aren't.
> Are there any clocks?   Yes, there are.
> Is there a TV?   Yes, there is.
> Are there any plants?   Yes, there are.
> Are there a lot of kitchen cupboards?   No, there aren't.

What do you think?

Ask students for a few examples of things they like and don't like about Cyril's home, and then allow them to continue exchanging opinions in pairs.

Ask students for any interesting opinions they or their partner gave and find out what they both liked and disliked.

Focus attention on the next question. Ask students for their ideas on the perfect home. Write the ideas on the board. If students show interest, give them time to discuss their ideas in pairs or smaller groups.

The aim is to generate some personalized discussion, so do not insist on complete accuracy.

LISTENING AND SPEAKING (SB p42)

Homes around the world

> **POSSIBLE PROBLEMS**
>
> The listening texts contain quite a lot of words that may be new, or that students might not remember. The listening task is designed to get students to pick out key information, so they should be encouraged not to worry about unknown words.

You *could* refer them to the tapescripts while they listen, or you could do this after they have listened once or twice, and then study the vocabulary. However, try if possible not to use the tapescripts while they listen – but only you know your class!

Even for listening for specific information, you will need to pre-teach/check the following words first: *centre, village, church, verandah, bed and breakfast, blinds, capital city, exciting, light* (n), *alone,*

1 Focus attention on the photos of the four places and get students to match the correct names.

Answers
1 New England   2 Samoa   3 Seoul   4 Lisbon

2 **T 5.5** [CD 1: Track 54] Students listen to the five people talking about where they live and fill in the chart, adding any extra information they have understood. Encourage them to pool information for the last part of the chart. With a weaker class, listen to extract 1 and elicit the information about Manola as an example. Also be prepared to pause the recording between extracts.

Answers

	Candy and Bert	Alise	Kwan	Manola
House or flat?	house	house	flat	flat
Old or modern?	quite old	in the old style	we don't know	old
Where?	in centre of village	near the sea	in centre of city	old town, near the sea
How many bedrooms?	three	one	one	one
Live(s) with?	each other	her family	alone	alone (with her cat)

T 5.5
Homes around the world
Candy and Bert from New England
C Our house is quite old, about fifty years old. It's in the centre of the village near the church. All the houses here are white. We have a living room, quite a big kitchen and three bedrooms, and a big verandah all around the house.
B Our children aren't at home now. They both have jobs in the city, so most of the time it's just Candy and me.
C Yes, so in summer we do bed and breakfast for tourists. We have lovely visitors from all over the world.

Alise from Samoa
I live with my family in a house near the sea. We have an open house, ... er ... that is ... er ... our house doesn't have any walls. Houses in Samoa don't have walls because it is very, very hot, but we have blinds to stop the rain and sun. Our house is in the old style. We have only one room for living and sleeping, so it is both a bedroom and a living room. We have rugs and we sit and sleep on the floor.

Kwan from Korea
I live and work in Seoul, the capital city of Korea. It's a big, modern, exciting city, but it is quite expensive. My flat is very, very small. I have three rooms: a small kitchen, a bathroom, and a room for sitting, eating and sleeping. But I live in the centre of the city, and there are a lot of shops, restaurants and bars near my flat. My work place is near too. I live alone at the moment, but I want to marry my girlfriend next year.

Manola from Lisbon
I live in the old town near the sea. It is called the Alfama. I have a very beautiful flat. There's just one room in my flat, one very big room with one very big window. My bed's next to the window so I see the sea and all the lights of the city when I go to sleep. I live alone, but I have a cat and I'm near the shops and lots of friends come to visit me. I love my flat.

Extra information
Candy and Bert from New England: house is about fifty years old, near the church; all the houses are white; have a living room, quite a big kitchen, three bedrooms, and a big verandah; children aren't at home now, both have jobs in the city; in summer do bed and breakfast for tourists, have lovely visitors from all over world
Alise from Samoa: house doesn't have any walls because is very, very hot in Samoa; have blinds to stop the rain and sun; one room for living and sleeping; have rugs – sit and sleep on the floor
Kwan from Seoul: lives and works in Seoul, capital city of Korea; big, modern, exciting city, but quite expensive; flat is very, very small – three rooms: a small kitchen, a bathroom, and a room for sitting, eating, and sleeping; a lot of shops, restaurants and bars near flat; work place is near too; lives alone at the moment, but wants to marry girlfriend next year
Manola from Lisbon: lives in an old town called the Alfama; has beautiful flat – one very big room with one very big window; bed next to window so can see the sea and lights of city when she goes to sleep; has a cat and lives near shops; lots of friends visit her; loves flat

3 Focus attention on the example about Candy and Bert and Alise. Elicit further examples, using the information in the table and making sure students produce the correct third person singular forms when talking about Alise, Kwan, and Manola. Divide the class into pairs and get students to continue talking about the people. Remind students to stress the 'important' words as shown in the example.

4 Focus attention on the examples in the Student's Book and then get students to ask you questions about where you live. Then get students to continue in pairs or groups of three. Elicit any interesting information from the whole class in a short feedback session.

ADDITIONAL MATERIAL

Workbook Unit 5
Exercise 9 Vocabulary of rooms and activities

WRITING SB (p116)

Describing where you live

Linking words – *and, so, but, because*

Being able to link ideas is an essential skill for students. It's important to give a good grounding in understanding and using linkers, and so the writing syllabus continues with a focus on key linking words for elementary students.

1 Focus attention on the table and elicit an example with *and*: *I like New York and I like Chicago.* Students continue making sentences. Check the answers.

Answers
I like New York and I like Chicago.
I like New York, so I go there a lot.
I like New York, but I don't like Los Angeles.
I like New York because it's an exciting city.

2 Students write similar sentences about where they live starting as shown. You could ask one or two students to read their sentences to the class.

3 Focus attention on the example and then get students to complete the sentences working individually. Give them time to check in pairs before checking with the class.

Answers
2 so   3 because   4 but   5 so   6 but

4 Focus attention on the photos and elicit basic information (*Her name's Suzie. She has a new flat.*) Elicit the first linking word in the text (*but*) and then get students to continue the task. Check answers.

Answers
1 but	5 so	8 and
2 and	6 but	9 and/but
3 and	7 because	10 because
4 but		

5 Give an example by answering the questions in exercise 4 about where you live. Then give students time to write notes about their home, using the questions as prompts. Divide the class into pairs and get students to exchange information about their homes, using the questions in the exercise and their notes.

6 Draw up a paragraph plan from the questions in exercise 4 for students to follow when they write their own description:
Paragraph 1: Where is it?
　　　　　　　Is it old or new?
　　　　　　　How many rooms are there?
Paragraph 2: Who do you live with?
　　　　　　　What is near your home?
Paragraph 3: Do you like it? What do you like best of all?

With weaker classes, go back to the model text in exercise 3 and get students to underline the key structures they will need to use, e.g. *I live* … ., *there's* …, etc.

Give students time to write their description in class or set it for homework. If possible, display the descriptions on the classroom wall or noticeboard to allow students to read each other's work. When you check the students' description, point out errors but allow students to correct them themselves and try to limit correction to major problems to avoid demoralizing.

EVERYDAY ENGLISH (SB p43)

Directions 1

1 Remind students of Suzie and her new flat from pp36–38. Make sure they understand the names of the places and shops on the map. As a class, ask where you can do the things on the list.

POSSIBLE PROBLEMS

Students may query the use of 's in words like *chemist's* and *newsagent's*. Explain that this means the *chemist's/newsagent's shop* but we don't need to say the word *shop*. There might not be the direct equivalent of *newsagent's* in your students' countries. A newsagent sells newspapers, magazines, cigarettes, sweets, and little items such as birthday cards and soft drinks.

Answers

buy: aspirin **at a chemist('s) or supermarket**
a book **at a bookshop (sometimes at a supermarket)**
a DVD **at a music shop or at a supermarket**
some bread **at a baker's or a supermarket**
some milk **at a newsagent's or at a supermarket**
stamps **at a post office (sometimes at a supermarket or newsagent's)**
send an email **at an Internet café**
go for a walk **in the park**
see a film **at the cinema**
have a drink: **at a café, or a pub**
catch a bus: **at a bus stop**

2 **T 5.6** [CD 1: Track 55] Play conversation 1 and elicit the answers from the class as an example. Play conversations 2 and 3, pausing the recording after each one, and get students to complete their answers. With weaker classes, you could play the conversations through first, before students begin to write. Play the recording again to check the answers.

POSSIBLE PROBLEMS

If students query *one* in conversation 3, explain briefly that it's a way of avoiding the repetition of *café*.

Answers and tapescript

1 A **Excuse** me! Is there a **newsagent's** near here?
   B Yes. **It's in** Church Street. Take the first **street on the** right. It's **next to** the music shop.
   A OK. Thanks.
2 A Is there a post office near here?
   B Go straight ahead, and it's **on the** left, **next to** the pub.
   A Thanks a lot.
3 A Excuse me! Is there a **café** near here?
   B There's an Internet café in Park Lane **next to** the bank, and there's an Italian restaurant in Church Street next to the **travel agent's**.
   A Is that one **far**?
   B No. Just two minutes, that's all.

Check that the class understand *Excuse me!*, *over there*, *first/second*, and *near/far*. If necessary, explain the difference between *next to* and *near* (*next to* is two-dimensional, whereas *near* is three-dimensional).

MUSIC OF ENGLISH

T 5.7 [CD 1: Track 56] Read the *Music of English* box as a class. Check students' understanding of *on the corner* by asking them to find the baker's on the map and say where it is. Draw students' attention to the intonation arrows. Write *Excuse me! Is there a chemist's near here? Yes, it's over there.* on the board [with intonation arrows].

Play the recording, following the words with your finger as the recording plays. Students listen and repeat.

Explain to them that this is the 'music of English'. Encourage them to copy the model as closely as possible, and to exaggerate the intonation and stress. Practise the second example. Drill the questions and answers in open pairs across the class. Students continue practising in pairs.

3 Students work in pairs to practise the conversations. Go round the class monitoring, and ensure that students are attempting the polite intonation.

4 Focus students' attention on the expressions in the box. Drill the pronunciation of the places in the list. Point out that we say **the railway station**, not **a railway station**, as there is usually only one in each town. Get students to practise one or two conversations in open pairs across the class. Students continue to work in closed pairs. You could ask some of the pairs to act out their dialogues for the rest of the class. Encourage each student to attempt to use the appropriate intonation and stress pattern, even if the result is not exactly according to the model.

5 Students talk about their own situation. You could do this as a group activity or as a class.

Don't forget!

Workbook Unit 5
Exercise 10 Listening practice on giving directions
Exercise 11 Translation

Grammar Reference
Look at the exercises on SB p140 as a class, or set for homework. The answers are on TB p176.

Word list
Remind students of the Word list on SB p154. They could translate the words, learn them at home, or transfer some of the words to their vocabulary notebook.

Pronunciation Book Unit 5

DVD/Video Episode 2 To the rescue

6 can/can't/could/couldn't • was/were
Words that sound the same
On the phone

Can you speak English?

Introduction to the unit

Skills and ability are the themes of this unit. These are particularly suitable topics to introduce and practise *can/can't* (ability). However, the unit has two main aims in that we also introduce some past tenses for the first time: the past of *can* (ability) – *could*, and the Past Simple of the verb *to be* – *was/were*. The skills work includes a jigsaw reading about two talented teenagers and provides a further context for and practice of the grammar.

Language aims

Grammar – *can/can't* Students have already met the form *can* in the *Everyday English* section of Unit 2, but it is used only as a polite request *Can I have … ?* In Unit 2 it was introduced idiomatically because it is a useful expression.

Here, in Unit 6, the use is extended to ability, and all aspects of the form (statements, questions, negatives) are fully explored and practised.

> **POSSIBLE PROBLEMS**
> 1 Sometimes after all the practising of the Present Simple, students want to use *do/don't* and *does/doesn't* to form the question and negative.
> **Do you can swim?*
> **I don't can swim.*
> 2 A major problem with *can* and *can't* is the pronunciation. Often students find the different realizations of the vowel sounds (/ə/ or /æ/ in *can* and /ɑː/ in *can't*) confusing and, because the final *t* in *can't* tends to get lost, they can't recognize whether the sentence is positive or negative and they have difficulty producing the correct sounds themselves.
>
> | | |
> |---|---|
> | *I can swim.* | /aɪ kən swɪm/ |
> | *Can you swim?* | /kən ju swɪm/ |
> | *Yes, I can.* | /jes aɪ kæn/ |
> | *I can't come.* | /aɪ kɑːŋ kʌm/ |
>
> For these reasons we give special attention to the pronunciation in the unit by including exercises for recognition *and* production.

was/were and could/couldn't These forms are the first introduction to a past tense. We have chosen to present them in a simple and straightforward manner by having students complete a table about the present and past.

> **POSSIBLE PROBLEMS**
> Again pronunciation is a problem. The vowel sounds in *was* and *were* have both weak and strong realizations: *was* /ə/ and /ɒ/; and *were* /ə/ and /ɜː/.
> *He was at home.* /hiː wəz ət həʊm/
> *Was he at home?* /wəz hiː ət həʊm/
> *Yes, he was./No, he wasn't.* /jes hiː wɒz/ /nəʊ hiː wɒznt/
> *Were they at home?* /wə ðeɪ ət həʊm/
> *Yes, they were./No, they weren't.* /jes ðeɪ wɜː/ /nəʊ ðeɪ wɜːnt/
> The pronunciation is focused on and practised in the unit.

Vocabulary and pronunciation We focus on words that sound the same but have a different spelling and meaning, i.e. homophones; for example *see* and *sea*. This provides the opportunity to give more practice of phonetic script.

There are many homophones in English (because of the non-phonetic spelling), and students confuse the two meanings, especially when hearing them (as opposed to seeing them when reading).

Everyday English Language useful for making phone calls is introduced and practised.

Writing The syllabus continues with work on simple formal letters.

Workbook There is further practice on *can/can't*, *was/were*, and *could/couldn't*. The question *How much … ?* is practised with *is* and *was*.

In the *Vocabulary* section, more words that commonly go together are practised (*ask a question*, *get up early*).

There is an exercise to revise and extend coverage of prepositions and a *Check it* section with a translation exercise and further listening practice.

Notes on the unit

STARTER (SB p44)

1   Briefly check the pronunciation of the languages and focus attention on the example. If necessary, drill the pronunciation of the countries and languages in pairs, especially where there is a change in stress, e.g. *Japan*, *Japanese*

Students work in pairs and say where each language is spoken. Check the answers.

> **Answers**
> They also speak French in Switzerland, Belgium, and some parts of Africa.
> They speak Spanish in Spain, Mexico, parts of South and Central America, Cuba, and the USA.
> They speak German in Germany, Austria, and Switzerland.
> They speak Italian in Italy and Switzerland.
> They speak Portuguese in Portugal, Brazil, Angola, and Mozambique.
> They speak Japanese in Japan.
> They speak English in Great Britain, the USA, Canada, Australia, New Zealand, Singapore, the West Indies, and India (and in many other countries as the language of tourism, business, and technology).

2   Tell the class which languages you can speak and focus attention on the example. Students continue to work in pairs or small groups. If you have a small group, allow each student to tell the rest of the class about their language skills. If you have a big group, select just a few students to feed back, but make sure you choose different students at the next feedback stage, so that everyone gets a chance.

WHAT CAN YOU DO? (SB p44)

can/can't

1   This is quite a simple presentation. The aim of the photos is to illustrate the meaning of *can* and *can't*. The sentences are recorded to provide models of the different realizations of the vowel sounds and to raise students' awareness of these from the start.

First, ask students to look at the photos and elicit basic information about the Brady family. (*How many children are there in the Brady family? How old are they? What nationality is the father? And the mother?*)

Ask students to read the sentences. (Most of the vocabulary should be familiar or obvious from the picture, but check that there are no isolated difficulties.) Check comprehension of *quite well* and *really well* by giving personal examples. Students then match the sentences to the photos and write the appropriate sentence number in the boxes provided.

T 6.1 [CD 1: Track 57] Students can discuss their answers with a partner before listening to check. Then check the answers with the whole class. Ask students to repeat the sentences after listening to each one.

> **Answers**
> 1c 2e 3a 4b 5d

GRAMMAR SPOT

1   Focus attention on the *Grammar Spot*. Students work in pairs and say all the persons of *can/can't*. Ask them what they notice about the verb form for each person. Check students are clear about the answer.

> **Answer**
> *Can/can't* are the same for all persons, so there is no *-s* added in the *he/she/it* forms. We do not use the auxiliary *don't/doesn't* to form the negative.

Pronunciation

2   **T 6.2** [CD 1: Track 58] This activity focuses on the pronunciation of *can/can't* in the positive, questions, and short answers. Play the recording and get your students to read and listen very carefully to the pronunciation of *can* and *can't*. First, ask generally *Can you hear differences?* If necessary, repeat the sentences yourself, exaggerating the vowel sounds in *can* and *can't* and isolating them /ə/, /æ/, /ɑː/, so that your students can fully appreciate the differences. Focus attention on the stress highlighting. Ask *When is 'can' pronounced /kən/? (When it is unstressed.)* Play the recording again and get students to repeat chorally and individually.

3 Focus attention again on the sentence stress in the positive and negative sentences. Drill the sentences and then get students to practise in pairs.

Read Grammar Reference 6.1 on p141 together in class, and/or ask students to read it at home. Encourage them to ask you questions about it.

SUGGESTION

If your students need more practice with the pronunciation of *can/can't*, play the sentences from exercise 1 again and get students to repeat. (The sentences are produced below in phonetic script.)

1 /ʃi: kən wɔ:k naʊ/
2 /wi: kən drɔ: bət wi: kɑ:nt raɪt/
3 /aɪ kən sɪŋ kwaɪt wel/
4 /kən ju: pleɪ ðə drʌmz/ /jes aɪ kæn/ /nəʊ hi: kɑ:nt/
5 /kən ðeɪ dɑ:ns/ /jes ðeɪ kæn maɪ dædz əʊkeɪ ənd maɪ mʌm kən dɑ:ns fləmeŋkəʊ rɪəli wel/

---

2 **T 6.3** [CD 1: Track 59] This is a dictation to check that your students can recognize what they hear. Pre-teach/check *cook* and *drive*. Play the first sentence and elicit the answers as an example with the whole class. Ask students to listen and write in the answers. Pause the recording after each sentence. Then ask them to check their answers with a partner. Play the recording again as you conduct a full class feedback. (You could also give them the tapescript.)

Answers and tapescript
1 I **can speak French**, but I **can't speak German**.
2 He **can't dance**, but he **can sing**.
3 '**Can** you **cook**?' 'Yes, I **can**.'
4 They **can ski**, but they **can't swim**.
5 We **can dance** and we **can sing**.
6 '**Can** she **drive**?' 'No, she **can't**.'

Play the recording again and get students to repeat chorally and individually.

PRACTICE (SB p45)

Lucía can't cook. Can you?

1 This is a recognition exercise that moves into a production stage. This time the recording is much more natural-sounding, not being a series of sentences for dictation, but a girl talking about her abilities.

T 6.4 [CD 1: Track 60] Ask your students to listen to Lucia and put a ✔ next to things she can do or a ✘ next to the things she can't do in the first column in the chart. Play the first sentence of the recording as an example. Then play the rest of the recording and get students to complete the task.

Put students into pairs to compare their answers. Then conduct a full class feedback to establish the correct answers. Let students listen again if necessary.

Answers

drive a car	✘	ski	✔
speak French	✘	swim	✔
speak Spanish	✔	play the guitar	✘
cook	✘	dance	✔
play tennis	✔	use a computer	✔

T 6.4 Lucia
Well, there are a lot of things I can't do. I can't drive a car, of course, I'm only 14. Languages? Well, I can't speak French, but I can speak Spanish. My mother's Spanish, and we often go to Spain. My mum's a really good cook. She can cook really well, not just Spanish food, all kinds of food, but I can't cook at all. I just love eating! What about sports? Er … I think I'm good at quite a lot of sports. I can play tennis, and I can ski. Sometimes we go skiing in the Spanish Pyrenees. And of course I can swim. But musical instruments – no – I can't play any at all. But I can dance! I dance flamenco with my mum sometimes. I love it. And I can use a computer, of course. All my friends can.

---

2 The exercise now becomes personalized. Students complete column 2 of the chart about themselves.

3 This is the productive phase of the activity. Practise the questions in the Student's Book in open and closed pairs. Encourage students to distinguish between the strong and weak forms of *can*, and to stress the words that are highlighted. Focusing their attention on the stressed words should help them produce any weak forms.

SUGGESTION
1 Make sure students use appropriate rising intonation with the *Yes/No* questions, and falling intonation with the short answers.

Can you ski? Yes, I can.

2 Make sure that they pronounce the *t* on the end of the negatives. The two consonants *nt* together are difficult for many nationalities.

Students work in pairs and ask and answer questions about each of the activities in the chart. Go round and monitor and help as they do this.

Then round off the activity by asking a few members of the class to tell the others about their and their partner's abilities. Focus on the highlighted contrastive stress in the speech bubble.

What can computers do?

> **NOTE**
> This can be quite a contentious activity because students tend to disagree about what exactly computers can do, and/or the degree to which they can do it.

4 Check comprehension of the key vocabulary: *poetry, feel ill, laugh, play chess, hear, fall in love.* Put your students into pairs to do this activity. (We are hoping that discussion and disagreement will generate some freer speaking in English, in which case the activity can last some while. However, be grateful for any efforts at students expressing their opinions and don't worry if the activity is quite short.)

In the sample answers we have included an extra section (*They can ... but ...*), which is for your information only. You can choose how/if you deal with this extra information.

> **Sample answers**
> **They can ...**
> translate (but word for word, not overall meaning), check spellings, speak English (only in limited fashion with unnatural intonation), make music (but not like Mozart!), play chess, have conversations (but limited and misunderstanding context), hear (they can recognize some speech, but limited)
> **They can't ...**
> write poetry, feel ill, laugh, think (because they work completely in numbers), fall in love

Conduct a feedback session with the whole class. Elicit other examples of what you can/can't do with a computer, e.g. *You can buy things, but you can't touch the things you want to buy.*

Ask students to imagine they live in 2050. In small groups or pairs students think of examples of what computers can do in 2050. e.g. *have interesting conversations, organise the home and housework, look after the children.*

ADDITIONAL MATERIAL

Workbook Unit 6
Exercises 1 and 2 These practise *can* and *can't*.

WHERE WERE YOU YESTERDAY? (SB p46)

was/were, can/could

This is a very direct presentation of the past of the verbs *to be* and *can.* It revises the present of the verbs and then moves straight to the past tense equivalents.

Pre-teach/check *yesterday,* by looking at the first example with the class.

T 6.5 [CD 1: Track 61] Play the recording. Students listen and write in the answers. When they have finished, go through the exercise with them, modelling the questions and answers for them to repeat, and focusing on the weak vowel sounds of *was* and *were* (/wəz/ and /wə/) in statements and questions, and the strong vowel sounds (/wɒz/, /wɒznt/, /wɜː/, /wɜːnt/) in short answers and negatives.

> **POSSIBLE PROBLEM**
> **The negatives**
> The groups of consonants in the negatives *wasn't* /wɒznt/, *weren't* /wɜːnt/ and *couldn't* /kʊdnt/ may be difficult for some students and may need extra choral and individual repetition.

As you go through the presentation, keep backtracking by asking individual students to answer the earlier questions again.

Finally, get your students to ask and answer the questions in open pairs across the class. Use the opportunity to check and correct them carefully. You can move on to practice in closed pairs, unless you think this may prove too laborious.

GRAMMAR SPOT

1 Focus attention on the examples. Then put your students into pairs to complete the table with the past of *to be.* Quickly check through the answers with the whole class.

> **Answers**
>
> | | Positive | Negative |
> | --- | --- | --- |
> | I | was | wasn't |
> | You | were | weren't |
> | He/She/It | was | wasn't |
> | We | were | weren't |
> | They | were | weren't |

Pronunciation

2 **T 6.6** [CD 1: Track 62] This is a repetition exercise with some more questions and answers to help consolidate the pronunciation. As with *can,* focus attention on the stress highlighting. Ask *When are was/were* pronounced /wəz/, /wə/? (*When they are unstressed.*) Insist on accurate pronunciation of the strong and weak forms.

3 Students complete the positive and negative forms of the past of *can.*

> **Answers**
> **Positive could** (all persons)
> **Negative couldn't** (all persons)

Read Grammar Reference 6.1 and 6.2 on p141 together in class, and/or ask students to read it at home. Encourage them to ask you questions about it.

PRACTICE (SB p47)

Talking about you

1 Drill the first question and answer in open pairs. Students continue asking and answering the questions in closed pairs. Monitor and help. Encourage them to ask about times other than those listed in the book. Round the activity off by asking one or two students to tell the others about their partner.

2 Focus attention on the photo and ask students *Who can you see?* (Emma and Marco.) Set the scene of the conversation by telling students that the two friends are talking about parties they've been to. Check that they realize that they can only use *was, were, wasn't, weren't,* and *couldn't* to fill the gaps. Elicit the answer to go in the first gap as an example.

Ask students to work in pairs to do the exercise. Play the recording for them to listen and check their answers.

Play it again and ask students to focus on the pronunciation, not only of *was* and *were,* but of the stress and intonation of the questions and answers.

T 6.7 [CD 1: Track 63] Play the recording for students to check their answers.

Ask one or two pairs of students to take the parts of Emma and Marco and read the conversation aloud across the class. Encourage lively and natural pronunciation.

Answers and tapescript
E=Emma, M=Marco
E **Were** you at Charlotte's party last Saturday?
M Yes, I **was**.
E **Was** it good?
M Well, it **was** OK.
E **Were** there many people?
M Yes, there **were**.
E **Was** Pascal there?
M No, he **wasn't**. And where **were** you? Why **weren't** you there?
E Oh . . . I **couldn't** go because I **was** at Sergio's party! It **was** brilliant!
M Oh!

Now ask the class to practise the conversation again in closed pairs. Monitor and help as they do this. (Don't let this go on too long otherwise it will become boring!)

SUGGESTION
Try to personalize the language as much as possible by getting students to use real parties or other events they have been to recently as the basis for similar conversations, e.g. a rock concert, John's party last Sunday, the disco last Friday evening, the football match last week.

Put some skeleton dialogue prompts on the blackboard and ask pairs of students to come to the front of the class and act out their ideas, e.g.

... *the rock concert last Sunday?*   ... *(Tom) there?*
... *good?*   ... *brilliant!*
... *many people?*

Four geniuses!

This section brings together *could, couldn't,* and *was,* and it also introduces *to be born* and *until.* It continues the theme of skills and talents, but this time focuses on some famous characters. Students are also given the opportunity to personalize the language.

3 In pairs students discuss what each person is famous for. Divide the class into small groups to check their ideas, before confirming the answers with the whole class.

Answers (left to right)
Salvador Dalí – art, Charlotte Brontë – writing plays/stories, Tiger Woods – playing golf, Albert Einstein – science

POSSIBLE PROBLEM
(I) was born is taught here as an expression, not as an example of the passive. Don't be tempted to go into the grammar. Some students translate from their own language and want to say **I am born.*

4 Focus attention on the example. Check comprehension of *was born* and *until* and drill the pronunciation. Ask students to give you a complete sentence about Salvador Dalí, matching lines in columns A, B, and C.

Check the rest of the answers with the whole class. (It is true that Einstein couldn't speak until he was eight!)

Answers
1 Salvador Dalí was born in Spain in 1904. He could paint when he was one.
2 Charlotte Brontë was born in England in 1816. She could write plays when she was four.
3 Tiger Woods was born in the USA in 1975. He could play golf when he was three.
4 Albert Einstein was born in Germany in 1879. He couldn't speak until he was eight!

5 Drill the questions in the Student's Book, highlighting the falling intonation in the *wh-* questions. Students continue working in pairs, asking and answering about the geniuses.

6 This is the personalization stage. Drill the questions in the *you* form, getting students to repeat them in chorus and individually. Make sure the students can hear the difference between *where* and *were*, and again insist on accurate intonation.

Students work in small groups and ask and answer the questions. At the end of the activity, ask a few students to tell you what they can remember, e.g. *Laura was born in Madrid in 1985. She could read when she was five.*

SUGGESTION
Students could think of some famous talented people that they know and make similar sentences about where/when they were born and what skills they had at different ages.

Check it

This exercise practises the grammar of the unit.

7 Ask students to work in pairs or small groups to choose the correct sentence. Ask them to work quite quickly, then conduct a full class feedback on which are the correct answers. Try to get students to correct each other and explain any mistakes they hear.

Answers
1 I can't use a computer.
2 I can speak English very well.
3 I'm sorry. I can't go to the party.
4 He could play chess when he was five.
5 Were they at the party?
6 She wasn't at home.

ADDITIONAL MATERIAL

Workbook Unit 6
Exercises 3–5 These practise *was* and *were*. Exercise 4 is suitable for oral work and could be used in class. Exercise 5 practises past and present tense forms covered so far.
Exercise 6 This practises *could* and *couldn't* with *was*, *were*, and *can/can't*.

READING AND SPEAKING (SB p48)

Talented teenagers

This activity is a jigsaw reading. This means it should result in not only reading practice, but also some freer speaking.

The class divides into two groups and each group reads a different, but similar text about a talented teenager and answers the questions. After this, students from the different groups get together to exchange information about the person in their text. This means that they should get some speaking practice whilst their main attention is on the completion of the reading task.

These texts are based on real people and have been written to include examples of the grammar taught in this and previous units.

You need to be very clear when giving instructions for any jigsaw activity. If necessary and possible, give them in L1.

1 Discuss the questions in exercise 1 with the whole class. Focus attention on the photographs of the two teenagers and elicit guesses about what they can do.

2 Divide the class into two groups. Tell Group A to read about the singer and Group B to read about the writer. Ask each group to read through their text as quickly as possible to get a general understanding of it and to check if their guesses about the teenagers were correct.

3 Get students to read the text again more slowly and find the information in their text to answer the questions about Joss or Christopher. Most of the vocabulary in the texts should be known, but allow students to use dictionaries if they can't guess from the context. With weaker classes, you could pre-teach/check the following items: the soul singer – *soul, blues, shy, voice, note, worried*; the fantasy writer – *bestseller, magic, characters, story*.

When they have read the texts, the students could either go through the questions on their own and then check with others from the same group, or work with a partner from the same group to answer the questions. Each group has the same questions to answer.

Check the answers with Group A students and Group B students separately. The main idea of these questions is to check understanding, therefore short answers are perfectly acceptable. However, when you have a full class feedback you might want to encourage further language production, such as in the brackets below.

Answers
Group A – Joss Stone
1 She's seventeen.
2 She sings soul and the blues.
3 (She was born) in Devon (in the south of England).
4 (She lives) in a small village in the English countryside.
5 (She lives) with her family.
6 Yes, she does.
7 She could sing very well.
8 No-one in her family can sing. (Her mum can't sing a note.)
9 She was in New York.
10 (She was in New York) to make a record.

Group B – Christopher Paolini

1 He's fifteen.
2 He can write very well/bestsellers.
3 (He was born) in Montana in the USA.
4 (He lives) in Paradise Valley.
5 (He lives) with his family.
6 No, he doesn't. (His parents teach him at home.)
7 He couldn't read very well.
8 (They were surprised) that *Eragon* (his first book) was so good.
9 He was in New York.
10 (He was in New York) for interviews.

4 Tell each student to find a partner from the other group and go through the questions and answers together, telling each other about the teenager in their article. Try not to offer help at this stage – let students exchange the information themselves as far as possible.

SUGGESTION

If possible, play a short section of a song by Joss Stone and/or show students the cover of a CD by Joss Stone or a book by Christopher Paolini. This will help to put the information in the texts into a broader context.

5 This stage allows students to summarize the information from both texts and also provides useful consolidation of the *he/she* and *they* forms with various structures. Focus attention on the examples in the Student's Book and then get students to continue discussing similarities and differences in pairs.

Sample answers

They both live with their families. Both Joss's and Christopher's parents were surprised at their child's talent. They were both in New York last month.

Joss is 17 but Christopher is 15. Joss goes to school but Christopher's parents teach him at home. Christopher lives in the USA, but Joss lives in England.

Conduct a general feedback session with the whole class. If appropriate, ask students if they know of any other very talented teenagers, or to comment on Joss's and Christopher's lifestyle.

POSSIBLE PROBLEM

If students become involved in discussion activities, they often start to talk in L1 in their frustration to get their point across. Don't worry too much if this happens, at least it shows that they are interested! Gently encourage them to try and express something in English as this is such good practice, and don't correct them too much. The aim of this activity is fluency, not accuracy.

Roleplay

SUGGESTION

You might find that time is short for the roleplay or that it might be too difficult for your students as it stands, so an alternative approach is included here. Photocopy the interview on TB p141 and ask your students to complete the gaps either in class or for homework. They can choose which teenager is being interviewed.

Answers

1 ask 2 are 3 go 4 who 5 were 6 were 7 what
8 go/travel

6 Assign roles of the journalist and Joss or Christopher, or allow students to choose the role they want. Focus attention on the examples in the Student's Book and then get students to prepare the interview, using the questions in exercise 3 to help them. Allow sufficient time for students to make notes, but discourage them from writing out the interview word for word. Get students to practise the interview in pairs and then act it out in class. (If time is short, use the alternative approach in the *Suggestion* above.)

VOCABULARY AND PRONUNCIATION (SB p50)

Words that sound the same

This activity introduces your students to homophones: words that have different spellings and meanings, but which sound the same. Of course, it is not important that your students learn the linguistic term *homophone*, but it is important that they are aware of such words, as there are so many in English and they can be particularly confusing when listening. The use of phonetic script in the activity serves not only to continue the process of getting to know it, but also to highlight the fact that there is often no relation between sounds and spellings in English.

1 This is to illustrate what is meant by words that sound the same. Ask your students to read aloud the sentences to themselves and then ask for suggestions about the words in bold. They should easily notice that the words sound the same but are spelt differently and have different meanings.

/raɪt/ = *write* and *right*

/aɪ/ = *eye* and *I*

/nəʊ/ = *no* and *know*

2. Ask students to work in pairs to do this. Most of the words are taken from previous units and should be familiar, but allow them to check new words. Whilst they are doing the exercise, write the words in A on the board in a column.

Bring the class together to go through the exercise and invite students, in turn, up to the board to write the words that sound the same next to each other.

3 This exercise puts some of the words which have the same sound but different spelling in context and should be good fun to do. Focus attention on the example and then ask students to work in pairs to complete the task. Then check through with the whole class, asking individuals to spell the correct words.

T 6.8 [CD 1: Track 64] Play the recording. Students listen and repeat.

Answers and tapescript
1 I can **hear** you, but I can't **see** you.
2 **There** are three bedrooms in **our** house.
3 I don't **know where** Jill lives.
4 My **son** lives near the **sea**.
5 Don't **wear** that hat, **buy** a new one!
6 **No**, **I** can't come to your party.
7 You were **right**. Sally can't come **for** dinner.
8 **Their** daughter could **write** when she was three.
9 I **know** my answers are **right**.

4 You could begin this by asking the class to chant through the phonetic transcriptions together to check their progress in reading them.

Remind students of the phonetic symbols chart on SB p159. Ask them to work on their own to do the exercise and then check their answers with a partner before you go through it.

Answers

1	/nəʊ/	know	no	4	/raɪt/	write	right
2	/sʌn/	son	sun	5	/hɪə/	hear	here
3	/tuː/	too	two	6	/weə/	wear	where

ADDITIONAL MATERIAL

Workbook Unit 6
Exercise 7 Words that go together, e.g. *paint pictures*

EVERYDAY ENGLISH (SB p50)

On the phone

1 Explain that this section focuses on the language needed to get phone numbers through International Directory Enquiries. Focus attention on the cards and explain that they show the names and addresses of people that the students want to phone.

T 6.9 [CD 1: Track 65] Focus attention on the first person (Lisa Jefferson) and on the example in the conversation. Check/pre-teach *initial*. Students listen and answer the operator's questions and get Lisa's telephone number. Do this as a class activity, getting students to call out the answers.

Answers and tapescript
Operator International Directory Enquiries. Which country, please?
You The USA.
Operator And which town?
You Boston.
Operator Can I have the last name, please?
You Jefferson.
Operator And the initial?
You L.
Operator What's the address?
You 89 Franklin Street.
Recorded message The number you require is **001 616 326 1204**.

Check students have written Lisa's phone number down correctly.

Roleplay

2 Divide the class into pairs and get Students A to turn to p148 and the Students B to p150. Students work in pairs to roleplay the operator and someone wanting Yoshi and Fernando's telephone number.

Briefly check students have exchanged the information correctly.

Answers
Yoshi: Tel/fax: (75) 842 2209
Fernando: Tel/fax: (998) 764 9832

3 **SUGGESTION**
This activity includes some of the typical expressions used over the phone in English. Make sure students understand that each language uses different expressions over the phone and if they translate from their own language, they may cause confusion or surprise! Point out in particular that in English you cannot say *I'm (Jo)* when saying who is speaking.

Check comprehension of: *Great!*, *get someone* (as in 'fetch'), *Never mind*, *ring back*, *message*. Focus attention on the *Caution Box* on p51 and the use of *will* to make offers or promises. (Do not focus on other uses of *will*, e.g. simple future, at this stage, as this may confuse students.) Ask students to look at the photos and say if the situations shown are formal or informal. Elicit the correct line for the first gap in conversation 1. Students work individually to complete the conversations and then discuss their answers in pairs.

4 **T 6.10** [CD 1: Track 66] Students listen and check.

> **Answers and tapescript**
> **T 6.10**
> 1 A Hello.
>   B Hello. Can I speak to Jo, please?
>   A This *is* Jo.
>   B Oh! Hi, Jo. This is Emma. Is Sunday still OK for tennis?
>   A Yes. That's fine.
>   B Great! I'll see you on Sunday at ten, then. Bye!
>   A Bye!
> 2 A Hello.
>   B Hello. Is that Emma?
>   A No, it isn't. I'll just get her.
>   C Hello, Emma here.
>   B Hi, Emma. It's Marco. Listen! There's a party at my house on Saturday. Can you come?
>   C Oh sorry, Marco. I can't. It's my sister's wedding.
>   B Oh, never mind. Perhaps next time. Bye!
>   C Bye!
> 3 A Good morning. Barclays Bank, Watford. How can I help you?
>   B Good morning. Can I speak to the manager, please?
>   A I'm afraid Mr Smith isn't in his office at the moment. Can I take a message?
>   B Don't worry. I'll ring back later.
>   A All right. Goodbye.
>   B Goodbye.

> ## MUSIC OF ENGLISH
>
> **T 6.11** [CD 1: Track 67] Read through the *Music of English* box as a class, focusing on the stress highlighting, linking lines, and intonation arrows. Play the recording. Students listen and repeat, producing the stress, word linking and intonation in a natural way.

5 Students practise the conversations in pairs, then invent more telephone conversations, based on the ones in the Student's Book. They can change the names, times, arrangements, etc. but should keep the basic format of each conversation.

Formal letters

Applying for a job

Unit 6 introduces some of the key conventions of formal letters including layout, greetings and endings, and overall style. Students get the opportunity to analyse a model letter written in reply to a job advertisement and then complete a guided writing task. This is the type of letter students may well need to write at some stage in their learning.

1 Give students time to read the advertisement and answer the questions.

> **Answers**
> The job is a receptionist.
> It's at The Oxford International School.

2 Focus attention on the information about Carol and ask students if they think she is the right person for the job. Elicit reasons (*Carol is a good candidate, because she has experience of working with people, she speaks two foreign languages, she knows Oxford well, and she probably used a computer in her last job.*)

3 Focus attention on Carol's letter and elicit the answers to the first two gaps as examples. Then give students time to complete the letter, using the information about Carol. Check the answers with the class.

> **Answers**
>
> | 1 | Road | 5 | live | 9 | can |
> |---|---|---|---|---|---|
> | 2 | Street | 6 | am a | 10 | languages |
> | 3 | receptionist | 7 | was | 11 | use |
> | 4 | am 28 | 8 | like | 12 | was |

Briefly review the content of Unit 4 on SB p115 by eliciting the key parts of a letter: date, address(es), *Dear …*, ending, signature. Focus attention on the model letter and on the guidance notes about formal letters on SB p117 again. Give students time to read through each note and then ask check questions, e.g. *How many addresses are there?* (two), *Which one is on the right?* (the writer's), *Where does the date go?* (under the reader's address), *How do you begin the letter?* (*Dear…*), *How do you end the letter?* (*Yours sincerely*).

Ask students why Carol uses *Ms* in the greeting (because she doesn't know if Anne is married or not). Elicit the difference between *Miss* (for a single woman) and *Mrs* (for a married woman). At this stage, do not explain the difference between *Yours faithfully* and *Yours sincerely* as this is covered in Unit 9.

Focus attention on the paragraph labels. Point out that *I look forward to hearing from you* is a standard expression that can be used in any formal letter to request a reply.

4 Focus attention on the advertisement and elicit the job (*tourist guide*). Check comprehension of the details, e.g. *Who do you write to?* (Peter Mann), *Where?* (Happy Holidays, Central Office, 89 Brook Street, London, W1 5PW), *What are the 'qualifications'?* (over 18, like talking to people, know your town well, speak English, free from July to September). Get students to answer the questions in the advertisement about themselves.

Remind students to use Carol's letter in exercise 3 as a model and to follow the paragraph plan. Give students time to write their letter in class or set it for homework. If possible, allow students to read and check each other's letters, both for interest and to help each other with mistakes. When you collect in the letters, check for the correct layout and use of greeting, ending, and full forms. Point out errors but allow students to correct them themselves and try to limit correction to major problems to avoid demoralizing.

Don't forget!

Workbook Unit 6
Exercise 8 Prepositions
Exercise 9 Translation
Exercise 10 Listening practice on telephone language

Grammar Reference
Look at the exercises on SB p141 as a class, or set for homework. The answers are on TB p176.

Word list
Remind students of the Word list on SB p154. They could translate the words, learn them at home, or transfer some of the words to their vocabulary notebook.

Pronunciation Book Unit 6

Video/DVD Episode 2 To the rescue

Past Simple 1 – regular verbs
Irregular verbs • Words that go together
What's the date?

Then and now

Introduction to the unit

The past (the early part of the 20th century) and more recent past (the 1980s) are the themes of this unit. Within these contexts both regular and irregular forms of the Past Simple are presented. The formation of the question and negative is introduced, but the latter is only minimally practised because it is one of the main grammatical aims of Unit 8. The skills work includes a jigsaw reading with texts on two famous 'firsts' – Amelia Earhart and Yuri Gagarin – which provides further practice of the Past Simple.

Language aims

Grammar – Past Simple 1 The learning of the Past Simple is facilitated by students' knowledge of the Present Simple, in that both tenses use a form of *do* as an auxiliary in the question and negative. It is not such a big leap to learn that the same auxiliary is used in its past tense form, *did*, to make the Past Simple tense, especially as this form remains constant in all persons.

Many of the exercises in this unit provide opportunities to contrast the Present and Past Simple tenses.

POSSIBLE PROBLEMS

1   Although students should be helped by their knowledge of the Present Simple (see above), the use of *did* still causes problems and students forget to use it, for example:
    * *Where you went last night?*
    * *When she start school?*
    * *She no liked her job.*

2   There are a large number of irregular verbs to learn. From now on students should be encouraged to consult the irregular verb list on SB p159 and learn the irregular verbs as and when needed. You could start setting some to learn for homework and giving short tests on them at the beginning of some lessons!

3   The different realizations of the pronunciation of *-ed* at the end of regular verbs is a problem. Students always want to pronounce the *-ed* in its entirety – /ed/ – and not the /t/, /d/, /ɪd/ endings, for example:
    cleaned */kliːned/ instead of /kliːnd/
    worked */wɜːked/ instead of /wɜːkt/
    visited */vɪzɪted/ instead of /vɪzɪtɪd/

    There is an exercise to help students perceive the different endings, but we suggest you avoid spending too much time getting students to produce the endings at this stage so as not to overload them.

Vocabulary and listening The focus of this section is words that go together, i.e. high-frequency collocations or word groupings. This includes verb + noun collocations, prepositions, and compounds nouns.

Everyday English This section introduces and practises ordinals and dates.

POSSIBLE PROBLEMS
The main problem that students face with ordinals is pronunciation. The sound /θ/ always causes difficulty, and there are a lot of consonant clusters, for example, *sixth* /sɪksθ/, *twelfth* /twelfθ/. In rapid speech, sounds are often dropped, for example /twelθ/ instead of /twelfθ/ and /fɪθ/ instead of /fɪfθ/. Saying dates also causes problems of form. We can begin with the month

(*April the third*) or the date (*the third of April*), but in both cases we need to add *the*, which is never written, and in the latter case we need to add *of*, which is also never written. Years beginning 20– can also be read in two ways, e.g. 2010 = *two thousand and ten* or *twenty ten*.

Note that in American English, 3/8/99 means the eighth of March 1999, whereas in British English it means the third of August 1999.

Writing The syllabus continues with a description of a recent holiday.

Workbook More irregular verbs are introduced. There are exercises to revise the Present Simple alongside the Past Simple.
In the *Vocabulary* section, there is an exercise on recognizing parts of speech.
Numbers 100–1,000 are also practised.

Notes on the unit

STARTER (SB p52)

Check comprehension of great-grandparents. Demonstrate the activity by telling the class about your own grandparents and great-grandparents, giving as much information as you can about when and where they were born, their names, and their jobs. Use photographs you have brought to class if appropriate.

Students work in pairs and talk about what they know about their grandparents and great-grandparents.

WHEN I WAS YOUNG (SB p52)

Past Simple – regular verbs

1 Focus attention on the photos of Shirley Temple Black and ask students if they recognize her. Elicit any information/guesses about her as a child and now as an adult. Pre-teach/check *retired* (adj), *retire* (v), *politician*, *foreign*, *discuss*, *movie star*, *act*.

2 **T 7.1** [CD 1: Track 68] Ask students to read and listen about Shirley Temple Black in text **A** and complete the text. (This text is about her life now and revises the Present Simple before moving to the introduction of the Past Simple.) Play the recording and then check the answers. Make sure students have spelt *goes* correctly.

> **Answers and tapescript**
> Shirley Temple Black **is** a retired politician. She **lives** with her husband in California. She **likes** cooking and playing with her grandchildren. Also, she sometimes **works** at Stanford University for the Institute of International Studies. She **goes** there every month and **meets** foreign ministers. They **discuss** world problems.

Ask a few questions about Shirley's life now.
What does she do? (She's a retired politician.)
Where does she live? (In California.)
Does she live alone? (No, she doesn't.)
What does she like doing? (Cooking and playing with her grandchildren.)
Why does she go to Stanford University? (Because she sometimes works for the Institute of International Studies.)
What does she do there? (She meets foreign ministers and they discuss world problems.)

3 **T 7.2** [CD 1: Track 69] Tell your students that they are going to listen to and read about Shirley's past in text **B**. Play the recording and immediately go through the *Grammar Spot* exercises.

> **GRAMMAR SPOT**
>
> Go through the exercises one by one, establishing the answers after each exercise.
>
> 1 Refer students to text **B** and get them to find examples of the past of *is* and *can*. Check answers.
>
> > **Answers**
> > When she **was** very young, Shirley **was** a famous movie star. . . . when she **was** only three . . . She **could** act, she **was** a good singer, . . . But when she **was** 20, . . .
>
> 2 Students complete the sentence with the correct form of *work*. Check the answers.
>
> > **Answers**
> > Now she **works** at Stanford University.
> > When she was a child she **worked** in films.
>
> 3 Students work in pairs and find the Past Simple of *start*, *dance*, *like*, and *retire*. Get them to work out the rule for forming the Past Simple of regular verbs.
>
> > **Answers**
> > To form the Past Simple of regular verbs, add *-ed* or *-d* to the infinitive.
>
> Read Grammar Reference 7.1 on p142 together in class, and/or ask students to read it at home. Encourage them to ask you questions about it.

4 **T 7.3** [CD 1: Track 70] Check comprehension of *look after*, *earn*, and *study*. Students work in pairs to decide on the past form of the verbs in the box and practise the pronunciation. The order of the verbs reflects the pronunciation of the endings in the Past Simple (see *Answers* below).

Play the recording and let students check their answers. Get students to spell the past forms. Pay particular attention to the change of +*y* to -*ied* in *study*–*studied*.

Answers and tapescript
/t/   liked   looked   worked
/d/   earned   loved   studied
/ɪd/   acted   decided   wanted   started

Play the recording again and get students to repeat. You can point out that the endings can be grouped according to pronunciation, but do not spend too long on this, as students will focus on pronunciation on p54.

5   **T 7.4** [CD 1: Track 71] Explain that text **C** gives more information about Shirley's past and students have to complete it using the Past Simple forms of the verbs in the box from exercise 4. Elicit the verb for the first gap as an example. You could ask students to try and fill the gaps with the verbs before they listen, then to listen and check their answers with a partner. Or, if you think that it would be too difficult, let them listen to the text and fill in the answers as they go along.

Play the recording straight through without pausing.

Answers and tapescript
From the age of three Shirley **worked** very hard for 20th Century Fox.
'I **acted** in three or four movies every year. Fortunately I **liked** acting!' And the public **loved** her and her films. The films **earned** over $35 million.
She says, 'I didn't go to school. I **studied** at the studio and my mother **looked** after me there.'
So why did she stop acting? When she was 12, she finally **started** school. She was a good student and she **wanted** to go to university. She was still a good actor, but her films weren't so popular, because she wasn't a little girl any more. She **decided** to change her career. It was a big change – from actor to politician. She says, 'I was a politician for 35 years, but people only remember my movies!'

Go through the answers as a class, getting students to take turns at reading aloud part of the text. Correct their pronunciation of past tense verbs in preparation for the exercise on pronunciation in the *Practice* section on p54.

GRAMMAR SPOT

1   Refer students back to text **C** about Shirley and get them to find a question and negative.

Answers
So why **did** she **stop** acting?
I **didn't go** to school.

2/3 Go through the notes on the formation of questions and negatives with the whole class. Draw attention to the use of the past auxiliary *did*, followed by the stem of the main verb: *did ... stop* (not *did ... stopped*), and *didn't go* (not *didn't went*). Having the main verb in the Past Simple form, although incorrect, may seem more logical to students.

Read Grammar Reference 7.2 on p142 together in class, and/or ask students to read it at home. Encourage them to ask you questions about it.

6   This exercise focuses on *wh-* questions in the Past Simple. Focus attention on the example and then get students to work in pairs to complete the questions.
T 7.5 [CD 1: Track 72] Play the recording so that students can check their answers.

Answers and tapescript
1   When **did** she **start** in films? When she was only three years old.
2   How many films **did** she **act** in? Over 50.
3   Who **did** she **work** for? 20th Century Fox Film Studios.
4   How much money **did** her films **earn**? Over $35 million.
5   Where **did** she **study**? At the film studio. She didn't go to school.
6   When **did** she **start** school? When she was 12.
7   What **did** she **want** to do? Go to university.
8   Why **did** she **stop** acting? Because her movies weren't so popular any more.

Play the questions from the recording one by one (or say them yourself) and get students to repeat them both chorally and individually. Ask other students to provide the answers. These are all *wh-* questions, so encourage natural falling intonation on each one.

Where did she *study*?

Students continue practising the questions and answers in pairs. Monitor and check for accurate formation of Past Simple questions and negatives. Be prepared to drill the forms again if students have problems.

PRACTICE (SB p54)

Talking about you

1   This activity brings together the past of *to be*, *to be born*, and *did* in Past Simple questions, so that students become aware of the difference between the past of the verb *to be* and full verbs. Elicit the verb form for the first gap as an example. Get students to complete the sentences on their own first and then check in pairs.

Check the answers with the whole class, asking individuals to read out their answers.

Drill the questions, reminding students to use falling intonation in questions 1–6 but rising intonation in 7.

2 If you have room, ask students to get up and walk round the class asking two or three other students the questions, and answering about themselves in return. Or, if you don't mind a lot of movement, get students to ask each question to a different student. Tell them that you are going to see how much they can remember when they sit down.

3 After a few minutes, students sit down and tell you what information they can remember. Remind them to use the third-person singular forms *was* and *was born*.

For consolidation, you could ask students to write a short paragraph about themselves for homework.

ADDITIONAL MATERIAL

Workbook Unit 7
Exercises 1 and 2 Past Simple: regular verbs, *Yes/No* questions, and short answers

Irregular verbs

Now the theme moves to the more recent past with a focus on life in the year 1984. This provides the context for the introduction of irregular verbs.

1 Refer students to the irregular verb list on SB p159. Make sure they understand that it is an important resource that they should refer to regularly.

Elicit one or two examples of the Past Simple forms. Ask students to work with a partner. Ask them to use their dictionaries to look up new words and check the list to find out which verb is regular and what the irregular forms of the others are.

Ask students to read out the correct answers.

2 **T 7.8** [CD 1: Track 75] Play the recording (and/or model the verbs yourself) and ask students to listen and repeat. Check pronunciation of the more difficult forms, e.g. *bought* /bɔːt/. (See Answers above for tapescript.)

3 Briefly review how to say 19– dates and if you think your students need to practise dates, ask the class to chant the years from 1990 to 2000.

Write *1984* in large numbers on the board and refer students to the photos to elicit ideas about the worlds of politics, sport, science, and music. You could put them into groups to do this if you have time and if you feel that your students would respond well. Elicit some examples from the class to set the scene for the recording and James's conversation with his parents about 1984.

Let students read the texts first and check for any unknown vocabulary. Encourage students to use the context to help them, but with weaker classes, you could pre-teach/check *prime minister, president, leader, athlete, gold medal, champion, album,* and *hit record,* referring to the photos as appropriate. Explain that *president* is used for the official leader of a country that does not have a king or queen as head of state.

Tell students that the recording is in the form of a conversation between James and his parents and that the texts in the Student's Book are a summary of what the speakers talk about. Students are required only to select key points to practise certain verbs.

T 7.9 **[CD 1: Track 76]** Play the recording. Students listen and complete as much of the texts as they can, then compare their answers in pairs.

Play the recording again so that students can complete or check their answers. Elicit any further information students can remember.

Answers

James: left, came, got	Science: made, bought
Politics: was, began, died	Music: sold, sang, had
Sports: won, became	

T 7.9

1984 The year I was born
J=James, D=Dad, M=Mum

J Dad, tell me about when I was born. When did you leave Hong Kong?

D Erm … you were born in January, and we left later that year and came back to Britain.

M Yes, you got a job in London, didn't you, Robert?

D That's right. Remember Margaret Thatcher was Prime Minister, then.

M Of course. She was Europe's first woman Prime Minister, James.

J I know that, Mum. But who was in the White House?

D Ronald Reagan. Actually, he began his second four years then.

M He was an actor before. Did you know that, James?

J No, I didn't, Mum!

D And that was the year that the Soviet leader, Yuri Andropov, died.

M Oh, yes. He was only leader for a year. Oh, and I remember – the Soviet Union didn't go to the Olympic Games that year. Isn't that right, Robert? The 1984 Games – were they in Los Angeles?

D Yes, they were. Remember Carl Lewis won four gold medals that year.

J That was in athletics, wasn't it?

M That's right.

D Oh, and remember little Tiger Woods?

J The golfer?

D Yes. He became junior champion that year. He was only eight years old.

J Wow. Hey, 1984 was a busy year. Did anything else happen?

M Well … Apple Macintosh made a new computer. I remember because I bought one. Millions of people bought one.

J And what about music? Was Michael Jackson famous then?

D Yes, he was. His album *Thriller* came out that year. It sold millions.

J 43 million, actually. It's the best-selling album of all time!

D Really?

M Oh, and remember, Robert? Madonna sang *Holiday!* (sings)

J Oh, no! Stop it, Mum! You sing that every time we go on holiday!

M I know. I like it. Anyway, who else was famous, then, Robert?

D Let's see. Paul McCartney … Tina Turner, David Bowie – they all had hit records that year.

J Wow, that's amazing! They're all still famous today.

4 Ask students to give the first question and answer as an example. Students work in pairs to ask and answer the rest of the questions. Insist on full answers so that they get practice with the irregular past forms. Check for accurate question formation and falling intonation. If students have problems, drill the questions and answers in open pairs and then in closed pairs.

Check the answers with the whole class.

Answers

1 When did James and his parents leave Hong Kong? They left Hong Kong in 1984.

2 Where did his father get a job? He got a job in London.

3 How many medals did Carl Lewis win? He won four gold medals.

4 What did Apple Macintosh make? They made a personal computer.

5 Which song did Madonna sing? She sang *Holiday*.

6 How many albums did Michael Jackson's *Thriller* sell? It sold 43 million albums.

SUGGESTION
You could ask students to bring in photos of when they were babies to use as a springboard for exercise 5.

---

5 Tell students where you were born and give examples of key people/events/trends in that year, e.g. *world leaders, sports events, science, popular songs/artists/films, trends in cars/fashion/design, famous people*, etc. Write the above categories on the board and get students to find out information about the year they were born for homework. If you have access to online computers, students could do this during class time.

With weaker classes, build a skeleton on the board with the students to help them with the writing task, e.g.

I was born on … in … . In that year … was the leader of my country. Other important leaders were… . In sport … won … and … became world champion in … . In science … made … . Millions of people bought a … . In music, … sang … and … all had hit records.

When students have written about the year they were born, put them into pairs or small groups to exchange information. Elicit any interesting examples during class feedback.

When did it happen?

1 Set up this activity by giving the class a few cues of major events and getting students to form the question and give the corresponding dates, e.g.
the Berlin Wall/fall – When did the Berlin Wall fall? In 1989.
the First World War/end – When did the First World War end? In 1918.

Refer students to the examples in the Student's Book and elicit the answers to the questions (*the Second World War began in 1939 and ended in 1945; the first person walked on the moon in 1969*). Drill the questions, focusing on the highlighted stress pattern in the speech bubbles.

Students work in small groups and list other major events of the 20th century, both nationally and internationally. They then form questions to 'test' the other groups.

Pre-teach expressions like *in the (1950s), in about (1995)* to enable students to give an answer if they can't give an exact year. Get students to ask their questions to another group. Conduct brief feedback with students saying sentences about the most interesting/popular events.

What did you do?

Focus attention on the phrases in the box, pointing out that we can't use *last* with parts of a day, except *night*. Check pronunciation and then get students to give a few examples of the phrases in context, e.g. *I went to the cinema last night.*

2 Check comprehension of the vocabulary in the list of verb phrases. Drill the questions chorally and individually, and then get students to ask and answer in pairs. You could suggest that they take notes about each other. Go round the class monitoring and helping.

Bring the class together and briefly check the past form of the verbs, as students will need these to report back. Students say what they learned about their partner.

Check it

3 Ask students to do this exercise on their own and then check with a partner before you go through the exercise as a class.

Answers
1 He bought some new shoes.
2 Where did you go yesterday?
3 Did you see Jane last week?
4 Did she get the job?
5 I went out yesterday evening.
6 He studied French at school.
7 What did you have for breakfast?
8 I was in New York last week.

Describing a holiday

This unit takes students through the key stages of preparing to write a short description of a holiday. They focus on key information and note-taking, completing a gapped model paragraph before writing their own description.

1 Pre-teach/check *bed and breakfast*, *countryside*, and *temple*. Give students time to read the notes and check any other vocabulary before completing the table with their own notes. Be prepared to feed in new vocabulary.

2 Focus attention on the examples and then get students to continue asking and answering in pairs.

3 Focus attention on the examples, and then get students to complete the questions and give short answers.

Answers
2 When did she go? Last October.
3 How long did she stay? Three weeks.
4 How did she travel? By plane.
5 Where did she stay? With friends.
6 What did she do? She visited Tokyo and Kyoto.
7 What did she see? Some beautiful temples, but not Mount Fuji.
8 Did she enjoy the holiday?

4 This task puts the information about Daniella into a connected paragraph and consolidates Past Simple forms. It also provides a model for exercise 5. Elicit the answer to the first gap and then get students to complete the task. Check the spelling of the Past Simple forms, as students will need to use them in their own writing.

Answers

1	had	5	met	9	took
2	went	6	drove	10	saw
3	travelled	7	stayed	11	enjoyed
4	was	8	visited	12	didn't see

5 Give a brief description of your last holiday as an example. In pairs, get students to talk about their last holiday. Give students time to write their description in class or set it for homework. If possible, display the descriptions on the classroom wall or noticeboard to allow students to read each other's work. You could ask them to vote for the most interesting holiday. When you check the students' descriptions, point out errors but allow students to correct them themselves and try to limit correction to major problems to avoid demoralizing.

ADDITIONAL MATERIAL

Workbook Unit 7
Exercises 3–5 Past Simple: irregular verbs
Exercise 6 This practises question formation.
Exercise 7 This contrasts Present Simple and Past Simple.

Two famous firsts

This is another 'jigsaw' reading activity, so make sure students are clear about which text they should read and how to exchange their information. The mechanics of the activity are made easier by students working on the same true–false statements, irrespective of whether they read about Amelia Earhart or Yuri Gagarin.

1   Check students understand the terms *nouns, verbs,* and *adjectives* by translating into L1 or using a simple example sentence and getting students to name the noun, verb, and adjective, e.g. *The young man left yesterday.* Get students to translate the words into L1 using their dictionaries. Check answers as a class.

2   Focus attention on the photos. Check students recognize the two people and can pronounce their names (/əˈmiːliə ˈeəhɑːt/, /ˈjuːriː gəˈgɑːrɪn/.) Get students to complete the sentences referring to the texts if necessary.

> **Answers**
> Amelia Mary Earhart was the first **woman to fly across the Atlantic**.
> Yuri Gagarin was the first **man in space**.

Elicit any further information or impressions students have of the two 'firsts'.

3   Divide the class into two groups. Tell Group A to read about Amelia Earhart and Group B to read about Yuri Gagarin. Ask each group to read through their text as quickly as possible to get a general understanding.

4   Get students to read the text again more slowly and find the information in their text to do the true–false task. Exercise 1 covers the key vocabulary in the text, so encourage students to use the context and not to worry about individual words that don't relate to the task. If students query it, highlight the difference between *travel to Europe* (as in question 7) and *travel around the world* (as appears in the texts) with simple board drawings. Remind students to correct the statements that are false.

When students have read the texts, they could either go through the statements on their own and then check with others from the same group, or work with a partner from the same group to do the exercise. Each group has the same statements to work on.

Check the answers with Group A students and Group B students separately.

> **Answers**
> **Group A – Amelia Earhart**
> 1   True
> 2   True
> 3   False. She worked in a hospital in World War I.
> 4   False. She wanted to be a pilot when she was 23.
> 5   False. The text doesn't mention the type of plane she flew.
> 6   True
> 7   False. She travelled around the world.
> 8   True
>
> **Group B – Yuri Gagarin**
> 1   False. His family was very poor.
> 2   True
> 3   False. He saw his first plane in World War II.
> 4   False. He wanted to be a pilot when he was a teenager.
> 5   True
> 6   False. He was a father.
> 7   False. He travelled around the world.
> 8   True

5   Tell each student to find a partner from the other group and go through the statements together, telling each other about the person in their text. Encourage students to exchange their information in a meaningful way, by comparing and contrasting the two 'firsts', rather than simply saying true/false about each statement, e.g.

A   *Amelia Earhart came from a rich family. What about Yuri Gagarin?*
B   *No, his family was very poor.*

Check the answers with the class. Again, get students to give complete sentences, comparing and contrasting the two people, using *They both …/Neither of them … .*

> **Answers**
> 1   Amelia Earhart came from a rich family, but Yuri Gagarin didn't.
> 2   They both had a short but exciting life.
> 3   Neither of them fought in a World War.
> 4   Amelia Earhart wanted to be a pilot when she was 23 and Yuri Gagarin wanted to be a pilot when he was a teenager.
> 5   Yuri Gagarin flew fighter jets, but Amelia Earhart didn't.
> 6   They both married and Yuri Gagarin had children, but Amelia Earhart didn't.
> 7   They both travelled around the world to talk about their experiences.
> 8   They both died in a plane crash.

6   Get students to complete the questions about the other person, i.e. Group A complete the questions about Yuri Gagarin, and Group B about Amelia Earhart. Students can work in pairs or small groups to do this. If students have problems finding the correct words, you could put them on the board in two groups clearly headed Amelia Earhart and Yuri Gagarin (the words are in **bold** below).

Check the answers with Group A students and Group B students separately.

Answers
About Amelia Earhart
1 Where **was** she born?
2 What **did** she study first?
3 When **did** she **go** up in a plane?
4 When **did** she **break** her first record?
5 **Did** she marry? **Did** she **have** any children?
6 What **did** she do in 1935?
7 Where **did** her plane disappear?

About Yuri Gagarin
8 Where **was** he born?
9 When **did** he see his first plane?
10 Why **did** he **join** the Russian Air Force?
11 Why **did** the doctors choose Yuri to be an astronaut?
12 What **did** he do in 1961?
13 Why **did** he **travel** around the world?
14 How **did** he die?

Students then work with the same partner as in exercise 5 and ask and answer the questions. Check the answers with the whole class, getting students to give full statements where possible in order to practise past forms, e.g. *Amelia Earhart was born in Kansas.*

Answers
About Amelia Earhart
1 Amelia Earhart was born in Kansas.
2 She studied nursing first.
3 She went up in a plane when she was 23.
4 She broke her first record in 1921.
5 Yes, she did. No, she didn't.
6 She became the first person to fly alone across the Pacific.
7 Her plane disappeared near Howland Island in the Pacific Ocean.

About Yuri Gagarin
8 He was born on a farm.
9 He saw his first plane in World War II.
10 He joined the Russian Air Force because his teachers thought he was a natural pilot.
11 They chose Yuri to be an astronaut because he was the best in all the tests.
12 He finally went into space.
13 He travelled around the world to talk about his experiences.
14 He died when his fighter jet crashed on a test flight.

What do you think?

Get one or two students to give an example and then ask students to continue talking about famous people from history. Allow the discussion to continue for as long as students' interest is held, and exchanges are taking place in English, <u>not</u> in L1!

Words that go together

Collocation and word groupings are a key feature of English and it's important that students start to become familiar with them as early in their learning as possible. This vocabulary section focuses on verb + noun collocation, the use of prepositions in a range of high-frequency phrases/structures, and compound nouns (noun + noun combinations).

Verbs and nouns

1 Explain that this task has verbs in list A and nouns in B and that some of the words appeared in the reading texts on p57. Focus attention on the example and then get students to complete the task. Remind students that more than one answer may be possible. Let students check in pairs before checking with the whole class.

Answers

drink a cup of tea	watch television
drive a car	win a medal/a lot of money
eat a sandwich/a meal	speak Spanish
break a record	ride a bike
cook a meal	earn a lot of money
play the guitar	

Focus attention on the example questions and answers in the Student's Book. Students practise them in open pairs following the highlighted stress patterns. Students continue asking and answering in closed pairs. With weaker classes, elicit other possible questions before the pairwork stage, e.g. *Can you speak Spanish? Do you watch television every day? When did you last ride a bike?*

Prepositions

2 Read the example sentence in class. Give students time to complete the task before getting class feedback.

Answers

2	to, with	5	at, on	8	at, at
3	on	6	in, in	9	on
4	around	7	of, in	10	to

Personalize the language by asking students to choose three of the statements and make them true for themselves. They should change the details of the sentences but keep the language around the preposition the same, e.g. *I like listening to pop music.*

Compound nouns

3 Explain that this task focuses on noun + noun combinations, and focus attention on the examples. Point out that the first is written as two words and the second as one. Focus attention on stress highlighting.

Ask students where the main stress usually falls, on the first or second word (*the first word*). Drill the words as necessary.

Get students to write their answers to the task, so that they can focus on whether to write them as one or two words.

T 7.10 [CD 1: Track 77] Play the recording. Students listen, check their answers, and repeat the compound noun, putting the stress on the first word in each.

Answers and tapescript

orange juice	boyfriend	washing machine
railway station	newspaper	living room
swimming pool	film star	car park
handbag	birthday card	

Focus attention on the examples in the book and get students to say the exchanges in open pairs. Elicit one or two more example definitions and then get students to test each other in pairs.

4 **T 7.11** [CD 1: Track 78] Tell the students they will hear four short conversations and that they should listen for the compound nouns for each which appear in exercise 3.

Answers and tapescript

1 **A** I can't find my **handbag**.
  B Here it is!
  A Oh yes, thank you. Where did you find it?
  B In the **living room** where you left it!
2 **A** Would you like some **chocolate cake**?
  B No, thanks, just **orange juice** for me.
  A But I made this cake for you.
  B Did you? I'm sorry! I don't like chocolate cake.
3 **A** I have nothing to wear for your **boyfriend**'s party.
  B What about your white jeans?
  A They aren't clean.
  B Well, wash them. You have a **washing machine**, don't you?
4 **A** Do you want anything from the shops?
  B A **newspaper**, please. *The Times*, I think.
  A OK.
  B Oh, and can you take this letter to the **post office**?
  A Sure.

Ask students to turn to the tapescript on SB p130 and practise the conversations with a partner.

SUGGESTION
You can consolidate the verbs and nouns, and compound nouns, with the photocopiable activity on TB p142. Photocopy enough pages for your students to work in pairs. The activity is divided into two sections – a matching activity and a gap-fill to practise the vocabulary. Divide the students into pairs. Give each pair a set of words and explain that they have to match them to form verb + noun collocations and compound nouns. Elicit an example, e.g. *become a pilot*. If

appropriate, do the activity as a race with the fastest students to match the words correctly as winners. Hand out a copy of the gap-fill to each pair of students. Focus attention on the example, and get students to complete the task. Check the answers, getting students to say which compound noun is written as one word.

Answers

2	railway station	8	film star
3	drive a car	9	Did … win a medal
4	orange juice	10	ride a bike
5	birthday card	11	car park
6	play the guitar	12	newspaper
7	break a record		

EVERYDAY ENGLISH (SB p59)

What's the date?

1 Students work in pairs to match the ordinals to the correct numbers.

Answers and tapescript

1st	first	6th	sixth	17th	seventeenth
2nd	second	10th	tenth	20th	twentieth
3rd	third	12th	twelfth	21st	twenty-first
4th	fourth	13th	thirteenth	30th	thirtieth
5th	fifth	16th	sixteenth	31st	thirty-first

T 7.12 [CD 1: Track 79] Students listen and practise saying the ordinals. Pause the recording after each one and drill them around the class, correcting carefully.

2 Focus attention on the example and then get students to ask and answer questions about the other months of the year. You don't need to let this go on for very long.

3 Focus attention on the *Caution Box* and explain the different ways of writing and saying the dates. Elicit an example and then get students to practise saying the dates. For the first five dates, they should practise saying them both ways. Students often have a lot of difficulties saying dates, so do the activity as a class and correct mistakes very carefully.

T 7.13 [CD 1: Track 80] Students listen and check.

Answers and tapescript

1 The first of April
  April the first
2 The second of March
  March the second
3 The seventeenth of September
  September the seventeenth
4 The nineteenth of November
  November the nineteenth

5 The twenty-third of June
   June the twenty-third
6 The twenty-ninth of February, nineteen seventy-six
7 The nineteenth of December, nineteen eighty-three
8 The third of October, nineteen ninety-nine
9 The thirty-first of May, two thousand
10 The fifteenth of July, two thousand and seven

4 **T 7.14** [CD 1: Track 81] Students listen and write down the dates they hear. Tell them there are seven dates in total. With weaker classes, play the first one or two dates as examples first. Let them check in pairs before you give the answers.

Answers and tapescript
1 The fourth of January
2 May the seventh, 1997
3 The fifteenth of August, 2001
4 **A** It was a Friday.
  B No, it wasn't. It was a Thursday.
  A No, I remember. It was **Friday the thirteenth. The thirteenth of July**.
5 **A** Oh no! I forgot your birthday.
  B It doesn't matter, really.
  A It was last Sunday, wasn't it? The thirtieth. **November the thirtieth.**
6 **A** Hey! Did you know that Shakespeare was born and died on the same day?
  B That's not possible!
  A Yes, it is. He was born on **April the twenty-third, fifteen sixty-four** and he died on **April the twenty-third, sixteen sixteen**.

5 Students work in pairs to ask and answer the questions about dates. Monitor and feed back on any common errors before checking the answers with the whole class.

Answers
(We can only give some of the answers.)
3 25 December
4 14 February
5 In the UK, it is always on a Sunday towards the end of March.

Don't forget!

Workbook Unit 7
Exercise 8 Parts of speech, such as *adjective*, *noun*
Exercise 9 Translation
Exercise 10 Listening practice on an amazing journey
Exercises 11–13 Practice of numbers 100–1,000
Exercise 14 Prepositions: *about*, *after*, *for*

Grammar Reference
Look at the exercises on SB p142 as a class, or set for homework. The answers are on TB p176.

Word list
Remind students of the Word list on SB p155. They could translate the words, learn them at home, or transfer some of the words to their vocabulary notebook.

Pronunciation Book Unit 7

Video/DVD Episode 3 An old friend

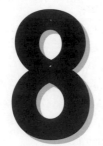

Past Simple 2 – negatives – *ago*
Spelling and silent letters
Special occasions

A date to remember

Introduction to the unit

This is the second unit on the Past Simple tense, and it provides further practice and reinforcement of the input in Unit 7, focusing particularly on the negative. The title of this unit is 'A date to remember' and the topics in the unit lend themselves to practice of the Past Simple and *ago*. The unifying theme of the unit is how things began, with reading texts on inventions, and listening texts on the start of two different relationships. This main listening exercise is one of the first extensive listening exercises where students do not have the support of the written word.

NOTE
Recordings for Unit 8 are split across CD1 and CD2. CD2 recordings begin with T8.5 . Vocabulary and Pronunciation on SB p64. Cassette 1 contains all the recordings for units 1–8.

Language aims

Grammar – Past Simple 2 See the introduction to the Past Simple and problems associated with it on TB p51. There is considerable practice of the positive in this unit, but there is also much emphasis on question forms and negatives. These present few problems of concept, but there can inevitably be mistakes of form.

Common mistakes
*When you went home? *Where did go Peter?
*When did you went home? *I no went out last night.

ago *Ago* is an adverb which is used when the point of reference is the present. It means 'before now', and is used only with past tenses, not present tenses or present perfect tenses. *Ago* always comes after an expression of time.

Different languages realize this concept in various ways.
two years ago – *il y a deux ans* (French)
          – *vor zwei Jahren* (German)
          – *hace dos años* (Spanish)
          – *due anni fa* (Italian)

Common mistakes
*I went there ago two weeks.
*I went there before two weeks.
*My cat died for two years.

Time expressions There is a focus on preposition and noun collocations, such as *on Saturday* and *in summer*. These prepositions can cause a lot of confusion and so will need a lot of practice and regular reviewing.

Vocabulary Words with silent letters are focused on and practised, e.g. *talk*, *know*, *listen*. Again, the emphasis is that English spelling is not phonetic. The phonetic script is further practised to introduce words with silent letters.

Everyday English Common expressions for special occasions, such as *Happy birthday* and *Happy New Year* are introduced and practised. This provides the opportunity for some very interesting discussion on cross-cultural traditions, especially if you have a multilingual class. What occasions different nationalities celebrate, and how they celebrate them, is fascinating!

Writing There is further practice on linking words including *because*, *when*, and *until*. Students write about an old friend.

Workbook Past Simple and past time expressions are further practised. In the *Vocabulary* section, there is a focus on words which are both nouns and verbs, e.g. *dance*, and revision and extension of machines and inventions. There is also a short story in two parts with accompanying comprehension questions.

Notes on the unit

STARTER (SB p60)

> **POSSIBLE PROBLEMS**
>
> Students often confuse *eat* /iːt/ and its past form *ate* /et, eɪt/, so these will need careful highlighting. The past of *wear* – *wore* /wɔː/ can also present pronunciation problems.
>
> Students may try and look for patterns in the past forms, expecting *take* to work in the same way as *make*, so take the opportunity to remind them that the past forms have to be learned!

Students work in pairs and say the Past Simple of the verbs in the box. If they have problems with the form of any of the irregular verbs, refer them to the irregular verb list on SB p158.

Check the answers with the whole class, getting students to spell the past forms and making sure they can pronounce them correctly. Elicit the regular verbs (*listen to* and *watch*).

> **Answers**
>
> | | | | |
> |---|---|---|---|
> | eat | ate | make | made |
> | drink | drank | ride | rode |
> | drive | drove | take | took |
> | fly | flew | watch | watched |
> | listen to | listened to | wear | wore |

FAMOUS INVENTIONS (SB p60)

Past Simple: negatives – *ago*

1 Focus attention on the photos, ask *What can you see?* and elicit any relevant vocabulary. Check pronunciation carefully, especially of the 'international' words which are the same or very similar in other languages, e.g. *hamburger* /ˈhæmbɜːgə/, *Coca-Cola* /ˈkəʊkə ˈkəʊlə/, *jeans* /dʒiːnz/, *television* /ˈtelɪvɪʒn/, and *photograph* /ˈfəʊtəɡrɑːf/. Check students stress the noun form *record* correctly /ˈrekɔːd/.

Students work in pairs and match the verbs in the *Starter* activity with the photos.

Check the answers with the whole class.

> **Answers**
>
> | | |
> |---|---|
> | 1 watch television | 6 eat hamburgers |
> | 2 drink Coca-Cola | 7 take photographs |
> | 3 make phone calls | 8 fly planes |
> | 4 drive cars | 9 ride bikes |
> | 5 listen to records | 10 wear jeans |

2
> **SUGGESTION**
>
> You might want to pre-teach *ago*. You could ask questions such as the following to feed this in:
>
> *When was your last English lesson?* (On Tuesday.)
> *How many days ago was that?* (Two days ago.)
> *When did you last have a holiday?* (In June.)
> *How many months ago was that?* (Five months ago.)
> *When did you last go to the cinema?* (Last Friday.)
> *How many days ago was that?* (Five days ago.)
>
> Focus students' attention on *ago* and explain its use (see *Language aims* on TB p66).

Model the example question yourself exaggerating the stress pattern. Get lots of repetition practice. Then practise the question and the sample answers in open pairs. Do the same for five of the photographs. Students ask and answer questions about the remaining photos in closed pairs.

3 Students give you their opinions about what people did and didn't do a hundred years ago following the highlighted stress pattern in the example.

Getting information

4
> **NOTE**
>
> This activity requires students to use the Past Simple passive in the question: *When was/were … invented?* Point out that students will need to use *was* to ask about examples in the singular, e.g. *Coca-Cola* and *television*. You can drill the question forms, but do not do a full presentation of the passive at this stage.

Divide the class into pairs and get the A students to turn to p149 and the B students to p150. Explain that they each have different information and they have to ask questions to complete what's missing. Remind them not to show each other their information. Elicit one or two examples using the model in the Student's Book. Get students to write the dates down and work out how long ago the item was invented. You may get some surprised reactions and even disagreement from students, as there is a big difference between, say, the invention of the car and when cars became generally available.

> **Answers** (The number of years ago will depend on the year you are using the course.)
>
> 1 Coca-Cola was invented in 1886.
> 2 The camera was invented in 1826.
> 3 The record player was invented in 1878.
> 4 The first plane was invented in 1903. (The first flight across the Channel was in 1909.)
> 5 Jeans were invented in 1873 (made by Levi Strauss).
> 6 Hamburgers were invented in 1895.
> 7 Cars were invented in 1893. (A Benz went at 18 miles an hour.)
> 8 The telephone was invented in 1876.
> 9 The television was invented in 1926.
> 10 Bicycles were invented in about 1840.

1 Focus attention on the *Grammar Spot*. Get students to work through the answers in the table orally first. Then check the answers with the whole class, writing the sentences on the board for students to copy.

Answers

Present Simple	Past Simple
He lives in London.	**He lived in London.**
Do you live in London?	**Did you live in London?**
Does she live in London?	**Did she live in London?**
I don't live in London.	**I didn't live in London.**
He doesn't live in London.	**He didn't live in London.**

Highlight that *he/she/it* has a different form in the Present Simple from the other persons, but that all forms in the Past Simple are the same.

2 Get students to complete the sentences to consolidate the meaning of *ago*. (The answers will depend on the year you are using the course.)

Read Grammar Reference 8.1 and 8.2 on p142 together in class, and/or ask students to read it at home. Encourage them to ask you questions about it.

PRACTICE (SB p61)

Time expressions

1 Ask students to identify the correct preposition for the time expressions. Some they will know, some will be new. If mistake follows mistake, you can expect some frustration, and possibly amusement, from students. Give them these rules to help:

on + day/day of the week plus part of the day, e.g. *on Saturday morning*

in + part of the day (except *night*)/month/season/year/century

at + time

This leaves only *at night* and *at weekends* that do not fit any of the categories. Check the answers.

Answers

at seven o'clock	in the morning
on Saturday	on Sunday evening
at night	in September
in 2002	at weekends
in summer	in the nineteenth century

2 Demonstrate the activity by getting students to practise the examples in the Student's Book in open pairs following the highlighted stress pattern in the example. Students continue in closed pairs asking questions with *when*, and answering the questions in the two different

ways. Monitor and check that the questions are well formed, and that the voice starts high. Feed back on any common errors in grammar or pronunciation.

3 Give an example by telling students about your day so far and then get students to tell the class about their day. If you have a small group and sufficient time, you could ask each student to give their example. If you have a lot of students, you could get students to work simultaneously in small groups, making sure the students who worked together in exercise 2 talk to different students.

PRACTICE (SB p62)

Three inventions

1 Ask students to look at the texts and the three photos and say what they can see. You will probably need to pre-teach/check *windscreen wiper*. Students read the three texts, checking new words in their dictionaries. The following words will probably be new: *painter, opera, idea, government, studio, notice* (v), *clean* (v), *design* (v/n), *laugh* (v), *draw/drew, hear*.

Tell students they are going to listen and read the texts correcting dates as they listen.

2 **T 8.1** [CD 1: Track 82] Students listen and correct the dates. You could either play the recording all the way through, or stop it after each text. Check pronunciation of the names of the inventors, especially Daguerre /dæˈgeə/.

Drill the example sentence in the Student's Book chorally and individually, focusing attention on the highlighted contrastive stress:

Daguerre didn't start his experiments in the 19 20s.
He started them in the 18 20s.

Ask students to make a negative and a positive sentence about each date. Remind them that they will need to change the order of information in sentences that begin with the date (see *Answers* below). Check the answers with the whole class, either by getting students to read out the pairs of sentences with the correct stress or by asking different students to read the texts aloud with the correct information. Correct any pronunciation mistakes.

Answers and tapescript

Daguerre didn't start his experiments in the 1920s. He started them in the 1820s.

He didn't sell his idea to the French government in 1935. He sold it to them in 1839.

There weren't 70 studios by 1940. There were 70 daguerreotype studios in New York City by 1850.

Mary Anderson didn't begin designing something to clean the windows from inside the car in 1893. She began in 1903. She didn't invent the windscreen wiper in 1925. She invented it in 1905.

All American cars didn't have them by 1960. Only American cars had them by 1916.

Leonardo da Vinci didn't draw a design for the modern bicycle in 1540. He drew it in 1490.

Kirkpatrick Macmillan didn't make a bicycle in 1789. He made it in 1839.

The bike didn't become cheap in 1825. It became cheap in 1895.

T 8.1

The photograph
Louis Daguerre from France
Louis Daguerre was a painter for the French opera. But he wanted to make a new type of picture. He started his experiments in the 1820s. Twelve years later he invented the photograph. He sold his idea to the French government in 1839 and the government gave it to the world. Daguerre called the first photographs 'daguerreotypes'. They became popular very fast. By 1850, there were 70 daguerreotype studios in New York City.

The windscreen wiper
Mary Anderson from the USA
Mary Anderson often visited New York City by car. In winter she noticed that when it rained or snowed, drivers got out of their cars all the time to clean their windows. In 1903 she began designing something to clean windows from inside the car. People, especially men, laughed at her idea. But they didn't laugh for long. She invented the windscreen wiper in 1905. And by 1916 all American cars had them.

The bicycle
Kirkpatrick Macmillan from Scotland
Long ago in 1490, Leonardo da Vinci drew a design for the modern bicycle. But the first person to make a bicycle was Kirkpatrick Macmillan in 1839. He lived in Scotland, so people didn't hear about his invention for a long time. Twenty years later, another bicycle came from France. In 1895 the bike became cheap and everyone could have one. Now people, especially women, could travel to the next town. It helped them find someone to marry!

3   Focus attention on the example in the Student's Book, on the negative form, and the correct answer. Drill the pronunciation, focusing attention on the highlighted contrastive stress again.

T 8.2 [CD 1: Track 83] Students listen and check.

Answers and tapescript
1   He didn't invent the bicycle. He invented the photograph.
2   He didn't give his idea to the French government. He sold it to them.
3   She didn't live in New York City. She often visited New York City.
4   All cars didn't have windscreen wipers by 1916. Only American cars had them.
5   Leonardo da Vinci didn't make the first bicycle. Kirkpatrick Macmillan made it.
6   He didn't come from France. He came from Scotland.

Play the recording again and get students to practise the stress and intonation.

4   Elicit another incorrect sentence as an example, e.g. *Louis Daguerre was a designer. He wasn't a designer. He was a painter.* Divide the class into pairs. Get students to write more sentences and then exchange with a partner to correct them.

Did you know that?

5   **T 8.3** [CD 1: Track 84] Pre-teach/check the following vocabulary: *spaghetti, really, incredible, true, afraid,* and *believe.* Students read and listen to the conversations. Draw their attention to the wide voice range of the second speaker as he/she expresses incredulity. Practise the conversations in open pairs, and really encourage students to sound surprised! You could write the following on the board:

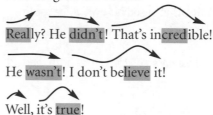

Really? He didn't! That's incredible!

He wasn't! I don't believe it!

Well, it's true!

6   Pre-teach/check the following vocabulary: *painting, alive, actress, millionaire, spell* (past tense *spelled*), *snow* (v), *wall, voice.*

Take care also with the pronunciation of these words:
van Gogh (in British English) /ˌvæn ˈgɒf/
spelled /speld/
Sahara Desert /səˈhɑːrə ˈdezət/
Louis /ˈluːi/

Also, point out how we say kings and queens in English. (Students might not understand Roman numerals.)
King Louis the fourteenth
King Henry the eighth
King Francis the first

Divide the class into pairs, getting students to work with a different partner than in exercise 4. Ask the A students to turn to p149 and the B students to p151. Do an example from Student A's information and one from Student B's. Remember that students may have difficulty in selecting the correct short response (*wasn't, didn't*), so you might want to go through them as a class first, especially with weaker groups. If students produce a good, wide voice range, and enjoy doing the exercise, do not insist on complete accuracy. (This is primarily a pronunciation exercise.)

Sample answers

Did you know that Vincent van Gogh sold only two of his paintings while he was alive?

Really (etc.)? He didn't! I don't believe it (etc.)!

Did you know that the actress Shirley Temple was a millionaire before she was ten?

Really? She wasn't!

Did you know that Shakespeare spelled his name in eleven different ways?

He didn't! Really? That's incredible!

Did you know that in 1979 it snowed in the Sahara Desert?

It didn't!

Did you know that King Louis XIV of France had a bath only three times in his life?

He didn't! I don't believe it!

Did you know that it took 1,700 years to build the Great Wall of China?

It didn't!

Did you know that Walt Disney used his own voice for the character of Mickey Mouse?

He didn't!

Did you know that Shakespeare and Cervantes both died on 23 April 1616?

They didn't! Really?

Did you know that King Francis I of France bought the painting *The Mona Lisa* to put in his bathroom?

He didn't! That's incredible!

Did you know when Shakespeare was alive, there were no actresses, only male actors?

There weren't! I don't believe it!

ADDITIONAL MATERIAL

Workbook Unit 8
Exercises 1–4 Past Simple: regular and irregular verbs, positives and negatives
Exercise 5 Past time expressions
Exercise 6 *ago*

LISTENING AND SPEAKING (SB p63)

How did you two meet?

> **POSSIBLE PROBLEMS**
>
> This is one of the first extensive listening exercises in *New Headway Elementary – the THIRD edition* where students are not encouraged to read and listen at the same time. They have to listen to the recording only. Students often find listening to recordings very difficult for the obvious reason that they have no visual support. They cannot see the speakers, or their lips. However, there are several pre-listening tasks, and students are guided to comprehension via the questions.

1 Get students to read the sentences and check any new vocabulary. Make sure they understand the difference between *get engaged*, *get married*, and *get divorced*. Students work in pairs to put the sentences in order. Ask for some feedback. You may get lots of different ideas!

> **Sample answers**
>
> 1 Jack and Jill met at a party.
> 2 They went out for a year.
> 3 They fell in love.
> 4 They got engaged.
> 5 They got married.
> 6 They had two children.
> 7 They got divorced.

2 Focus attention on the photos and elicit some basic information about the two couples: *What are their names?* (Ned and Carly; Eric and Lori) *How old are they?* (in their 20s). Students read the introductions to the stories. Elicit a range of ideas as to what happened next, e.g. Ned went away to study/Carly met a different person; Eric's mom introduced him to a lot of girls/found a dating agency for Eric, etc. Point out that students are not expected to give correct answers at this stage, so any suggestions they make are valid.

3 **T 8.4** [CD 1: Track 85] Tell students they are going to listen to each couple talking and they should try to understand just what happened next in each relationship and not to panic if they don't understand every word. Pause the recording after Carly and Ned and allow students to check in pairs. Then play the recording of Eric and Lori and again let students check in pairs.

> **SUGGESTION**
>
> Try to get students used to listening for gist from this first extensive listening exercise and so only repeat the recording if students have really failed to follow what happened next in the stories. They will probably tell you they didn't understand anything, but get them to pool their ideas in pairs or small groups before feeding back, as this will help build their confidence.

> **Answers and tapescript**
>
> Ned married his girlfriend and moved to London.
> Eric and Lori's mothers decided that they wanted them to meet.
>
> **T 8.4**
> **My very first love**
> **C=Carly, N=Ned**
>
> **C** I first met Ned when I was just ten years old. He was sixteen, er, very good-looking, and of course he had a girlfriend ... a really beautiful girlfriend. I hated her.
>
> **N** Hmm. I can remember Carly when she was only ten. She played in the street. She played on the corner near my house. I was sixteen. I had a girlfriend – she didn't like you, did she, Carly?
>
> **C** Hmm, no ... because she knew I liked you!!! You married her, didn't you? Four years later ... I was fourteen, I cried and cried ... I remember it well.

N Yeah – I was only twenty. I wasn't ready. It was a big mistake – a big mistake.

C You moved to London and had Michelle, your daughter.

N Yeah – my little Michelle, she's great …

C Yeah, she's lovely … And I finished school and then I went to college. I didn't marry … I had one or two boyfriends but nobody special. And two or three years later, my brother had a party. He invited you, and you came … And when I saw you, all the old feelings came back, and you told me you were divorced …

N Yeah, I was divorced and at my parents' house again. You were twenty-one, and just … wonderful. And we just fell in love.

C Yes, that's what happened. That was three years ago – now I'm twenty-four, we're married and we have a new baby, and Michelle is with us too. I'm so lucky … I married my very first love.

Do mothers know best?
E=Eric, L=Lori

E Our story is easy. We didn't do anything. It was our mothers who did it all!

L Yes. You see, our mothers are friends. They met one summer by the lake. They both have little summer houses there. And, of course, they talked a lot about their children …

E … and they decided that they wanted us to meet.

L We both thought this wasn't a very good idea!

E When my mom said to me 'I know a nice girl for you,' I just thought, 'No way.'

L Me, too! You see, my mom did this a lot, and it was usually terrible.

E But we finally said 'OK' – just for some peace.

L I took my sister with me …

E … and I took my best friend, Steve.

L But I was so surprised! Eric was wonderful!

E And of course, I thought the same about Lori. We all had a great time by the lake that summer. And at the end of the summer I knew I was in love with Lori.

L That was four years ago, and our wedding is in the fall. Our mothers are very happy, and we are, too!

E Yes. Sometimes mothers know best!

4 **T 8.4** [CD 1: Track 85] Get students to read through the questions and pre-teach/check *good-looking, lake, summer house, terrible*. Ask students to listen again for the information they need to answer the questions. Point out that they will need to listen carefully because the information is not always in the same order as the questions. Play both recordings again straight through and get students to complete their answers. Get them to check in pairs and exchange any information they missed. Only play the recording a third time if most of your students have missed a lot of key information. Check the answers with the whole class.

Answers
1 Carly was 10 and Ned was 16. Eric and Lori met four years ago.
2 She thought he was good-looking.
3 She didn't like Carly.
4 They met one summer by the lake. (They both have little summer houses there.)
5 It was terrible when their mums wanted them to meet a new girl or boy.
6 Eric thought Lori was wonderful, and Lori thought Eric was wonderful.
7 No, they don't. Only Carly and Ned have children.

5 Make sure students understand that they need to write the initial of the person who said the sentences and also think about the context. Elicit the answer to sentence **a** as an example. Then get students to complete the task, working in pairs or small groups. Again, encourage them to pool their knowledge and only play the recording again if they have real problems remembering the details.

Answers
a C When Ned married his girlfriend and moved to London.
b E When Eric and Lori first met.
c N When Ned married his girlfriend.
d E When Eric's mom said 'I know a nice girl for you.'
e C When Carly met Ned again at her brother's party.
f L When Lori went to meet Eric.
g C When Carly and Ned met again, and now.
h L Eric and Lori's wedding plans.

Speaking

6 Students work in pairs. Tell them they are going to roleplay being one of the characters from the listening. Let students choose their character. If you can, ask the boys/men to imagine they are Ned/Eric, and similarly the girls/women to imagine they are Carly/Lori. Make sure that each student is paired with the husband/wife of the other couple, i.e. Ned and Lori, and Eric and Carly. Students tell their partner about how they met their husband/wife from their character's point of view. The partner can ask them questions for more details and the student roleplaying must answer in character.

7 To encourage students to feel comfortable about talking about their own life, give an example about how your own relationship started and/or how your parents/grandparents met. Students continue in pairs.

Ask students to give the whole class examples of romantic, unusual, or amusing starts to a relationship.

Writing about a friend

Linking words – because, when, until

The writing syllabus continues with the second focus on linking words to include *because*, *when*, and *until*. Students do a matching and then a gap-fill exercise to practise the use of the linkers, before writing a short text about a friend. The writing task also consolidates the use of Present Simple and Past Simple.

1 Check comprehension of *because*, *when*, and *until* via translation or by getting students to check in dictionaries. Focus attention on the example and then give students time to complete the task working individually. Check the answers with the class.

> **Answers**
> 2 Peter couldn't speak until he was nearly four.
> 3 Tim didn't see the Colosseum when he was in Rome.
> 4 Eva didn't start learning English until she was thirty.
> 5 I didn't enjoy maths lessons when I was at school.
> 6 Sally didn't buy the red shoes because she couldn't afford them.
> 7 They didn't go to bed until after midnight.
> 8 We met Ken's wife last Saturday when they came for dinner.

2 Give an example by answering the questions in exercise 2 about a friend you had when you were young. Then give students time to write notes about their friend, using the questions as prompts. Divide the class into pairs and get students to exchange information about their friends, using the questions in the exercise and their notes. Check for correct use of Present Simple and Past Simple and, if necessary, briefly review the use of the tenses for present habits and past events.

3 Give students time to read through the text quickly to get a general idea of what it is about. Elicit the first two missing linking words as examples and then get students to complete the text. Check the answers with the class.

> **Answers**
> 1 when   6 but   11 but
> 2 and   7 when   12 and
> 3 because 8 and   13 and
> 4 and   9 because 14 so
> 5 until   10 so

4 Draw up a paragraph plan from the questions in exercise 2 for students to follow when they write their own text:
Paragraph 1: What is his/her name?
Where did you meet?
What did you do together?

Paragraph 2: How often do you meet now?
What do you do when you meet?
With weaker students, elicit the key structures needed to write the story, e.g. *My oldest friend is called … . We met in …* [place] *when we were …* [age]. *We … every week. Now we meet every … and we … .*

Give students time to write their text in class or set it for homework. If possible, display the texts on the classroom wall/noticeboard to allow students to read each other's work. You could ask them to vote for the most interesting text. When you check the students' work, point out errors but allow students to correct them themselves and try to limit correction to major problems to avoid demoralizing.

Song

The song *I just called to say I love you* appears in photocopiable format on TB p144. You will find the song after **T 8.4** on the Class Cassette/CD1 Track 86. Students choose the correct words to complete the song, then listen and check their answers. The answers are on TB p171.

END OF CD 1

ADDITIONAL MATERIAL

Workbook Unit 8
Exercise 7 Words that are nouns and verbs
Exercise 8 A puzzle activity on machines and inventions

You will need CD2 from this lesson onwards

Spelling and silent letters

The aim of this exercise is again to show students that English spelling is not phonetic through an exercise on silent letters. It is useful to have a convention when writing words on the board to show students a silent letter. This might be by writing the silent letter in a different coloured pen, or by crossing out the silent letter, e.g. *Xnow*.

You could encourage your students to do the same in their vocabulary notebooks.

The silent *r* in mid-position (e.g. *girl*) and in the end position (e.g. *daughter*) is practised. We do not advise you to explain the rule about the *r* being silent in end positions unless the following word begins with a vowel sound, e.g. *daughter and son*. This would probably overload students at this level.

Also, pronunciation work here and on the recording is based on RP. If you are a native-speaker teacher with a different accent, you may like to point this out and explain a little about the many and varying accents of spoken English!

1 Read the instructions as a class. Practise the words chorally and individually. Students work in pairs to cross out the silent letters.

T 8.5 [CD 2: Track 2] Students listen and check.

Answers and tapescript		
1 walk	5 eight	9 flight
2 listen	6 island	10 could
3 autumn	7 work	11 wrong
4 write	8 your	12 daughter

Students practise saying the words in pairs. Monitor and check.

2 Focus attention on the example. Students look at the phonetics and write in the words from exercise 1.

Answers		
2 could	4 autumn	6 island
3 listen	5 write	

3 Elicit the first word as an example. Students work in pairs to write other words with silent letters. They are all words students have met in earlier units or should recognize.

T 8.6 [CD 2: Track 3] Students listen and check.

Answers and tapescript		
1 born	3 world	5 cupboard
2 bought	4 answer	6 Christmas

Students practise saying the words in pairs. Monitor and check.

4 Elicit the first sentence as an example and then get students to continue reading the sentences in pairs.

T 8.7 [CD 2: Track 4] Students listen and check.

> **SUGGESTION**
> Students can write another three sentences using the words in exercises 1 and 3 and then exchange with a partner who should read them aloud. Alternatively, you could dictate, then practise saying the following sentences with your class:
> *She could walk to work in an hour.*
> *I thought they were in the cupboard.*

EVERYDAY ENGLISH (SB p64)

Special occasions

This exercise can provide a lot of fascinating information if you have students from different countries, or if some of your students know foreign countries.

1 Students look at the list and decide which are special days. They match the special days to a picture and/or object.

Answers	
1 birthday	6 wedding day
2 Valentine's Day	7 Mother's Day
3 Easter Day	8 Thanksgiving
4 New Year's Eve	9 Christmas Day
5 Hallowe'en	

2 Ask your students if they have similar celebrations for the same special days. Elicit some examples of how they celebrate, using the ideas given and their own ideas. Students work in small groups to describe to each other how they celebrate. Conduct a brief feedback session with the whole class. Write new vocabulary on the board for students to record in the vocabulary notebooks.

> **BACKGROUND NOTES**
> Here are some notes on how some British people celebrate the special days (though not all British people, of course).
>
> **Birthday**
> There is often a birthday cake, with candles to be blown out and everyone sings *Happy birthday*. People send birthday cards, and there is perhaps a birthday party with friends.
>
> **Mother's Day**
> This is on a Sunday towards the end of March (the fourth Sunday in Lent). Children give cards and a present such as some flowers or chocolates.
>
> **Wedding day**
> People get married in a church for a religious ceremony or a registry office for a civil ceremony. Rice or confetti is thrown at the bride and groom to wish them luck, and the bride often carries a horseshoe, again to symbolize good luck. There is a party afterwards called a *reception*, and the bride and groom may go on a holiday called a *honeymoon*.
>
> **Hallowe'en**
> This is the evening of 31 October, when it was believed that the spirits of dead people appeared. Customs associated with Hallowe'en in Britain and the US are fancy dress parties where people dress up as ghosts, witches, etc. Children often celebrate by wearing masks or costumes and going 'trick or treating' – going from house to house collecting sweets, fruit, or money.
>
> **Thanksgiving**
> This is a national holiday in the US (the fourth Thursday in November) and Canada (the second Monday in October) first celebrated by the Pilgrim settlers in Massachusetts after their first harvest in 1621. Most families enjoy a large meal together.
>
> **Easter Day**
> There is no fixed tradition of ways to celebrate Easter. Children receive chocolate Easter eggs and usually eat too many of them!

New Year's Eve

In Scotland this is called *Hogmanay* and it is a more important celebration than in the rest of Britain. People go to parties and wait for midnight to come, when they wish each other 'Happy New Year'. In London many thousands of people celebrate New Year in Trafalgar Square where they can hear Big Ben (the clock on the Houses of Parliament) strike midnight.

Valentine's Day

People send Valentine cards to the person they love. They are usually sent anonymously! People also put messages in newspapers to their loved one. These can often be quite funny!

Christmas Day

This is the 25 December, the main day for celebrating Christmas in Britain, when presents are exchanged. There is a large lunch, traditionally with turkey and Christmas pudding, which is made from dried fruit. People decorate the house, and have a Christmas tree. Young children believe that Santa Claus (or Father Christmas) visits during the early hours of Christmas morning and leaves presents by the children's beds or under the tree.

3   Students work in pairs to complete the conversations with the days, and match them to the occasions in exercise 1.

T 8.8 [CD 2: Track 5] Students listen and check their answers.

Answers and tapescript

1   **birthday**
    Happy **birthday** to you.
    Happy **birthday** to you.
    Happy **birthday**, dear Grandma,
    Happy **birthday** to you.

2   **Valentine's Day**
    A   Did you get any **Valentine** cards?
    B   Yes, I did. Listen to this.
        Roses are red. Violets are blue.
        You are my **Valentine**
        And I love you.
    A   Wow! Do you know who it's from?
    B   No idea!

3   **Mother's Day**
    A   Wake up, Mummy! Happy **Mother's Day**!
    B   Thank you, darling. Oh, what beautiful flowers, and a cup of tea!
    A   And I made you a card! Look!
    B   It's lovely. What a clever boy!

4   **wedding day**
    A   Congratulations!
    B   Thank you very much!
    A   When's the big day?
    B   Pardon?

    A   When's your **wedding** day?
    B   The 26th June. Didn't you get your invitation?

5   **New Year's Eve**
    A   It's midnight! Happy **New Year** everybody!
    B   Happy **New Year**!
    C   Happy **New Year**!

6   **weekend**
    A   Thank goodness! It's Friday!
    B   Yeah. Have a nice **weekend**!
    A   Same to you.

7   A   Ugh! Work again. I hate Monday mornings!
    B   Me, too. Did you have a good **weekend**?
    A   Yes, I did. It was great.

MUSIC OF ENGLISH

Read the *Music of English* box as a class. Using the recording as a model, drill the sentences in conversation 5, paying particular attention to stress and intonation. Get three students to take a role each and act out the conversation to the class.

Put students in pairs and ask them to choose a different conversation (avoid 1 as it is a song). With weaker students allocate conversations 2, 3, 4, 6 and 7. Students practise, paying close attention to stress and intonation. Students take it in turns to act out their conversations to the class.

Don't forget!

Workbook Unit 8

Exercise 9   A short gapped story in two parts with comprehension questions and listening practice

Exercise 10   Translation

Exercise 11   Listening practice on special occasions

Grammar Reference

Look at the exercises on SB p143 as a class, or set for homework. The answers are on TB p176.

Word list

Remind students of the Word list on SB p155. They could translate the words, or look at them at home, or transfer some of the words to their vocabulary notebook.

Pronunciation Book Unit 8

Video/DVD Episode 3 An old friend

PHOTOCOPIABLE MATERIAL: EXTRA IDEAS UNITS 5–8

Reading TB p143

The reading exercise is about a world champion memory man and revises Units 5–8. It could be done for homework.

Activities to exploit the reading are provided and the answers are on TB p171.

9

Count and uncount nouns
I like/I'd like • *some/any* • *much/many*
Food • **Polite requests**

Food you like!

Introduction to the unit

The theme of this unit is food and drink, which lends itself to the presentation and practice of the target items – count and uncount nouns with a review of the determiners *some* and *any* (in Unit 5 they were introduced with count nouns only) and a focus on *much/many*. The verb *like* is contrasted with *would like*, and the *Everyday English* focus *Polite requests* carries through the food and drink theme. The skills material includes a reading text about food around the world, and an invitation to discuss eating habits in different countries. There is also a *Listening and speaking* section on *My favourite national food*.

> **NOTE**
> Recordings for Units 9–14 are on Cassette 2.

Language aims

Grammar – count and uncount nouns Students often need help with the concept of count and uncount nouns, and need regular practice with the articles and determiners that can be used with them. Students also need to understand that a lot of nouns can be both countable and uncountable, depending on the context in which they are used, e.g.
Two coffees, please. (countable and meaning 'two cups of coffee')
Coffee is expensive. (uncountable and meaning 'coffee in general')
Students also have to get to grips with interference from their own language where some nouns which are uncount in English are countable. This can lead to misuse, e.g.
* *They gave me advices.*
* *I'd like some informations.*

like and would like *Would like* is introduced for the first time, and this is the first time that students have seen the modal verb *would*. It is easy for students to confuse *like* and *would like*. Here are some common mistakes.
* *Do you like a coffee?*
* *I like a cup of tea, please.*
Are you hungry? *You like a sandwich?*
It is relatively easy for students to perceive the difference between a general expression of liking and a specific request, but you can expect many mistakes for a long time as students confuse *like* and *would like*, especially the two auxiliary verbs *do* and *would*.

some/any *Some* and *any* were first introduced in Unit 5, but only with count nouns. This unit introduces them with uncount nouns as well.

The often-repeated rule that *some* is used in positive sentences and *any* in questions and negatives is not entirely true, but it's still useful at this level. However, in this unit the use of *some* in requests and offers is also introduced. It is quite a subtle concept for students to grasp that *some* can be used in questions when there is no doubt about the existence of the thing requested or offered. The use of L1 might help to clarify this.

As in Unit 5, we do not suggest that you explore the use of *any* to mean 'it doesn't matter which', as in *Take any book you want*.

much/many The focus on quantities is extended with a focus on *much/many*. The question forms *How much … ?* and *How many … ?* are also practised.

Vocabulary There is quite a heavy vocabulary load in this unit, largely to do with food and drink. Words to do with food and drink are introduced as part of the presentation of count/uncount nouns, and there is more lexis to do with food in the language practice and skills work. For this reason, there is no separate vocabulary section.

Everyday English Polite requests with *Can/Could you … ?* and *Can/Could I … ?* are introduced and practised.

Writing In this section there is a focus on filling in forms, and students write an email to book a hotel room.

Workbook There are exercises on count and uncount nouns, *I like/I'd like*, and *some/any, much/many*.

The vocabulary of the unit is recycled and extended through a menu and related activities.

Notes on the unit

STARTER (SB p66)

Give examples of your own favourite fruit, vegetable, and drink. Then get students to write their own answers. Students compare their answers in pairs.

Ask students to tell the rest of the class their answers, checking and drilling pronunciation as necessary. Revise the alphabet by getting students to spell each word. Build up lists on the board for each category and get students to copy them into their vocabulary notebooks.

FOOD AND DRINK (SB p66)

Count and uncount nouns

1 Students match the food and drink in columns **A** and **B** with the photos.

Focus students' attention on the two lists **A** and **B**, and ask them to identify which list has plural nouns. Elicit from students that these nouns can be counted – i.e. we can say two apples, three oranges, one strawberry, etc.

> **Answers**
>
> | **A** | | **B** | |
> |---|---|---|---|
> | p | apple juice | t | apples |
> | b | tea | e | oranges |
> | o | coffee | h | bananas |
> | a | milk | d | strawberries |
> | k | beer | g | carrots |
> | q | pizza | n | peas |
> | m | pasta | j | tomatoes |
> | i | cheese | s | hamburgers |
> | l | fish | c | chips |
> | f | chocolate | r | biscuits |
>
> List B has plural nouns.

2 The aim of exercises 2 and 3 is to revise *like* with count and uncount nouns, but more especially to reinforce the idea of *like* to express an 'all time' preference, in preparation for the presentation of *would like* in the next section which expresses a preference/request at a specific time.

T 9.1 [CD 2: Track 6] Focus on the photos. Tell students that they are going to listen to two children, Daisy and Piers, talking about what they like and don't like to eat and drink. Tell them they will need to refer to both lists **A** and **B** while doing the task and that the answers sometimes appear in a different order from in the lists. Play the first line to elicit an example about Daisy. Students listen and tick the things Daisy likes in lists **A** and **B** in exercise 1. Be prepared to play the script again so that students can make notes about Piers. Check the answers to what Daisy likes and Piers dislikes individually.

> **Answers** (also see exercise 1)
> Daisy likes: apple juice, tea, apples, oranges, bananas, strawberries, carrots, peas, tomatoes, pizza, pasta, cheese, fish and chips, chocolate.
> Piers doesn't like: apple juice, tea or coffee, oranges, fruit, vegetables (except potatoes), fish, peas, tomatoes.

T 9.1
D=Daisy, P=Piers

D Mmm, I love apple juice. Do you like it, Piers?
P No – it's disgusting. I like Cola, … and I love beer.
D Yuck! You don't! You don't drink beer!
P Yes, I do. Sometimes my dad gives me some of his beer – and I love it.
D Well, that's different … My dad drinks coffee – I don't like coffee at all. But my mum drinks tea and I love tea – with lots of milk and sugar.
P No, I don't like tea or coffee, just Cola – oh and orange juice. It's funny – I like orange juice, but I don't like oranges. I don't like fruit very much at all. Except bananas – I quite like bananas.
D Really? I like all fruit – apples, oranges, bananas, and I love strawberries. And … what about vegetables, do you like them?
P No – I don't eat vegetables.
D What? Never? Not even potatoes? You eat chips – I know you do.
P Yeah – OK, I eat potatoes – especially chips. Chips and hamburgers. I love that for my dinner.
D I don't like hamburgers – my favourite dinner is fish and chips with peas.
P Fish – yuck! Peas – yuck!
D I like vegetables – especially carrots and peas, oh and tomatoes. Hey, are tomatoes fruit or vegetable?
P I don't know. Anyway, I don't like tomatoes – except on pizza or with pasta and cheese. I love pizza and pasta.
D Me too.
P Anyway, I know your favourite food.
D No, you don't!
P Yes, I do. It's chocolate – all girls like chocolate!
D Boys like chocolate too! You ate all those chocolate biscuits at my house last week.
P They were biscuits. That's different. Anyway – you ate more than me …

D No, I didn't!

P Yes, you did!

D Didn't!

P Did!

3 **T 9.1** [CD 2: Track 6] Get students to decide who says which sentence, and write D for Daisy or P for Piers. Play the recording again if necessary. Check answers.

Answers
P=Piers, D=Daisy

D I don't like coffee at all.

P I like orange juice, but I don't like oranges.

P I don't like fruit very much at all.

P I quite like bananas.

D I like all fruit.

D I like vegetables, especially carrots and peas.

After students have listened, ask if they can remember what the teenagers said to express that they liked something or didn't like it, e.g. *delicious, fantastic, Yuck!, disgusting*. Ask what people say in other languages. Ask the class if they can remember any of the other things the teenagers said and what they disagreed about (*apple juice, tea, beer, fruit, vegetables, hamburgers, fish*).

4 Drill the pronunciation of the food and drink in the lists in exercise 1. Also practise the sentences in exercise 3, paying particular attention to stress highlighting.

Give an example of your own likes and dislikes, using the range of expressions from exercise 3, rather than simply *I like/I don't like …* . Students look at the lists of food and drink, and decide what they like and don't like. They then work in pairs and talk about their likes and dislikes, using the expressions from exercise 3. Monitor and check.

Get students to feed back briefly, encouraging them to talk about their partner and so practise the third person -*s*, e.g. *Ana likes fruit, but I don't*. Correct mistakes in grammar and pronunciation carefully.

GRAMMAR SPOT

Focus attention on the *Grammar Spot* and look at the questions as a class. Don't hurry this part. Allow students time to think. If one student knows and wants to give the answer before the others have had time to think, ask him or her to wait a little.

Answers

1 We cannot count the things in the sentences on the left, but we can count the things in the sentences on the right. (You might want to feed in the terms *count* and *uncount* nouns.)

2 We cannot count apple juice, but we can count apples.

Read Grammar Reference 9.1 on p143 together in class, and/or ask students to read it at home. Encourage them to ask you questions about it.

I like… and *I'd like*…

1 **T 9.2** [CD 2: Track 7] Focus attention on the photo of Piers and Daisy and tell students that they are going to read and listen to a conversation between Daisy's mum and Piers. Play the recording through once.

POSSIBLE PROBLEM

Point out that students may hear *Would you like a tea or a coffee?* instead of *Would you like some tea or coffee?* The meaning here is *Would you like a (cup of) tea or a (cup of) coffee?* and that is why the article is used with the uncount nouns. This form is a feature of spoken English and so encourage students to use *some* with plural and uncount nouns in offers and requests.

2 Students practise the conversation in exercise 1 following the stress pattern in the example, and then make similar conversations. If they have problems with pronunciation, play the recording again and get them to repeat.

You could record students' conversations and play them back for intensive correction. Pay attention to all aspects of pronunciation.

GRAMMAR SPOT

Look at the *Grammar Spot* questions as a class.

1 Question 1 is intended to guide students to the difference between *I like* and *I'd like*. Do not attempt to go into a full presentation of the uses of *would* at this stage, just introduce it as a polite way of making requests and offers.

Answer

The sentences in *Would you like some tea?* and *I'd like a biscuit* mean *Do you want …* and *I want …*

Point out that when we talk about things in general, we do not use an article/determiner with plural count nouns or with uncount nouns. You could write these examples on the board:

I like biscuits. (NOT *I like some biscuits.)*
I don't like tea very much. (NOT *I don't like any tea very much.)*
Do you like Chinese food? (NOT * *Do you like any Chinese food?)*

2 Question 2 focuses on the use of *some* with count and uncount nouns when saying what you want.

3 Question 3 demonstrates the special use of *some* in requests and offers, and *any* in other questions and negatives.

Read Grammar Reference 9.2 on p143 together in class, and/or ask students to read it at home. Encourage them to ask you questions about it.

PRACTICE (SB p67)

Questions and answers

1 Elicit the answer to question 1 as an example with the whole class. Students work in pairs or small groups to choose the correct form.

T 9.3 [CD 2: Track 8] Students listen and check.

Answers and tapescript
1 **Would** you like a ham sandwich?
  No, thanks. I'm not hungry.
2 **Do** you like Ella?
  Yes. She's very nice.
3 **Would** you like a cold drink?
  Yes, cola, please.
4 Can I help you?
  Yes. **I'd** like some stamps, please.
5 What sports do you do?
  Well, **I** like swimming very much.
6 Excuse me, are you ready to order?
  Yes. **I'd** like a steak, please.

Students practise the conversations in pairs. Monitor and check for pronunciation.

2 **T 9.4** [CD 2: Track 9] Play number 1 and elicit the correct answer as an example. Students listen to the rest of the sentences and complete the exercise. Let students discuss their answers in pairs. (See **T 9.5** below for the questions.)

T 9.5 [CD 2: Track 10] Students listen again and check their answers. Then get them to practise the conversations in pairs.

Answers and tapescript
1 A Good afternoon. Can I help you?
  B **Yes. I'd like some fruit, please.**
2 A Who's your favourite writer?
  B **I like books by John Grisham.**
3 A What would you like for your birthday?
  B **I'd like a new bike.**
4 A Do you like animals?
  B **I like cats, but I don't like dogs.**
5 A Here's the wine list, sir.
  B **We'd like a bottle of Italian red wine.**
6 A Have some ice-cream with your strawberries.
  B **No, thanks. I don't like ice-cream.**

a or *some*?

The aim of this section is to consolidate the concept of count and uncount nouns and practise the use of *a/an* and *some*. Use the section to check how well students have grasped the concept and be prepared to explain further, using L1 if possible.

3 Focus attention on the examples. Students then work in pairs to write *a*, *an*, or *some* before the nouns.

Answers
3	a banana	8	some toast
4	some bread	9	some money
5	some milk	10	a dollar
6	some meat	11	a notebook
7	an apple	12	some homework

4 Students work in pairs to write *a*, *an*, or *some*. The aim of this exercise is to show that some nouns (*coffee, cake,* and *ice-cream*) can be both countable and uncountable.

Answers
1	an egg	5	a coffee
2	some eggs	6	some coffee
3	a biscuit	7	an ice-cream
4	some biscuits	8	some ice-cream

ADDITIONAL MATERIAL

Workbook Unit 9
Exercises 1 and 2 Count and uncount nouns
Exercises 3 and 4 *like*
Exercises 5 and 6 *'d like*, and *like* or *would like*
Exercise 7 Food vocabulary and ordering a meal

AT THE MARKET (SB p68)

some/any, much/many

The aim of this section is to practise *some/any*, and introduce *(not) much/many* with both count and uncount nouns. Students also get to use *a lot* in short answers.

1 Read the instructions and focus attention on the photo. Make sure students understand *white/brown bread*, and briefly revise the other items in the picture (see *Answers* on p79). Focus attention on the examples. Drill the examples around the class. Students look at the picture and make positive and negative sentences, working as a class. Correct mistakes carefully, and pay attention to the weak pronunciation of *some* /səm/.

Answers

There aren't many cakes.
There's some cheese.
There's some apple juice.
There aren't many biscuits.
There are some eggs.
There isn't much butter.
There isn't any brown bread.
There isn't much white bread.
There aren't many strawberries.
There are some tomatoes.
There are some apples.
There aren't any potatoes.
There are some carrots.

GRAMMAR SPOT

Read the *Grammar Spot* as a class. Also point out to students the use of *many* with the plural verb *are* and *much* with the singular verb *is*.

Read Grammar Reference 9.3 on p143 together in class, and/or ask students to read it at home. Encourage them to ask you questions about it.

2 Before students work in pairs to ask and answer questions, draw attention to the use of *any* in the questions with both count and uncount nouns, *there is some, how much,* and *there isn't much* with uncount nouns (*bread*) and the use of *how many* with count nouns (*apples*).
Also point out the use of *a lot* in the answer with both count and uncount nouns, e.g. *Are there any apples? Yes, there are a lot. Is there any apple juice? Yes, there's a lot.*
Drill the questions in open and closed pairs following the stress patterns in the examples. Focus attention on the shopping list and check students understand that 'cheddar' is a type of English cheese. Students then continue asking about the items in the shopping list. Monitor and check for the accurate use of *some/any* and *much/many* and be prepared to review this as necessary.

3 **T 9.6** [CD 2: Track 11] Students listen to the conversation and tick what Piers and his mother buy. It is supposed to be funny, so if students laugh they are probably understanding it!

If necessary, play the recording a second time. Check the answers.

Answers

bread ✓	carrots ✗
eggs ✗	strawberries ✗
milk ✗	tomatoes ✓
butter ✗	apple juice ✓
apples ✓	cakes ✗
biscuits ✗	cheddar cheese ✓
potatoes ✗	tea ✗

T 9.6

At the market
M=Mum, P=Piers, S=seller
M Piers! Hurry up!
P Aw, Mum, I don't like shopping.
M Come on, Piers. I need your help.
P OK.
...
S Good morning Madam. How can I help you today?
M Well, I'd like some apple juice, please.
S How many bottles?
M Two, please.
P But Mum, ... I don't like apple juice.
M Shh Piers. It's good for you. Thank you. Here ... You can carry them.
P Oh no!
M And a kilo of tomatoes, please.
S No problem. Lovely and fresh these tomatoes are. There we are.
M And I'd like some of that cheddar cheese, please.
S This one? How much? Is this much OK?
M That's fine, thanks. And ... is there any brown bread? I can't see any.
S Sorry, no, there isn't – but there's some nice white bread. Look! It's homemade.
M Erm ...
P Mum, I really like white bread. Please can we have it?
M Oh, OK then. Yes, thanks.
S Anything else?
P Oh yeah! Mum! Look at those cakes!
M Shh Piers. ... Um ... oh yes, some apples.
S How many – one bag or two?
M Two bags, please.
P Oh yuck. Can't we have bananas?
M No, we can't. Here. Take these bags for me.
P Oh Mum! They're heavy!
M Thanks ... How much is all that?
S Let's see, that's ten pounds and eighty-five pence.
M Here you are.
S Thanks. And here's your change.
M Thanks. Bye!
...
P Phew! Is that everything?
M No, erm, ... I still need erm ...
P Mum, not more. I hate shopping!
M ... need to buy your new trainers, but if you don't want to ...
P New trainers – cool!
M ... But I thought you didn't like shopping ...
P Yeah, but...

4 **T 9.6** [CD 2: Track 11] Ask students to turn to the tapescript on SB p132. Divide students into groups and get them to practise the conversation. If they have problems with pronunciation and intonation, play the recording and get students to repeat key sentences before practising the conversation again.

much or many?

1 Pre-teach/check *petrol*. Students work in pairs to complete the questions using *much* or *many*.

> **Answers**
> 1 How **many** people are there in the room?
> 2 How **much** petrol is there in the car?
> 3 How **much** money do you have in your pocket?
> 4 How **many** eggs are there in the cupboard?
> 5 How **much** milk is there in the fridge?
> 6 How **many** apples do you want?

2 Students choose an answer for each question in exercise 1.

> **Answers**
> 1e 2f 3d 4c 5b 6a

3 Drill the first question-and-answer exchange chorally and individually. Make sure students can reproduce falling intonation in the questions. Students practise the questions and answers in pairs.

Check it

4 Focus attention on the example. Students work in pairs to correct the mistakes.

> **Answers**
> 2 I don't like ice-cream./I wouldn't like an ice-cream.
> 3 Can I have some bread, please?
> 4 I'm hungry. I'd like a sandwich.
> 5 There isn't much milk left.
> 6 I'd like some fruit, please.
> 7 How much money do you have?
> 8 We have a lot of homework today.

Roleplay

5 Demonstrate the activity by writing a shopping list on the board and getting two confident students to roleplay the conversation. Drill the language in the Student's Book following the stress patterns in the examples. Briefly revise realistic prices for a small amount of shopping. Then students continue in pairs. You could ask some of the pairs to act out the dialogue.

ADDITIONAL MATERIAL

Workbook Unit 9
Exercise 8 *some* or *any*?
Exercise 9 *How much … ?* or *How many … ?*

Food around the world

> **SUGGESTION**
> You might want to set some vocabulary for homework prior to this lesson – the pictures on the page can then be used to check vocabulary in the lesson.
>
> | | |
> |---|---|
> | *move on* | *herrings* |
> | *farm* (v) | *sardines* |
> | *land* (n) | *sausages* |
> | *control* (v) | *course (of a meal)* |
> | *environment* | *chopsticks* |
> | *depend on* | *fingers* |
> | *rice* | *pick up (food)* |
> | *noodles* | *transport* (v) |

1 In a monolingual group, answer the questions as a whole-class activity. In a multilingual group, students can work in pairs or small groups and exchange information about their countries.

2 Focus attention on the photos. Ask students to identify the places or nationalities represented in the photos and to name the food itself.

> **Answers** (clockwise from the left)
> England – fish and vegetables
> China – rice harvest
> East Europe – meat and sausages
> China – noodles
> Caribbean – bananas
> strawberries
> sardines
> Middle East

3 Get students to read the text through quickly and match the correct headings to paragraphs 2, 3, and 4. Encourage students to focus on just matching the headings and tell them not to worry about new vocabulary at this stage. (If they have done the above homework task, they should not have too many difficulties.) You might want to set a time limit to encourage students to scan the text for clues.

> **Answers**
> Paragraph 2: What do we eat?
> Paragraph 3: How do we eat?
> Paragraph 4: Where does our food come from?

Students read the text again, matching lines to the photos. Get class feedback photo by photo, and keep up the pace.

Possible answers

Girls at the table: *in North America, Australia, and Europe, ... people eat with knives and forks...*

Paddy (rice) fields: *... in the south of China they eat rice*

Butcher: *... in central Europe, away from the sea, ... they eat more meat and sausages; ... there are hundreds of different kinds of sausages.*

Child at the table: *... in the north they eat noodles ...*

Lorry with green bananas: *... nowadays it is possible to transport food ...; bananas come from the Caribbean or Africa ...*

Strawberries: *... strawberries come from Chile or Spain.*

Fish: *... in Scandinavia, they eat a lot of herrings; ... the Portuguese love sardines...*

Men sitting on the floor eating: *... in parts of India and the Middle East people use their fingers and bread to pick up the food.*

4 Students read the text again more slowly and answer the questions. Get them to check in pairs before checking answers with the whole class.

Answers

1 About I million years ago.
2 No, they don't. They eat noodles.
3 Because they live by the sea.
4 In central Europe, away from the sea.
5 Austria, Germany, and Poland.
6 Only one.
7 They use their fingers and bread to pick up the food.
8 Because it is easy to transport food from one part of the world to another.

SUGGESTION

If students are interested in the details of the text, get them to write more questions for a partner to answer.

What do you think?

5 Read through the questions as a class. Quickly revise the meaning and pronunciation of *breakfast*, *lunch*, and *dinner* and check comprehension of *main meal*.

Students work in small groups and discuss the questions. This will obviously be a very productive activity in a multilingual group, but students in a monolingual group can also discuss food habits in their own country and their own family, and compare with other countries they have visited.

Conduct a brief feedback session with the whole class, encouraging students to compare different eating habits in different countries.

Writing

6 Students write a short paragraph about meals in their country, using their ideas from exercise 5. This can be given as a homework activity if you do not have time to do it in class. Don't correct this too harshly; the idea is to give students an opportunity for some freer writing, and they may well make a lot of mistakes.

LISTENING AND SPEAKING (SB p72)

My favourite national food

1 As a lead-in to this section, elicit examples of famous national or regional dishes, e.g. pizza from Italy, paella from Spain, etc. Focus attention on the photographs. Students work in pairs and say which dish(es) they like and then match them with the countries.

Answers

1 Bruschetta – Italy
2 Bife de chorizo – Argentina
3 Sachertorte – Austria
4 Full English breakfast – England

2 This activity serves to pre-teach the key food vocabulary from the listening task. Get students to look for the food items. Check by getting students to point to the correct part of the photos.

3 **T 9.7** **[CD 2: Track 12]** Tell students they are going to hear the four people in the photographs talking about their national dish. The first time they hear the people, they only need to identify their nationality and match each speaker to the correct dish. Play the recording through once and then check the answers.

Play the recording again and get students to listen out for what each speaker says about their dish. Get students to pool their information before checking answers with the whole class. Ask them if they have tried/would like to try any of the dishes now that they know more about them.

Answers

Anke – Austrian; Sachertorte
Graham – English; English breakfast
Sergio – Italian; bruschetta
Madalena – Argentinian; bife de chorizo
Accept any relevant detail from the tapescript for the second stage of the listening task.

T 9.7

Anke
One dish that is very famous in my country is 'Sachertorte'. It is a kind of chocolate cake and you eat it with cream. I love it! The famous Café Sacher is in the centre of Vienna. They say a chef called Franz Sacher invented it there. When I am in Vienna, I always go to Café Sacher for some of their cake and a nice black coffee.

Graham

Now in my job, I travel the world, and I like all kinds of food ... but my favourite, my favourite is ... er ... I always have it as soon as I come home ... is a full English breakfast. Bacon, eggs, sausage, mushrooms, tomatoes, and of course, toast. I love it, not every day, but when I'm at home we have it every Sunday. Mmmm! I'd like it right now. Delicious.

Sergio

We love eating in my country! One of my favourite national dishes is called 'bruschetta'. This is actually toast, but you make it with special bread. You can eat it with a lot of things, but my favourite bruschetta has tomatoes, garlic, and olive oil on it. In my town there is a 'bruschetteria'. This is a small café – selling only toast! It's my favourite place to go.

Madalena

One kind of food that my country is very famous for is meat, especially beef. Everybody eats a lot of meat here. My family eats beef three or four times a week. There are a lot of different beef dishes, but my favourite is 'bife de chorizo.' This is a big steak! My mum cooks it with tomatoes and chilli. Delicious!

4 Focus attention on the questions about the people in exercise 3. Students work in pairs and answer as many questions as they can. If necessary, play the recording again to let students complete their answers. Check the answers with the whole class.

Answers

Graham travels a lot.
Sergio and Anke go to cafés to eat their favourite food.
Anke likes sweet things.
Madalena and Graham eat their favourite food at home.

2 In the centre of Vienna.
3 A chef (called Franz Sacher).
4 When he's at home on a Sunday.
5 You make bruschetta with special toasted bread and add tomatoes, garlic, and olive oil.
6 A small café in his town that sells only toast.
7 Three or four times a week.
8 Her mother.

What do you think?

Give examples of your own favourite national dishes and describe them in a natural way. Elicit one or two other examples from the class and then get students to continue talking about their national foods in pairs.

Get class feedback. Establish what type of dishes are the most popular with the class, e.g. breakfast/lunch/dinner dishes, sweets/cakes, snacks, etc.

Polite requests

POSSIBLE PROBLEMS

This section introduces *Can I ... ?/Could I ... ?* and *Can you ... ?/Could you ... ?* for the first time. If you think your students will not be familiar with it, present it yourself, using the classroom to illustrate meaning: *Jean, can you open the window, please? Maria, could you clean the board, please? Emma, could I borrow your pen, please?* etc.

You could tell students that *Can I ... ?* and *Could I ... ?* mean the same, but *could* is usually more polite. Point out that although *could* looks like the past tense, the concept is in fact present. However, if you think your class is strong enough, you could use the situations in the Student's Book as a vehicle for presentation.

1 Look at the photograph and get students to say what they can see. (A meal/dinner party with a group of adults; there is a range of dishes including meat, rice, vegetables, and lots of different types of fruit. There is also wine and water to drink.)

2 Pre-teach/check *pass (the salt)*, *sparkling/still (water)*. Ask students to match the questions and responses.

T 9.8 [CD 2: Track 13] Students listen and check their answers.

Answers and tapescript

1 Would you like some more rice?
   Yes, please. It's delicious.
2 Could you pass the salt, please?
   Yes, of course. Here you are.
3 Could I have a glass of water, please?
   Do you want sparkling or still?
4 Does anybody want more wine?
   Yes, please. I'd love some.
5 How would you like your coffee?
   Black, no sugar, please.
6 This is delicious! Can you give me the recipe?
   Yes, of course. I'm glad you like it.
7 Do you want help with the washing-up?
   No, of course not. We have a dishwasher.

Read the information in the Caution Box as a class.

MUSIC OF ENGLISH

T 9.9 [CD 2: Track 14] Read through the *Music of English* box as a class. Play the recording. Tell students to listen carefully, paying special attention to the intonation and stress highlighting. Students listen and repeat each request, closely following the polite intonation. If necessary, give students further practice with the questions and answers in exercise 2.

3 Elicit the answer to question 1 as an example and then get students to complete the task.

Check the answers.

> **Answers and tapescript**
> **T 9.10**
> 1 **A** Can I have a cheese sandwich, please?
>   **B** Yes, of course. That's £1.75.
> 2 **A** Could you tell me the time, please?
>   **B** It's just after ten.
> 3 **A** Can you take me to the station, please?
>   **B** Jump in.
> 4 **A** Can I see the menu, please?
>   **B** Here you are. And would you like a drink to start?
> 5 **A** Could you lend me some money, please?
>   **B** Not again! How much would you like this time?
> 6 **A** Can you help me with my homework, please?
>   **B** What is it? French? I can't speak a word of French.
> 7 **A** Can I borrow your dictionary, please?
>   **B** Yes, if I can find it. I think it's in my bag.

4 Focus attention on the example. Students work in pairs to practise the requests in exercise 3 and give an answer.

T 9.10 [CD 2: Track 15] Play the recording and get students to compare their answers with those given by the speakers.

> **SUGGESTION**
> You can give further practice in food and drink vocabulary, *like*, *would like*, and polite requests by using the photocopiable activity on TB p145. Photocopy enough sheets for each student.
>
> 1 Hand out the sheets and give students enough time to complete the lists. With weaker students, you could brainstorm food and drink vocabulary, and elicit examples of interesting guests first.
>
> 2 Divide the class into groups of three. Focus attention on the examples and then get students to discuss their preferences. Emphasize that they need to agree on what to eat/drink, and who to invite.
>
> 3 Review the language in the examples, drilling chorally as necessary. If possible, move chairs to create space, play music to give a party atmosphere, and bring in plastic cups of water to add authenticity. Give students time to roleplay their party. Monitor and join in, as appropriate. This is primarily a fluency activity, so only feed back on major errors that are common to the whole class.

WRITING (SB p120)

Filling in forms

Booking a hotel

The writing syllabus continues with a focus on filling in forms and writing emails. The context is booking a hotel room and students review the language of polite requests.

1 Ask students if they send emails, and who they send them to and why. Then get students to read the model email and answer the questions in pairs. Check the answers with the class.

> **Answers**
> • The email is from Peter West.
> • It is to the Liverpool Arms Hotel or bookings@liverpoolarms.co.uk
> • It is about booking a room.
> • It begins *Dear Sir or Madam* and ends *Yours faithfully*.

Briefly review the greeting and ending used in the formal letter in Unit 6 (*Dear Ms Watson* and *Yours sincerely*). Ask *Why does the writer use 'Yours faithfully' in the email?* (because he doesn't know the name of the person who will read the email).

2 Check comprehension of the lines from the email in exercise 2. Ask students to decide where they go in the email. Then check the answers.

> **Answers**
> 1c 2a 3b

Ask some questions about the language used in the email, e.g. Which expressions make the email sound polite? (*I would like …*, *Could I possibly have …?*, *I understand …*, *Could you tell me …?*, *Please let me know …*, *Thank you very much.*) Does the writer use contracted or full forms? (full forms – *I would like*). Which expression asks for a reply? (*I look forward to hearing from you.*)

3 Pre-teach/check *check-in*, *check-out*, *en suite*, *guest* and *additional information*. Get students to read the form through so that they understand what information they need to transfer from the email. Give students time to complete the form and then check the answers.

Answers	
Name	Peter West
Email	p.west@uktel.com
Tel/Fax	0207 566 4945
Address	15 Monarch Road
	London NW1 2TS
Country	England
Number of guests	1 Adults
Number of rooms	1 Single
Check-in	12/04/(relevant year)
Check-out	15/04/(relevant year)
Additional information	I would like a quiet room at the back of the hotel. What time does the restaurant close?

4   Get students to read the writing task in exercise 4. Ask
    them what they want to book (*a double room for four
    nights next month with a view of the sea*). Elicit what they
    need to ask about (*Internet and other facilities* (e.g.
    phone, television, room service, car parking)). Ask students
    to think of any other things they could ask about (e.g.
    pets, restaurant, late bar, etc.). Remind them to decide on
    the dates they want the room and to use the polite
    language from the model email (see notes for exercise 2
    above). With weaker classes, elicit the first paragraph of
    the email with the whole class.

    Give students time to write their email in class or set it
    for homework. If possible, allow students to read and
    check each other's emails to help each other with
    mistakes. When you collect in the students' work, check
    for the use of appropriate language and the correct
    greeting and ending. Point out errors but allow students
    to correct them themselves and try to limit correction to
    major problems to avoid demoralizing.

Don't forget!

Workbook Unit 9
Exercise 10 Translation

Grammar Reference
Look at the exercises on SB p143 as a class, or set for
homework. The answers are on TB p176.

Word list
Remind your students of the Word list for this unit on SB
p156. They could translate the words, learn them at home,
or transfer some of the words to their vocabulary notebook.

Pronunciation Book Unit 9

Video/DVD Episode 4 Dinner for two

10

Comparatives and superlatives • *have got*
City and country • Directions 2

Bigger and better!

Introduction to the unit

This unit is unusual in that it has three presentation sections, each one revising the grammar of the one before.

The theme is describing places: towns and cities, the countryside, and resorts. These are useful contexts to practise comparatives and superlatives. Now we introduce *have got* (see Note in Unit 3, TB p19) in a direct comparison with *have* (for possession), which students are already familiar with. The skills section includes a jigsaw reading about three cities which are famous for their links to dance, Buenos Aires, Havana, and Seville, and provides further practice of the grammatical aims.

Language aims

Grammar – comparative and superlative adjectives The following aspects of comparatives and superlatives are introduced:

- the use of *-er/-est* with short adjectives, e.g. *cheap, cheaper, cheapest*.
- the use of *-ier/-iest* with adjectives that end in *-y*, e.g. *noisy, noisier, noisiest*.
- the use of *more/most* with longer adjectives, e.g. *more expensive, most expensive*.
- irregular adjectives such as *good, better, best*.

The presentation of these is staged. In the first presentation, pairs of opposite adjectives are revised/introduced and this leads to the introduction of comparative forms. These forms are then revised in the second presentation when *have got* is introduced. Finally, superlatives are introduced in the third presentation and at the same time comparatives and *have got* are revised.

Students usually experience little difficulty with the concept of comparatives and superlatives but experience more difficulty in producing and pronouncing the forms because of all the different parts involved. Utterances often sound very laboured and unnatural because equal stress is given to each word and syllable. For this reason we practise natural-sounding connected speech.

Common mistakes

She's more tall than me.   *She's taller that me.*
He's the most tall student in the class.   *He's tallest student in the class.*

have got The verb *have* for possession was introduced in Unit 3. We purposely have delayed the introduction of *have got* for possession until now because of the complications of production it causes if introduced alongside the Present Simple of *have*, particularly in the question and negative. (See the Note in the *Language aims* of Unit 3, TB p19.) In this unit there are many exercises that contrast *have* and *have got*.

Vocabulary and pronunciation Pairs of opposite adjectives are introduced as part of the presentation of comparative adjectives.

In the *Vocabulary* section, town and country words are introduced and practised in contexts which allow review of comparatives and superlatives.

There is further practice in recognizing phonetic script.

Everyday English There is further practice of getting and giving directions, and prepositions of movement such as *along* and *down* are introduced.

Writing Simple relative pronouns are introduced. Then students study a model text about London before writing a short piece about their capital city.

Workbook There is further practice on comparatives and superlatives, and *have got*.

In the *Vocabulary* section, compound nouns to do with towns are introduced such as *town centre, railway station*.

Notes on the unit

STARTER (SB p74)

This activity introduces the topic of city and country life and gets students thinking of adjectives related to each way of life. It is intended to be light-hearted and brief, so don't worry too much if students make errors with comparative and superlative structures – there will be plenty of opportunities to practise these in the activities that follow.

1 Focus on the question and answers. Ask students to discuss with a partner which they prefer, city or country life, and to give reasons. Get class feedback and write adjectives on the board.

2 Students decide which place, the city or the country, is the most popular.

CITY LIFE (SB p74)

Comparative adjectives

> **SUGGESTION**
> You could set exercise 1 for homework if you need to save class time. If you do, begin the lesson by going through the answers and practising the pronunciation of each word.

1 If students haven't done this exercise as homework (see *Suggestion* above), put your students into pairs and get them to match the adjectives with their opposites. Check the answers and the pronunciation first before students categorize the words into 'city' and 'country'.

Be prepared for students to want to pronounce the *ie* of *friendly* separately */frɪendli/* and make sure they say it correctly, /frendli/.

> **Answers**
> In these pairs of words the opposite of *old* is *modern* (it could also be *new*) not *young*, because in the context of the presentation the adjectives are being used to talk about buildings, not people.
>
> | | | | |
> |---|---|---|---|
> | fast | /fɑːst/ | slow | /sləʊ/ |
> | modern | /'mɒdən/ | old | /əʊld/ |
> | expensive | /ɪk'spensɪv/ | cheap | /tʃiːp/ |
> | dangerous | /'deɪndʒərəs/ | safe | /seɪf/ |
> | dirty | /'dɜːti/ | clean | /kliːn/ |
> | unfriendly | /ʌn'frendli/ | friendly | /'frendli/ |
> | noisy | /'nɔɪzi/ | quiet | /'kwaɪət/ |
> | exciting | /ɪk'saɪtɪŋ/ | boring | /'bɔːrɪŋ/ |
> | busy | /'bɪzi/ | relaxing | /rɪ'læksɪŋ/ |

Ask students to think about which words describe city life and country life. You could put the headings CITY and COUNTRY on the board and write in your students' suggestions as to which adjectives belong where, or you could ask individual students to come up to the board to write in the suggestions themselves. Be prepared for some discussion as there are obviously no prescribed right answers. Welcome any freer speaking that results.

2 **T 10.1** [CD 2: Track 16] This short listening task contextualizes opinions about city and country life and also key comparative forms. Play the recording and elicit who lives where (Joel in the city and Andy in the country). Get students to say who prefers the city and who prefers the country and why (*Joel prefers city life because it's faster, more modern, and more exciting. He thinks country life is more boring. Andy prefers country life because it's slower, safer, and more relaxing. He thinks city life is more dangerous.*)

Ask students who they agree with.

> **Tapescript**
> **J=Joel, A=Andy**
> J I prefer city life. It's faster, more modern, and more exciting than country life.
> A Yes, but city life's also more dangerous. The country's slower and safer than the city. I prefer the country. It's more relaxing.
> J Well, it's certainly more relaxing, but that's because it's more boring!

3 **T 10.2** [CD 2: Track 17] Now is the moment to concentrate on the pronunciation. Ask your students to look at the example sentence in the Student's Book and say it in chorus, either using yourself or the recording as a model. Focus particularly on the /ə/ sounds. Ask students whether /ə/ is used on stressed or unstressed words/parts of words (*unstressed*). Tell students that the /ə/ sound is always present at the end of the *-er* comparative and in the pronunciation of *than* /ðən/. Isolate *safer* and *than* and then drill them together as connected speech: *safer than* /'seɪfəðən/.

Drill the other sentences from the recording or by saying them yourself. If necessary, break up the sentences to drill them, particularly the comparative forms + *than*. Try to get a natural 'flow' in the repetition of the sentences as on the recording.

4 This exercise focuses on the main target language for this section, so make it clear to your class that this is an important moment and that this is the structure in English that compares things. If necessary and possible, use translation to do this.

Ask students to work in pairs to make sentences comparing life in the city and country. (You may need to point out the use of *more* with longer adjectives, but don't go into the rules in too much detail at this stage. They are dealt with more fully later on.) Get students to discuss their opinions in pairs. Monitor and check for accurate use of comparatives and acceptable pronunciation.

5 Students share their opinions with the rest of the class. If most of your students had problems with the comparative forms, write their sentences on the board including the mistakes and get the class to correct them. Encourage students to use the schwa /ə/ sound where appropriate. Any major problems with pronunciation can be dealt with by drilling the sentences with the whole class.

GRAMMAR SPOT

1 This is to reinforce and make clear to your students the rules governing the formation of comparative adjectives. Students work individually to complete the comparative sentences and try to formulate any rules they can. They may have got a clear idea from doing exercise 4 or they may need prompting and guiding, but try not to just give them the rules. You could write the rules up on the board as you go along.

> **Answers**
> I'm **older** than you.
> Your class is **noisier** than my class.
> Your car was **more expensive** than my car.
>
> -er is used with short adjectives such as *old, older*.
> -ier with adjectives that end in -y such as *noisy, noisier*.
> more ... is used with longer adjectives such as *expensive, more expensive*.

2 Students work in pairs to write the comparative forms, using their dictionaries if appropriate. Some comparative forms were given in exercise 4.

Check the answers with the whole class, getting students to spell the comparative forms.

> **Answers**
> | fast | **faster** | slow | **slower** |
> | modern | **more modern** | old | **older** |
> | expensive | **more expensive** | cheap | **cheaper** |
> | dangerous | **more dangerous** | safe | **safer** |
> | dirty | **dirtier** | clean | **cleaner** |
> | unfriendly | **unfriendlier*** | friendly | **friendlier** |
> | noisy | **noisier** | quiet | **quieter** |
> | exciting | **more exciting** | boring | **more boring** |
> | busy | **busier** | relaxing | **more relaxing** |
>
> *This is the comparative usually given by dictionaries, but *more unfriendly* is also often used.

3 Ask students for the irregular forms of *good* and *bad*, and check the pronunciation of *worse* /wɜːs/ carefully.

> **Answers**
> good **better**   bad **worse**

Read Grammar Reference 10.1 on p144 together in class, and/or ask students to read it at home. Encourage them to ask you questions about it.

PRACTICE (SB p75)

Much more than ...

1 Put the conversations in a context and tell your students that two people are discussing different cities they know.

> **NOTE**
> In this exercise we bring in the use of *much* to emphasize comparatives. The students are only asked to recognize it at first, and not produce it until later.

Focus attention on the example. Then ask students to work in pairs to complete the conversations. Point out that the students have to fill in the opposite adjectives in B's comments to those A uses.

T 10.3 [CD 2: Track 18] Play the recording and get students to check their answers. Tell them to focus on pronunciation, particularly stress and intonation.

> **Answers and tapescript**
> **T 10.3**
> 1 A Life in the country is **slower than** city life.
>   B Yes, the city's much **faster**.
> 2 A New York is **safer than** Los Angeles.
>   B No, it isn't. New York is much **more dangerous**.
> 3 A Seoul is **bigger than** Beijing.
>   B No, it isn't! It's much **smaller**.
> 4 A Madrid is **more expensive than** Rome.
>   B No, it isn't. Madrid is much **cheaper**.
> 5 A The buildings in Rome are **more modern than** the buildings in Prague.
>   B No, they aren't. They're much **older**.
> 6 A Cafés in London are **better than** cafés in Paris.
>   B No! Cafés in London are much **worse**.

Get individual students to practise the conversations across the class in open pairs. Encourage the Bs to sound really indignant when they disagree with A. Give them exaggerated models yourself or play the recording again to make clear that you want them to produce good stress and intonation and connected speech:

Examples

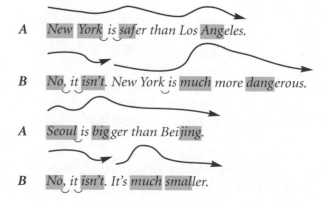

A   New York is safer than Los Angeles.

B   No, it isn't. New York is much more dangerous.

A   Seoul is bigger than Beijing.

B   No, it isn't. It's much smaller.

2 This is the personalization stage. Decide on two town/cities that you and all, or most, of the students know and demonstrate the activity. Students continue in pairs and decide which town/city they prefer. Monitor and check for accurate use of comparative forms and pronunciation.

Get a few students to feed back to the rest of the class. Discuss any common mistakes in grammar or pronunciation from the pairwork stage.

ADDITIONAL MATERIAL

Workbook Unit 10
Exercises 1 and 2 Consolidation of comparatives

COUNTRY LIFE (SB p75)

have got

In this presentation, comparatives are revised and *have got* is introduced in the context of a telephone conversation.

Focus attention on the photos of Joel and Andy and check students can remember their names. Read the introduction to the task aloud to the class to set the scene.

1 **T 10.4** [CD 2: Track 19] Tell students to close their books and listen to the telephone conversation between Joel and Andy. Play the recording through once. Ask students the gist questions.

> **Answers**
> Andy moved to the village of Appleton. Joel stayed in London.

2 Pre-teach/check *cottage* and *go surfing*. For the moment, don't focus on the examples of *have got* in the text – just tell students to complete the conversation with the missing adjectives. Make it clear that some of them are comparatives and some are not.

Play the recording for students to check their answers. Play the recording again for students to add in any answers they missed. Check the answers with the whole class.

> **Answers and tapescript**
> **J=Joel, A=Andy**
> **J** So, Andy, tell me, why did you leave London? You had a **good** job.
> **A** Yes, but I've got a **better** job here.
> **J** And you had a **nice** flat in London.
> **A** Well, I've got a **nicer** place here. It's a cottage!
> **J** Really? How many bedrooms has it got?
> **A** Three. And it's got a garden. It's **bigger** than my flat in London and it's **cheaper**.
> **J** But you haven't got any friends!
> **A** I've got a lot of new friends here. People are much **friendlier** than in London.
> **J** But the country's so **boring**!

> **A** No, it isn't. I've got a surfboard now and I go surfing at weekends. Appleton has got a cinema, restaurants, pubs, and a nightclub. And the air is **cleaner** and the streets are **safer**.
> **J** OK. OK. Everything is **better**! Can I come next weekend?
> **A** Of course you can!

3 Get students to practise the conversation in pairs. If necessary, play the recording again, drilling the sections students have problems with.

GRAMMAR SPOT

This *Grammar Spot* contrasts the form and use of *have got* with *have*.

1 Read through the notes with the whole class. You will need to point out the fact that the *have* in *have got* contracts, but that it doesn't in *have* for possession. Students may have trouble saying the contracted and negative forms, especially next to the following consonant, so practise saying the examples in the box. You could drill them chorally and individually.

I've got a dog.	/aɪv gɒt ə dɒg/
He's got a car.	/hi:z gɒt ə kɑ:/
Have you got a dog?	/hæv (həv) ju: gɒt ə dɒg/
Has she got a car?	/hæz (həs) ʃi: gɒt ə kɑ:/
They haven't got a flat.	/ðeɪ hævnt gɒt ə flæt/
It hasn't got a garden.	/ɪt hæznt gɒt ə gɑ:dn/

2 Introduce the past of *have* and *have got*. Elicit a few examples from the class of things they had when they were younger, e.g. *I had a dog. I had a bike.*

3 Ask your students to study the conversation and underline all the examples of *have got* and *had*. Make it clear that they are looking for questions and negatives, and not just the positive. Ask students to check in pairs, and then check with the whole class.

> **Answers**
> *have got*
> I**'ve got** a better job here.
> I**'ve got** a nicer place here.
> How many bedrooms **has** it **got**?
> And it**'s got** a garden.
> But you **haven't got** any friends!
> I**'ve got** a lot of friends here.
> I**'ve got** a surfboard now.
> Appleton **has got** a cinema…
> *had*
> You **had** a good job.
> And you **had** a nice flat in London.

Read the Grammar Reference 10.2 on p144 together in class, and/or ask students to read it at home. Encourage them to ask you questions about it.

have/have got

This is a very straightforward transformation exercise designed to focus students' attention solely on the difference in form between *have* and *have got* for possession. It is worth bearing in mind that focusing on the form of *have got* at this stage should help students when they meet the Present Perfect Simple in Unit 14.

1 We suggest that you refer students back to Grammar Reference 10.2 on p144 as they do this exercise. Focus attention on the examples and then get students to do the exercise on their own, writing the contracted forms where possible. Then get students to check with a partner, before you conduct a full class feedback.

> **Answers**
> 3 I've got a lot of homework tonight.
> 4 Have you got any homework?
> 5 Our school has got a good library, but it hasn't got many computers.
> 6 My parents have got a new DVD player.
> 7 Has your sister got a boyfriend?
> 8 I haven't got a problem with this exercise.

I've got more than you!

2 This roleplay should be a fun (and not very realistic!) activity. Focus attention on the cartoon and ask students *What have very rich people usually got?* and elicit a few suggestions from the whole class.

> **Possible answers**
> money; (big) houses; (fast) cars; planes; horses; boats; servants

Focus attention on the example in the Student's Book. Say the first line yourself and then in open pairs. Drill the sentences and encourage exaggerated stress and intonation as students boast about their possessions! If necessary, highlight the rise, rise, rise, rise, fall of the 'list' intonation in the second film star's reply.

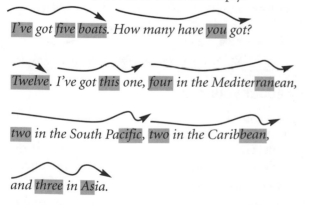

Ask your students to work in pairs. Get Student A in each pair to turn to p149 and Student B to p151. Elicit an example exchange from two confident students and then get the rest of the students to exchange information about their possessions. Go round the class checking grammar and pronunciation. Only correct where absolutely necessary, in order to encourage fluency. Then get feedback as to who is the richer!

ADDITIONAL MATERIAL

Workbook Unit 10
Exercises 3–5 *have/have got*
Exercise 6 Comparatives and *have got*

Superlative adjectives

This presentation of superlative adjectives includes revision of comparatives and *have got*.

1 Check comprehension of *holiday resort* and elicit whether students have ever visited one or whether they would like to. Focus attention on the photos of these luxury holiday resorts and the globes to show students the location of each one. Ask students to read the information about each place. Check comprehension of *seaplane flight, boat ride,* and *taxi ride*. Ask students to tell you which resort they like best and why. Here they could be revising *have got*, but don't insist on this, as the main aim is to generate interest in the theme and to take in some of the information about the resorts.

2 This exercise has been specially designed so that all the true sentences contain examples of superlative adjectives, thereby providing a means of illustrating the new structure. The false sentences contain examples of comparatives and *have got*.

Elicit the answers to numbers 1 and 2 as examples, explaining the superlative *the most expensive*, but not going into detail at this stage. Students work in pairs to decide which sentences are true and which are false, and to correct the information in the false ones.

> **POSSIBLE PROBLEMS**
> 1 You will have to draw attention to *the* in superlatives. It is common for students to omit this.
> 2 You will need to pre-teach/check *near* and *far* as opposites. Point out that the comparative and superlative forms of *far* are irregular: *further, the furthest*.
> 3 Draw attention to the prepositions in sentences 10 and 11: *the nearest **to**,* and *the furthest **from**.*

Check the answers with the whole class.

Elicit the number of correct sentences (six). Get students to work in pairs and focus on the correct sentences. Ask your class what is the same in all these sentences. Students should identify the *-est* endings in the short adjectives and *the most* form with longer adjectives, but be prepared to prompt them if necessary. (Do not go into a full explanation of the rules, as this is the focus of the *Grammar Spot* activity on p77.)

3   Check comprehension of *best* as the superlative of *good*. Get students to discuss which is the best hotel near where they live and to describe what it has got. Elicit a few interesting examples from the class.

GRAMMAR SPOT

1   Students complete the superlative sentences and try to work out the rules. Prompt and guide them if necessary. Write the rules up on the board as students work them out, taking the opportunity to remind them of the comparative forms.

> **Answers**
> The Palm Hotel is the **cheapest**.
> Bati Island is the **most expensive**.

–   *the … -est* is used with short adjectives such as *cheap*, (*cheaper*), *the cheapest*.
–   *the most* is used with longer adjectives such as *expensive*, (*more expensive*), *the most expensive*.

2   Students focus on the irregular forms and the dictionary entry for *good*. Elicit what information the dictionary gives (phonetic script, word category, and irregular comparative and superlative forms). Students complete the irregular forms for *bad* and *far*, using their dictionaries if appropriate.

> **Answers**
> bad   **worse**, **worst**   far   **further**, **furthest**

Read Grammar Reference 10.1 on p144 together in class, and/or ask students to read it at home. Encourage them to ask you questions about it.

The biggest and best!

This is another activity which integrates pronunciation work on stress and intonation.

1   Demonstrate the activity by reading the example aloud to the class. Then ask students to work on their own to complete the sentences.

T 10.5 [CD 2: Track 20] Play the recording and ask your students to check their answers. Ask them to listen carefully to the rhythm/stress and intonation of the sentences.

Answers and tapescript
T 10.5
1   That house is very big.
    Yes, **it's the biggest house** in the village.
2   The Ritz is a very expensive hotel.
    Yes, **it's the most expensive hotel** in London.
3   Appleton is a very pretty village.
    Yes, **it's the prettiest village** in England.
4   New York is a very cosmopolitan city.
    Yes, **it's the most cosmopolitan city** in the world.
5   Brad Pitt is a very popular film star.
    Yes, **he's the most popular film star** in America.
6   Miss Smith is a very funny teacher.
    Yes, **she's the funniest teacher** in our school.
7   Anna is a very intelligent student.
    Yes, **she's the most intelligent student** in the class.
8   This is a very easy exercise.
    Yes, **it's the easiest exercise** in the book.

2   **T 10.6** [CD 2: Track 21] Now ask students to close their books. Play the first lines again, pausing after each one so that your students can produce the reply. You could do this in chorus with the whole class, or ask individuals to respond, or mix the two approaches.

Really work hard to encourage good (probably exaggerated) stress and intonation in the replies, with the main stress on the superlative adjective.

Student(s):   *Yes, it's the biggest house in the village.*

Yes, it's the most expensive hotel in London.

Talking about your class

This is a freer speaking activity, which should be good fun, provided you warn students to be careful not to offend other people! Give them enough time to describe one or two other people, but do not let the activity go on too long.

You could put some other cues on the board to prompt comparative and superlative sentences: *lives near to/far from school*; *has a big bag*, etc.

3 Read the examples with students following the stress patterns in the example. Then put them into small groups and ask them to make sentences about the other students. Get the class to give you comments about each other.

4 Students write the name of their favourite film star and then tell the rest of the class. Write the names of the stars on the board and keep a score for each one. Students work in pairs and compare the stars, e.g. *(Brad Pitt) is more popular than (Tom Cruise)*. Then get students to say who is the most popular star in the class.

Check it

5 Ask students to work in pairs or small groups to correct the sentences. Ask them to work quite quickly, then conduct a full class feedback on the correct answers. Try to get students to correct each other and explain any mistakes they hear.

> **Answers**
> 1 Yesterday was **hotter** than today.
> 2 She's taller **than** her brother.
> 3 I'm the **youngest** in the class.
> 4 Last week was **busier** than this week.
> 5 He **hasn't** got/doesn't **have** any sisters.
> 6 Do you **have**/**Have you** got any bread?
> 7 My homework is the **worst** in the class.
> 8 This exercise is **the** most difficult in the book.

ADDITIONAL MATERIAL

Workbook Unit 10
Exercises 7–9 Comparatives and superlatives

> **SUGGESTION**
> You can give further practice in superlatives and talking about cities/regions by using the photocopiable activity on TB p146. Photocopy enough sheets for each student.
>
> **1** Hand out the sheets and focus attention on the example. Give students enough time to complete the gapped questions. Check the answers.
>
> > **Answers**
> > 2 the highest
> > 3 the best
> > 4 the busiest
> > 5 the friendliest
> > 6 the most modern
> > 7 the most interesting
> > 8 the most dangerous
> > 9 the worst
> > 10 the most beautiful
>
> Let students write the answers to the questions. Remind them when they are giving an opinion, they should not choose their own city/region.
>
> **2/3** Divide the class into groups of three. Pre-teach/check useful language for the discussion stage, e.g. *What did you put for question (1)?, I think …, I agree/don't agree with …, I prefer …,* etc. Get

students to discuss their answers. Monitor and check for accurate use of superlatives.

Elicit interesting examples in a short feedback stage. With monolingual classes, you could extend the activity by getting students to decide on the best/worst place to live in their country.

READING AND SPEAKING (SB p78)

Viva la danza!

This activity is a jigsaw reading. This means that it should result in not only reading practice, but also some freer speaking as in Unit 6.

The class divides into three groups and each group reads a different but similar text about a city and answers the questions. After this, students from the different groups get together to exchange information about the city in their text. This means that they should get some speaking practice whilst their main attention is on the reading task.

The texts are about three cities which are famous for dance – Buenos Aires, Havana, and Seville. These were chosen because they all have a very strong link to dance and are important tourist centres, but are different enough to make for interesting reading. The texts include examples of the grammar taught in this and previous units.

1 This exercise aims to generate some interest in the topic of dance and cities, and hopefully provide some motivation to read the texts.

> **T 10.7** [CD 2: Track 22] Tell students they are going to hear three types of Latin dance music. Play the recording and get students to answer the questions in pairs.

> **Answers**
> Flamenco – Seville   Tango – Buenos Aires   Salsa – Havana

2 Pre-teach/check *capital city, port, become independent, immigrants, slaves, tobacco fields, lead* (past *led*)*, socialist revolution, large, rule* (v). Students work in pairs and exchange what they know about the three cities. Get them to label the sentences BA (Buenos Aires), H (Havana), or S (Seville). If students have problems with some of the sentences, tell them not to worry at this stage. Explain that they will be able to find the correct information from one of the texts or from the other students in the class.

> **Answers**
> 2 BA   3 S   4 H   5 S   6 S   7 H   8 H   9 BA

3 Divide the class into three groups. Tell Group 1 to read about Buenos Aires, Group 2 to read about Havana, and Group 3 to read about Seville. Students should read and check the answers to exercise 2 that relate to the city they are reading about. Allow dictionaries to be used to check new words. Make sure that students understand that *the West* in the text on Havana refers to North America and the countries of Europe.

Regroup the students so that there is a Group 1, Group 2, and Group 3 student working together. Each group of three students should check the answers to exercise 2. Briefly check the answers with the whole class.

4 Students work individually. Ask them to read their text again and answer the questions about their city. Each group has the same questions to answer. When they have read the texts, they could either go through the questions on their own and then check with others from the same group, or work with a partner from the same group to answer the questions.

Check the answers with each group separately. The main idea of these questions is to check understanding, therefore short answers are perfectly acceptable.

Answers

Group 1 – Buenos Aires
1 3 million (10 million including Gran Buenos Aires).
2 River Plate.
3 It's called 'the Paris of the South' because of its lovely European buildings. It is also a big commercial centre and visitors love its beautiful shops.
4 It became independent from Spain in 1816. More than 4 million European immigrants came between 1840 and 1940 to work on the railways.
5 Astor Piazzolla lives there now.
6 Tango.
7 Flamenco guitar.
8 • buy things in beautiful shops ✓
   • visit Ernest Hemingway's house ✗
   • see a famous fiesta ✗
   • learn to dance in a club ✗
   • hear music by Piazzolla in his home country ✓
   • visit the Alcazar Palace ✗

Group 2 – Havana
1 2.2 million.
2 No, it doesn't have a river.
3 It is one of the oldest cities in Latin America. It is a very cultural city and has lots of beautiful old Spanish buildings.
4 In the 16th century it was Spain's most important port and city in Latin America.
   At the beginning of the 19th century it was one of the richest cities in the West.
   Ernest Hemingway lived there from 1940.
   In 1960 Fidel Castro led a socialist revolution and became president.
5 Ernest Hemingway.
6 Salsa.
7 Spanish guitar and African drums.

8 • buy things in beautiful shops ✗
   • visit Ernest Hemingway's house ✓
   • see a famous fiesta ✗
   • learn to dance in a club ✓
   • hear music by Piazzolla in his home country ✗
   • visit the Alcazar Palace ✗

Group 3 – Seville
1 750,000.
2 The Guadalquivir river.
3 It's one of Europe's largest historical centres with many beautiful old buildings. Tourists also come for its fiesta.
4 The Arabs ruled the city from 711 to 1248.
   In 1503 Seville became the most important port in Spain.
   The famous painter Diego Velázquez was born there in 1599.
   There were two international exhibitions in 1929 and 1992.
5 Diego Velázquez.
6 Flamenco.
7 Arabs and gypsies.
8 • buy things in beautiful shops ✗
   • visit Ernest Hemingway's house ✗
   • see a famous fiesta ✓
   • learn to dance in a club ✗
   • hear music by Piazzolla in his home country ✗
   • visit the Alcazar Palace ✓

5 Tell each student to find partners from the other two groups and compare the cities, using their answers from exercise 4. Encourage students to exchange information using comparative and superlative forms and *have/have got* where possible, e.g.
   Buenos Aires has got the biggest population.
   Buenos Aires is more commercial than the other cities.
   Seville has a fiesta, but the other cities don't.
   All three cities have got beautiful buildings.

   However, do not stop the group work to insist on these forms, as this will limit students' confidence.

   Conduct a full class feedback and get information about all three cities, encouraging your students to compare and contrast. This way you might get some freer use of comparatives, superlatives, and *have got*, but don't force this; just be pleased if it happens! The aim of this feedback is to encourage some fluency practice.

VOCABULARY AND PRONUNCIATION (SB p80)

City and country words

1 Focus attention on the photographs and elicit the correct words for numbers 1 and 2 (*theatre, museum*). Students work in pairs and continue matching. They can use their dictionaries or they can ask you about words they don't know.

   Check the answers and correct pronunciation as you go.

Elicit examples of what you usually find only in the country. Students may disagree here based on their own experience, so be prepared to accept a range of reasonable answers.

2 **T 10.8** [CD 2: Track 23] This exercise aims to consolidate the vocabulary in exercise 1 and review superlative and comparative forms. Make sure students realize that numbers 2 and 5 each require the same word, but that students should decide which one needs a capital letter. Give students time to complete the sentences. Then play the recording so that they can check their answers.

3 This exercise gives more practice on phonetic transcription, again using words that students have already seen. Always encourage your students to consult the phonetic symbols chart on SB p159 when they do an exercise like this. Ask them to do it on their own and then check answers with a partner.

T 10.9 [CD 2: Track 24] Play the recording and get students to check their answers. Play the recording again and get students to listen and repeat, looking at the phonetic transcription as they do so.

4 This is a fun activity to give further practice with the city and country vocabulary. Demonstrate the activity by getting students to say the examples chorally and individually. Encourage them to deliver the sentences rhythmically following the stress pattern in the examples. Give a new sentence with five or six examples to demonstrate 'list' intonation, e.g.

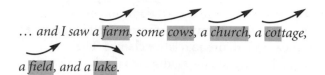

… and I saw a farm, *some* cows, *a* church, *a* cottage, *a* field, *and a* lake.

Get students to divide themselves into a 'country' and a 'city' group, according to which they prefer. If you have one group with a lot more students than the other, you may have to ask some students to switch. Get each set of students to play the game. The group that can continue the longest without forgetting a word is the winner.

ADDITIONAL MATERIAL

Workbook Unit 10
Exercise 10 Revision of compound nouns connected with town life, such as *town centre* and *railway station*

WRITING (SB p121)

Describing a place

Linking words – *which, where*

This unit introduces the relative pronouns *which* and *where*. Students will be familiar with these as question words and so should not have too much difficulty with the controlled practice. Exercise 3 serves to consolidate *which* and *where* as relatives and also as a model for students' own description of their capital city.

Write *which* and *where* on the board and ask *Things or places?* Get students to match the correct words (*which* – things, *where* – places). Focus attention on the *Caution Box*. Read the examples with the whole class. Point out that the reference to place in *in it* in the second sentence is replaced by *where* and so is not repeated. This is also true of *here* in sentence 3 of exercise 1.

1 Elicit the answer to number 1 and then get students to complete the task individually. Check the answers.

2 Brainstorm things to say about a capital city, e.g. population, history, buildings, tourist attractions, problems, etc. Elicit a few example statements from students about their capital or give some examples about yours. Divide the class into pairs and get them to talk about their capital. Elicit any interesting facts/opinions in a short feedback session.

NOTE

Exercise 3 contains examples of non-defining relative clauses, as well defining relative clauses. The punctuation needed for students to do the task is already in place, so do not go into an explanation of the difference between the two types of clause at this stage.

3 Get students to read through the text about London, ignoring the gaps, just to get an idea of the content. Check comprehension of: *land* (v), *lie* (v, of a river), *ride*, *big wheel*, *traffic*, *pollution*. Point to the photo of the London Eye to explain *ride on the big wheel*.

Elicit the answer to number 1, pointing out the use of *ago* to help students choose the past tense to answer *where the Romans landed*. Give students time to complete the exercise working in pairs. Encourage them to pool their knowledge of London. Check the answers.

Answers
1 d   2 c   3 a   4 f   5 e   6 b

4 Read the instructions as a class. Focus attention on the paragraph plan and elicit possible answers to each of the questions. With weaker classes, draft a sample first paragraph on the board with the whole class.

Give students time to write their description in class or set it for homework. Point out that students should try to write four paragraphs of roughly equal length. If possible, display the descriptions on the classroom wall or noticeboard to allow students to read each other's work. When you check the students' description, point out errors, but allow students to correct them themselves and try to limit correction to major problems to avoid demoralizing.

EVERYDAY ENGLISH (SB p81)

Directions 2

The listening text and the pictures provide the context for the introduction of prepositions of movement.

1 **T 10.10** [CD 2: Track 25] Refer students back to p74 to remind them of Andy and Joel. Check they can remember who lives where (Joel in the city and Andy in the country.) Briefly revise *left* and *right*. Focus attention on the map and get students to find the A34's exit for Apple Cross. Play the recording and tell students to mark the route to Andy's cottage with a pencil (or a finger).

Now ask them to work with a partner to fill in the gaps. Play the recording again for a final check.

Answers and tapescript
J=Joel, A=Andy
J So how do I find your cottage, then?
A Have you got a pen and paper?
J Erm . . . yes, I have.
A OK. Well, leave the A34 at Apple Cross. **Turn** left at the traffic lights. Then go **down** the hill, and **under** the first bridge. OK? Then go **over** the second bridge, and **along** the road by the river. Go **past** the pub, and **turn** right **up** the hill. Go **round** the corner past the farm, and my cottage is **on the** right. It's easy!
J OK. Got that. See you tomorrow afternoon!
A Bye. Safe journey. Oh, don't forget your surfboard!

2 Focus attention on the pictures of Joel's car and ask students where Joel is going (Andy's house). How do they know? (The route is the same as in the map above.) Complete the first sentence as a class, using the prepositions from the box. Students work in pairs to complete the rest of the text, using the information in the pictures.

T 10.11 [CD 2: Track 26] Students listen and check.

Answers and tapescript
Joel drove **down** the hill, **under** the first bridge, and **over** the second bridge. Then he drove **along** the road by the river, **past** the pub, and **up** the hill. Next he drove **round** the corner, off the road, **through** some apple trees, and **into** a lot of mud!

T 10.11
A=Andy, J=Joel
A Look at you! What happened? Where's your car?
J I had a small problem ...
A What? How?
J Well, I did what you said. I drove down the hill, under the first bridge, and over the second bridge, then I drove along the road by the river, past the pub, and up the hill. Next I drove round the corner, but I saw some big cows in front of me. So I turned quickly, drove off the road, through some apple trees, and into a lot of mud.
A Oh no! Are you all right?
J I'm fine. But now I can't move the car. Come and help me.
A Of course. But why didn't you just stop?
J Well, there were a lot of cows and they didn't look very friendly.
A But cows aren't dangerous.
J OK, OK! ... I still don't like the country very much ...

3 Get students to cover the text, look at the pictures, and tell Joel's story in pairs. As an alternative or extension to students telling the story in the third person, it can be fun to ask them to pretend to be Joel. This practises natural stress and intonation. Ask one or two students to do this for the others.

4 Demonstrate the activity by giving some directions to a few places near your school and getting students to call out when they think they know the answer.

Students continue working in pairs. Monitor and check.

Don't forget!

Workbook Unit 10

Exercise 11 Translation

Exercise 12 Listening and writing practice on places and
giving directions

Grammar Reference

Look at the exercises on SB p144 as a class, or set for
homework. The answers are on TB p176.

Word list

Remind your students of the Word list for this unit on
SB p156. They could translate the words, learn them at
home, or transfer some of the words to their vocabulary
notebook.

Pronunciation Book Unit 10

Video/DVD Episode 4 Dinner for two

11

Present Continuous • *Whose?*
Clothes • Words that rhyme
In a clothes shop

Looking good!

Introduction to the unit

This is the first unit where students encounter the Present Continuous. The Present Simple was introduced and practised much earlier in *New Headway Elementary – the THIRD edition* because it is used far more frequently, but by this stage of the course students should be ready to compare and contrast the two present tenses.

The theme of this unit is describing people, and there is a lot of related vocabulary input. The unit also practises *Whose … ?* in conjunction with possessive pronouns. There is a song, 'Flying without wings', by *Westlife*.

Language aims

Grammar – Present Continuous In this unit, we aim to teach the Present Continuous as though the present participle were just another adjective used after the verb *to be*, for example,
She's tall, pretty, hungry. → *She's working, cooking, thinking.*

> **POSSIBLE PROBLEMS**
>
> The Present Continuous has no equivalent form in many other languages, which use the present tense to convey the two concepts of 'action which relates to all time' and 'activity happening now'. For example, in French, *il fume dix cigarettes par jour* (he smokes ten cigarettes a day) and *il fume en ce moment* (he is smoking now), the present tense *fume* expresses both ideas.
>
> Students not only confuse the two concepts of the Present Simple and the Present Continuous, they also confuse the forms. When they have seen the *am/is/are* in the Present Continuous, they tend to try to use it in the Present Simple.
>
> The use of the Present Continuous for activities happening in the near future can seem strange, so the unit also introduces and practises this.
>
> **Common mistakes**
> **She's come from Spain.*
> **She's coming from Spain.*
> **I'm come to school by bus.*
> **What does he doing?*
> **Does he wearing a suit?*

Whose is it? It's mine.

> **POSSIBLE PROBLEMS**
>
> The question *Whose … ?* and possessive pronouns present few problems of concept, but learners do confuse *who's* and *whose*. Possessive pronouns simply have to be learned. They are practised in this unit in conjunction with *Whose … ?* and there is also a complete overview of subject and object pronouns, and possessive adjectives and pronouns in the *Grammar Spot* on p85.

Vocabulary There is a lot of vocabulary to do with describing people – colours, clothes, adjectives. There is also an exercise on words that rhyme and further practice of the phonetic script.

Everyday English Language used in a clothes shop is introduced and practised, as is the use of *will* to express a spontaneous decision.

Writing There is more work on linking words, and students are invited to write a short comparison of two people in their family.

Workbook The spelling of the present participle is practised. There is a section on the Present Continuous, and the Present Simple and the Present Continuous are further compared and contrasted.

Whose … ? and possessive pronouns are further practised.

In the *Vocabulary* section, some names for parts of the body are taught.

Notes on the unit

STARTER (SB p82)

1 Ask students to look around the classroom and try to find the items of clothing. You might need to bring in pictures of the items that might not be present in the classroom, e.g. a suit, a hat.

Focus attention on the examples *shorts, trousers, jeans, shoes, boots,* and *trainers*. Ask students what they notice about these words (they are all plural in English).

Drill the pronunciation of the words and briefly revise colours. Ask students to make sentences such as *It's a white T-shirt, They're black shoes*, but avoid the Present Continuous at this stage.

2 | **NOTE**
Exercise 2 aims to give initial practice in the Present Continuous with just one simple sentence. Do not go into a full presentation of the tense at this stage.

Drill the examples in the Student's Book. Get students to give two or three examples in open pairs to practise the *I* and *you* forms. Students continue in closed pairs and then get a few students to tell the whole class about themselves and you.

DESCRIBING PEOPLE (SB p82)

Present Continuous

1 This exercise introduces simple descriptions with *be* and *have got*. Pre-teach/check *pretty* and *fair/dark/grey (hair)*. Explain the difference between *good-looking* (general), *handsome* (for men), and *pretty* (for girls/women). Focus attention on the photo of Sofia and on the description. Elicit one or two other descriptions from the whole class and then drill the sentences chorally and individually. Students continue in pairs.

Possible answers
Andy's tall. He's got short grey hair.
Alison's tall.
Alison and Ella have got dark hair. Alfie has got fair hair.
Poppy's pretty. She's got long hair and blue eyes.
Kate and Sofia are good-looking. Kate's got long fair hair.
Dan, John, Clifford, and Albert are tall. John's got short grey hair.
Simon is tall and handsome.

Naomi has got short dark hair.
Colin is tall and handsome. He's got short dark hair.

2 Pre-teach/check the verbs in the list. Use the photos and mime to demonstrate the verbs if necessary. Ask the question for the example in the Student's Book and get students to read the answer, *Ella's smiling*. Elicit a plural example, e.g. *Who's laughing? Kate and Sofia are laughing*. Ask the students each of the questions in the list and get them to reply using the correct form of the third person of the Present Continuous.

Drill the questions and answers. Students ask and answer the questions in the list in pairs.

Answers
Ella and Simon are smiling.
Kate and Sofia are laughing.
Poppy's eating.
Andy, Alison, Ella, Alfie, Poppy, John, and Clifford are standing up.
Naomi is drawing.
Kate and Sofia are reading.
John and Albert are playing the guitar. (Dan is playing the violin, and Clifford is playing the mouth organ.)
Kate, Dan, Albert, Naomi, and Colin are sitting down.
Colin's using a computer.
Andy's painting.
Simon's walking.

3 Say the names of two or three people in the photos and get students to describe what they are wearing. Drill the sentences and then get students to continue in pairs.

Get students to continue practising the *he/she* form by talking about the other students, e.g. *Mario's wearing jeans and a white T-shirt.*

GRAMMAR SPOT

1 Read the notes with the whole class. Elicit other examples by pointing to people and objects in the class, e.g. *He's tall. It's new. We're happy*, etc.

2 Read the notes with the whole class and then get students to complete the table, using contracted forms. Check the answers with the whole class.

Answers

I	'm (am)	
You	're (are)	learning English.
He/She	's (is)	sitting in a classroom.
We	're (are)	listening to the teacher.
They	're (are)	

Name the tense and then get students to work out the negative and question forms. Get students to do this in pairs and then write up the answers on the board, or refer students to Grammar Reference 11.1 and 11.2 on p145.

3 Focus attention on the sentences. Get students to work out the difference between the two tenses. Make sure they understand that the Present Simple describes things that are always true, or true for a long time, and that the Present Continuous describes activities happening now and temporary activities. (Do not overload students by focusing on the use of the Present Continuous for activities happening in the near future. This is covered later in the unit.)

You could put sentences on the board to discuss with the whole class, e.g.

Present Simple	**Present Continuous**
She usually wears jeans.	*She's wearing a dress today.*
He works in a bank.	*He's working in the garden today.*
They speak French.	*They're speaking English at the moment.*
I like music.	Not possible: **I'm liking music ... .*

Read Grammar Reference 11.1 and 11.2 on p145 together in class, and/or ask students to read it at home. Encourage them to ask you questions about it.

PRACTICE (SB p83)

Talking about you

1 This activity aims to practise the Present Continuous in a personalized way. Demonstrate the activity by giving two or three examples about yourself. Get students to work individually and write their answers.

Get students to work in pairs and exchange their answers. Monitor and check for correct use of the Present Continuous and for appropriate linking, e.g. *I'm not wearing a jacket.* If necessary, drill pronunciation before eliciting a range of answers from students.

2 Make sure that students are clear what *Yes/No* questions are. Demonstrate the activity by drilling the questions and answers in the Student's Book chorally and individually. Get students to follow the stress patterns in the examples.

Ask a student to think of someone in the room, and ask a few *Yes/No* questions yourself. Drill these questions as much as necessary. When you feel students are ready, ask them to work in pairs. Remind them not to ask questions that are too personal!

3 This exercise gives students the opportunity to practise the Present Continuous in a connected way by describing a scene. Look out of the window and give a brief description of the scenery and any actions people are doing, e.g. *I can see the street and a small park. Some people are talking and two children are eating ice-creams.*

Pre-teach the expression *I can see ...* and get two confident students to look out of different windows if possible and give a description of the scene. Encourage them to be as detailed as possible and include colours and other adjectives in their description.

> **NOTE**
> If you have a large group, you will have to choose just three or four students to do this activity. With a smaller group, you could do this as a pairwork activity, with Student A describing the scene and Student B with his/her back to the window and listening.
>
> If you have a classroom with no windows, you can do this activity by getting students to imagine the scene.

Monitor and check for accurate use of the Present Continuous. Point out errors and drill the new forms and pronunciation as necessary.

Who's at the party?

4 **T 11.1** [CD 2: Track 27] This activity aims to practise the difference between the two present tenses, first in a recognition exercise, then in a productive one. Pre-teach/check the following vocabulary items: *musician, rich, stories, cigar, pilot, upstairs.*

Read the instructions with the whole class. Students listen and write the names next to the correct people.

Answers and tapescript
From top to bottom: Roz Sam Fiona George Harry Mandy

T 11.1
Who's at the party?

A Oh dear, Monica! I don't know any of these people. Who are they?

B Don't worry, Oliver. They're all very nice. Can you see that man over there? He's sitting down. That's Harry. He's a musician. He works in LA.

A Sorry, where?

B You know, LA. Los Angeles.

A Oh, yeah.

B And he's talking to Mandy. She's wearing a red dress. She's very nice and very rich! She lives in a beautiful old house in the country.

A Rich, eh?

B Yes. Rich and married! Next to her is Fiona. She's drinking a glass of red wine. Fiona's my oldest friend, she and I were at school together.

A And what does Fiona do?

B She's a writer. She writes children's stories – they're not very good but ... anyway, she's talking to George. He's laughing and smoking a cigar. He's a pilot. He travels the world, thousands of miles every week.

A And who are those two over there? They're dancing. Mmmm. They know each other very well.

B Oh, that's Roz and Sam. They're married. They live in the flat upstairs.

A So ... um ... that's Harry and Mandy and ... um ... it's no good, I can't remember all those names.

5 Focus attention on the table and on the names of the guests in the first column. Play the recording again as far as *He works in LA* and get students to read the example.

Ask students to work in pairs to complete the table. Play the recording again before you provide the answers.

Answers

	Present Continuous	Present Simple
Mandy	She's wearing a red dress.	She lives in a beautiful old house.
Fiona	She's drinking a glass of red wine. She's talking to George.	She writes children's stories.
George	He's laughing and smoking a cigar.	He travels the world.
Roz and Sam	They're dancing.	They live in the flat upstairs.

SUGGESTION
You might want to get some further practice of the two present tenses from this exercise. You could ask questions such as the following:
Where is Harry sitting? Where does he work?
What is Mandy wearing? Where does she live?
What is Fiona drinking? What does she write?

What is George smoking? Where does he travel?
What are Roz and Sam doing? Where do they live?

You could begin by asking a few questions yourself, and then encourage students to ask and answer the other questions in open and/or closed pairs.

Getting information

6 This is a 'spot the difference' activity based on two pictures of a party. Divide the class into pairs. Get Student A in each pair to turn to p149 and Student B to p151. Students should be familiar with such information-gap activities by now, but still be careful with instructions. Use L1 if necessary. Focus attention on the examples in the Student's Book. You could also elicit one or two examples with the class first. Pay attention to all aspects of pronunciation – sounds, stress and intonation.

You may need to give students some vocabulary before the exercise, or, if the class is small enough, let them ask you for words when the need arises.

Answers
Picture A
1 Three people are dancing.
2 The girl standing up with dark hair is wearing a black dress.
3 The boy with the cap is eating a sandwich.
4 There's a boy taking a photo.
5 There are two people kissing on the right.
6 The girl with the brown dress has long dark hair.
7 There's a girl writing.
8 Two girls are sitting down and talking.
9 Two people next to the sofa are eating a sandwich.
10 There's a boy with short fair hair wearing trousers.

Picture B
1 Four people are dancing.
2 The girl standing up with dark hair is wearing a red dress.
3 The boy with the cap is drinking.
4 There's a boy using a camcorder.
5 There are two people talking on the right.
6 The girl with the brown dress has short fair hair.
7 There's a girl reading.
8 Two girls are standing up and talking.
9 Two people next to the sofa are eating a pizza.
10 There's a boy with short fair hair wearing shorts.

ADDITIONAL MATERIAL

Workbook Unit 11
Exercises 1–5 Present Continuous
Exercises 6–7 Present Continuous and Present Simple

THE HOUSE IS A MESS! (SB p84)

Whose is it?

> **SUGGESTION**
>
> You could introduce *Whose is it?* and possessive pronouns using the classroom situation and use the Student's Book for further practice and consolidation.
>
> Take some personal possessions from the students and put them on the floor where everyone can see them. Hold something up and ask *Whose is this? Is it Karl's?* The aim is to convey the concept of possession.
>
> You could use the board and write up the question *Whose is this?*, pointing out that *whose* is not the same as *who's*. Then hold up a possession of your own, and ask *Whose is this?* Teach *It's mine.* Write this on the board. Then do the same for the other possessive pronouns, *yours, his, hers, ours,* and *theirs.*

1 Focus attention on the words in the box. Students work in pairs and locate the items in the room and then on the people on p85. Drill the words chorally and individually.

2 If you haven't presented *Whose?* using the classroom situation, do so now using the technique in the *Suggestion* above. Do not present all the possessive pronouns, as this can be done from the book. Just focus on *Whose is this?*, making sure students understand the concept by translating into L1 if possible.

T 11.2 [CD 2: Track 28] Play the recording. Students listen to the questions and then complete the answers.

> **Answers and tapescript**
> | | | |
> |---|---|---|
> | 1 | Whose is the baseball cap? | It's **his**. |
> | 2 | Whose are the boots? | They're **hers**. |
> | 3 | Whose is the baby? | It's **theirs**. |

Drill the questions and answers from the recording. If students query the use of *the* in the questions compared with *a* in exercise 1, explain briefly that *Whose is/are the …?* is used to ask who owns each specific item. Demonstrate the singular and plural question forms, using words from the box in exercise 1, e.g. *Whose is the tie? Whose are the sunglasses?* Students ask and answer questions about the other things in exercise 1.

> **Answers**
> | | |
> |---|---|
> | Whose is the plant? | It's hers. |
> | Whose is the coat? | It's his. |
> | Whose are the trainers? | They're his. |
> | Whose are the sunglasses? | They're hers. |
> | Whose is the tie? | It's his. |
> | Whose is the bag? | It's hers. |
> | Whose is the football? | It's theirs. |
> | Whose is the briefcase? | It's his. |

3 Focus attention on the examples and elicit the question form for plural nouns, e.g. *Whose sunglasses are these?* Get students to give you some objects that belong to them. Practise questions with *Whose?* in open pairs, making sure that the objects will generate each of the possessive pronouns in the box. Correct errors and drill the correct versions. Students continue in pairs.

> **GRAMMAR SPOT**
>
> 1 Make sure students understand the different categories in the table by putting simple sentences on the board and asking students to circle the key word, e.g.
> (We) speak English. (subject pronoun)
> *They are helping* (us). (object pronoun)
> (Our) *classroom is large.* (possessive adjective)
> *Those books are* (ours). (possessive pronoun)
>
> > **Answers**
> > | Subject | Object | Adjective | Pronoun |
> > |---|---|---|---|
> > | I | me | my | mine |
> > | You | you | **your** | **yours** |
> > | He | **him** | his | **his** |
> > | She | **her** | **her** | hers |
> > | We | us | our | **ours** |
> > | They | them | **their** | **theirs** |
>
> 2 Read the notes with the class. Point out that there are two ways of asking the question, *Whose + noun + is this?*, or *Whose + is this + noun?*, and that possessive pronouns replace possessive adjectives + noun.
>
> 3 Highlight the difference between *Whose?* (possession) and *Who's = (Who is).* Tell students the pronunciation is the same, but the meaning is different.
>
> Read Grammar Reference 11.3 on p145 together in class, and/or ask students to read it at home. Encourage them to ask you questions about it.

PRACTICE (SB p85)

who's or whose?

1 Students work individually and choose the correct word. Get students to compare with a partner before checking the answers with the whole class.

> **Answers**
> | | | |
> |---|---|---|
> | 1 your | 4 My, hers | 7 Whose, his |
> | 2 Our, theirs | 5 Who's, your | 8 Who's |
> | 3 their, ours | 6 mine, yours | 9 Whose, our |

2 **T 11.3** [CD 2: Track 29] Read the instructions. Remind students that *Who's …?* can be *Who is …?* or *Who has (got) …?*

Demonstrate the activity by playing the first two sentences and eliciting the answers. Students shout out

'1' if they think the word is *Whose ... ?* and '2' if they think it is *Who's ... ?* This is not an easy exercise, so go slowly, and repeat each sentence as often as necessary.

Answers and tapescript
1 Who's on the phone? **2**
2 I'm going to the pub. Who's coming? **2**
3 Wow! Look at that sports car. Whose is it? **1**
4 Whose dictionary is this? It's not mine. **1**
5 There are books all over the floor. Whose are they? **1**
6 Who's the most intelligent in our class? **2**
7 Who's got my book? **2**
8 Do you know whose jacket this is? **1**

What a mess!

NOTE

This exercise introduces the use of the Present Continuous to refer to arrangements in the near future. You might decide that this use merits a full presentation from you, but you could also decide to downplay it. Students are introduced to the *going to* future in Unit 12. The area of future forms and the concepts that they express in English is very complex, and we do not suggest that you explore it at this level.

It is not such a leap for students to be told that the Present Continuous can be used to describe activities happening in the near future, even though in their own language this concept may be expressed by the equivalent of the Present Simple. You can also mention that to express an arrangement in the near future, the Present Continuous usually needs a future time reference, e.g. *I'm doing my homework (now)* versus *I'm doing my homework tonight.*

3 **T 11.4** [CD 2: Track 30] Students listen and complete the conversation. Check the answers.

Answers and tapescript
A **Whose** is this tennis racket?
B It's **mine**.
A What's it doing here?
B I'm **playing** tennis this afternoon.

Read the information in the *Caution Box* as a class. Use L1 to translate and explain if you can.

T 11.4 [CD 2: Track 30] Play the recording again. Students listen and repeat.

4 Elicit the first conversation as an example and highlight the changes needed with plural nouns, e.g. *Whose are these ...? They're ... What are they doing here?*

T 11.5 [CD 2: Track 31] Students listen and check.

Answers and tapescript
1 Whose are these football boots?
They're John's. He's playing football later.
2 Whose are these ballet shoes?
They're Mary's. She's going dancing tonight.
3 Whose is this suitcase?
It's mine. I'm going on holiday tomorrow.
4 Whose is this coat?
It's Jane's. She's going for a walk soon.
5 Whose is this plane ticket?
It's Jo's. She's flying to Rome this afternoon.
6 Whose are all these glasses?
They're ours. We're having a party tonight.

Students work in pairs to make similar dialogues. Follow up the activity by asking them what they are doing this afternoon, tonight, tomorrow, later, soon.

Check it

5 Students work individually to correct the mistakes, and then check in pairs. Check answers with the class.

Answers
1 Alice is tall and she's got long, black **hair**.
2 **Whose** boots are these?
3 I'm wearing **jeans**.
4 Look at Roger. He**'s standing** next to Jeremy.
5 **He works** in a bank. He's the manager.
6 What**'s Suzie drinking**?
7 **Who's** that man in the garden?
8 Where **are** you going tonight?
9 What **are you doing** after school today?

ADDITIONAL MATERIAL

Workbook Unit 11
Exercise 8 Auxiliary verbs
Exercises 9 and 10 *Whose ... ?* and possessive pronouns
Exercise 11 Error-correction exercise

LISTENING AND SPEAKING (SB p86)

Looking for that something

SUGGESTION
Ask students what they know about the band *Westlife*. They are one of the most popular boy bands in the history of pop music. Originally from Ireland, they are in the *Guinness Book of World Records* as the only band to have been at number 1 in the charts seven times in a row. At the time of writing, the band has sold over 30 million records worldwide. *Westlife*'s 'Flying without wings' went to number 1 in April 1999. It has examples of the Present Continuous and consolidates language from earlier units.

1 Give two or three examples of what makes you happy. This helps students to see their teacher as a real person and also encourages them to talk about themselves more openly. Elicit further examples from the class. Get students to write their five examples and be prepared to help them with vocabulary. Students compare in pairs.

2 Get students to select the thing that makes them happiest and then compare with the rest of the class.

3 Ask students to close their books. Play the recording through once and let students just listen. Ask if they have heard the song before and if they like it.

4 Students open their books. Ask them to read through the song just to get an idea of its content. Tell them not to worry about words they don't recognize. Ask students what type of song it is (*a love song*) and what makes the songwriter happiest (*his wife/girlfriend*).

Focus attention on the words in the box and get students to refer back to the song to match the first word with its meaning. Elicit the answer. Get students to continue the matching task and to check their answers in pairs.

Check the answers with the class.

Answers
joy – happiness
to cherish – to love
to deny – to say no to something
solitary – alone, lonely
the sunrise – when the sun comes up

Deal with other vocabulary queries as they arise or let students use dictionaries to help them. If possible, be prepared to translate the lines that contain more complex structures, e.g. in verse 5.

5 **T 11.6** [CD 2: Track 32] Elicit the answers to the first two gaps and then get students to continue the task working in pairs. Encourage them to think about the meaning of the line, the grammatical context, and the rhyme to help them choose the answers. Play the recording to let students check/complete their answers.

Answers and tapescript
Everybody's **looking** for that something
One thing that makes it all complete
You find it in the strangest **places**
Places you never knew it could be
Some find it in the faces of their **children**
Some find it in their lover's **eyes**
Who can deny the joy it brings
When you find that **special** thing
You're flying without wings
Some find it sharing every **morning**
Some in their solitary lives
You find it in the words of others
A simple line can make you **laugh** or cry

You find it in the deepest **friendship**
The kind you cherish all your life
And when you know how **much** that means
You've found that special thing
You're flying without wings
So impossible as it may seem
You've got to **fight** for every dream
'Cause who's to **know** which one you let go
Would have made you complete
Well, for me it's waking up beside **you**
To watch the sunrise on your face
To know that I can say I **love** you
At any given time or place
It's little things that only I know
Those are the things that make you **mine**
And it's like flying without wings
'Cause you're my special **thing**
I'm flying without wings
You're the place my life **begins**
And you'll be where it ends
I'm flying without wings
And that's the joy you **bring**
I'm flying without wings

What do you think?

Elicit a range of ideas as to the meaning of 'flying without wings' before confirming the answer (*feeling elated or very happy*). Ask students if any of the things in their list in exercise 1 appeared in the song.

Ask students what they thought of the song. If in general they enjoyed it, you could ask them to choose a favourite verse and/or elicit other examples of songs about love and happiness in English or the student's own language.

Speaking

6 This questionnaire and mingling task gives students the opportunity to discuss favourite people/things and find out what they have in common with other students.

Ask students to read through the questions. Give a few examples of your own favourite things/people and then give students time to write their own answers. Elicit a sample exchange, e.g.
What's your favourite food? Chocolate.
What are your favourite things to do at weekends?
Relaxing and being with my family.
Who's your favourite film star or actor? Johnny Depp.

Drill exchanges in open pairs as necessary, highlighting the falling intonation in the *wh-* questions.

Get students to stand up and try to find other students with the same answers. If they don't find anyone, ask them to move on to the next question so that the activity doesn't go on too long.

7 When students have answered as many questions as possible, get them to sit down and feed back. Focus attention on the example in the Student's Book, highlighting the sentence stress:

Johann and I both like blue.   Stella and I both like trainers.
Elicit further examples from the class.

WRITING (SB p122)

Describing people

Linking words – *although, but*

The writing syllabus continues with a focus on two linkers of contrast – *although* and *but* – and how they can be used to join sentences. Students do two gap-fill exercises using *although, but*, and other linking words before going on to write a short comparison of two people in their family.

Read the *Caution Box* with the class. Ask what the linking words express (*contrast*) and check the answers.

> **Answers**
> *But* joins two clauses, often divided by a comma.
> *Although* often starts a sentence.
> *Although* is more formal than *but*.

Point out that we cannot use *but* to start a sentence, i.e. we can't say **But I like him a lot, I don't love him.*

1 Elicit the answer to number 1 as an example and then get students to complete the sentences, working individually. Check the answers with the class.

> **Answers**
> 1 but
> 2 because
> 3 Although
> 4 both
> 5 too
> 6 For example

2 Focus attention on the photo and elicit some basic details about the children. Get students to read the text through quickly to get an idea of the content. Focus attention on the example and then get students to continue the task, working individually. Students check in pairs before checking with the class.

> **Answers**
> 2 but
> 3 both
> 4 but
> 5 too
> 6 For example
> 7 Although
> 8 both
> 9 For example
> 10 because
> 11 Although
> 12 because

3 Give a brief example by describing the similarities and differences between your brothers and sisters and/or your parents/children. Briefly review some structures, e.g. *My (brother and sister) both (have blue eyes); My (mum) likes (classical music), but my (dad) prefers (jazz); Although my (sister) is sometimes (annoying), I love (her) very much.* Divide the class into pairs to talk about their family.

4 Before getting students to write their own comparison, elicit some of the useful structures in the model text, e.g. Expressing similarities: *They both have/are/like …; X is/has/likes … and Y is/has/likes … too.* Expressing differences: *Although X is/has/likes …, Y is/has/likes …; X is/likes/has …, but Y isn't/doesn't.* Also elicit the linking words for giving reasons (*because*) and examples (*for example*).

Focus attention on the writing plan and elicit possible sentences for each point. Remind students to write paragraphs of roughly equal length. Give students time to write their description in class or set it for homework. If possible, display the descriptions on the classroom wall or noticeboard to allow students to read each other's work. When you check the students' description, point out errors but allow students to correct them themselves and try to limit correction to major problems to avoid demoralizing.

VOCABULARY AND PRONUNCIATION (SB p88)

Words that rhyme

> **POSSIBLE PROBLEMS**
> Students find the different pronunciations of the spelling *ea* difficult.
> *mean* /iː/   *near* /ɪə/   *wear* /eə/
> The silent *gh* in *bought* can also cause problems.

1 The aim of these exercises is to show that English spelling is not phonetic, and so the same sound can be spelled in different ways. Most or all of the vocabulary should be known, but do check comprehension.

T 11.7 [CD 2: Track 33] Put students in AB pairs to read the short exchange aloud and decide together which words rhyme. Play the recording. Students listen and check their answers. Get class feedback. Students practise the lines with their partner, paying particular attention to the stress highlighting. Again the pronunciation in the book and on the recording are based on English RP. If, as a native speaker teacher, your accent differs (and some pairs don't rhyme for you), point this out to your students.

> **Answers**
> A knows, rose(s), those,
> B flowers, ours

2 Focus attention on the example and elicit one or two more answers. Students work in pairs to match the words that rhyme. Check the answers with the class.

Answers

green	mean	eyes	size
hat	that	those	knows
short	bought	ours	flowers
park	dark	hair	wear
list	kissed	near	beer
whose	shoes	grey	pay

Ask students to practise the words in rhyming pairs. Do this first as a class so that you can monitor pronunciation. Correct mistakes very carefully! Then students can practise the words again with a partner.

3 Check first that students know the symbols by referring to the phonetic symbols chart on SB p159. Note that the symbols are in three groups – single sounds, long sounds, and diphthongs.

T 11.8 [CD 2: Track 34] Students listen and check.

Answers and tapescript
Vowels

1	/e/	red	said	5	/ɑ:/	park	dark
2	/æ/	hat	that	6	/u:/	whose	shoes
3	/ɪ/	list	kissed	7	/ɔ:/	short	bought
4	/i:/	green	mean				

Diphthongs

1	/aɪ/	eyes	size	4	/eə/	hair	wear
2	/ɪə/	near	beer	5	/əʊ/	those	knows
3	/eɪ/	grey	pay	6	/aʊ/	ours	flowers

4 Students work in pairs and think of more words to add to the lists. They could use dictionaries if you wish. Build up a set of answers on the board.

Sample answers
Vowels

1	/e/	bread, head, when, again, ten
2	/æ/	ham, cat, sat, stamp, map
3	/ɪ/	fish, give, lived, his, it
4	/i:/	meat, feet, leave, see, be
5	/ɑ:/	heart, part, start, large, card
6	/u:/	boot, suit, you, true, blue
7	/ɔ:/	ball, door, caught, floor, or

Diphthongs

1	/aɪ/	buy, light, right, shy, die
2	/ɪə/	here, dear, clear, real, hear
3	/eɪ/	say, way, main, game, shake
4	/eə/	where, fair, care, pear, rare
5	/əʊ/	clothes, soap, hope, no, show
6	/aʊ/	hour, shower, now, how, cow

> **SUGGESTION**
> You can give further practice in words that rhyme by using the photocopiable activity on TB p147. Photocopy enough sheets for each pair of students and divide them along the cut lines.
>
> Divide the class into pairs. Give each pair a set of word cards to place face down on the desk. Students take it in turns to turn over two cards to try to find a pair of words that rhyme. If they find a rhyming pair, they keep the cards; if the words don't rhyme, the students replace them on the desk. Encourage students to say the words aloud to check if they have a rhyming pair.
>
> Pre-teach useful language for the game, e.g. … and … rhyme/don't rhyme, Put the cards back, I/You can keep the cards, I'm/You're the winner. The student who finds the most pairs of rhyming words is the winner.

Tongue twisters

5 **T 11.9** [CD 2: Track 35] Read the instructions with the whole class. Check comprehension of the vocabulary and then play the recording. Students listen and repeat.

Students work in pairs and say the tongue twisters to each other. Make sure students try and say them quickly, rather than read each word off the page.

6 Students learn two of the tongue twisters and say them to the rest of the class. You could introduce a little light-hearted competition and get students to vote for the 'tongue twister champion'. Allow students to 'get their own back' by asking you to say a tongue twister from their language! If you have a multilingual group, choose a few examples from the languages represented.

EVERYDAY ENGLISH (SB p89)

In a clothes shop

> **SUGGESTION**
> The final activity works best if you have some props! Bring in clothes for students to try on.

1 Focus attention on the example and then get students to look at the other lines of the conversation and decide who says them. You could do this as a class to sort out any unknown vocabulary. Point out that I'm afraid can also mean I'm sorry, as it does in this exercise. This is the first time that students may have come across the use of will for spontaneous decisions. Do not go into a full presentation of this use of will at this stage.

Answers

c SA	g C	j C	m SA
d C	h C	k C	n SA
e C	i SA	l SA	o SA
f SA			

2 Focus attention on photo 1 and on the lines that go with it. Students then match photos 2–4 with the lines from the conversation. Check the answers in the key below.

3 Students work in pairs and try to put all the lines of the conversation in the correct order.

T 11.10 [CD 2: Track 36] Students listen and check.

Answers and tapescript
SA=shop assistant, C=customer
Photo 1
SA Can I help you?
C Yes, please. I'm looking for a shirt to go with my new jeans.
SA What colour are you looking for?
C Blue.
Photo 2
SA What about this one? Do you like this?
C No, it isn't the right blue.
SA Well, what about this one? It's a bit darker blue.
C Oh yes. I like that one much better. Can I try it on?
SA Yes, of course. The changing rooms are over there.
Photo 3
SA Is the size OK?
C No, it's a bit too big. Have you got a smaller size?
SA That's the last blue one we've got, I'm afraid. But we've got it in green.
Photo 4
C OK. I'll take the green. How much is it?
SA £39.99. How do you want to pay?
C Can I pay by credit card?
SA Credit card's fine. Thank you very much.

MUSIC OF ENGLISH

Read through the *Music of English* box as a class. Play the recording again, pausing at the end of each line. Encourage students to follow the intonation and highlighted stress patterns in the Students Book. Students practise the conversation in pairs.

4 Students make similar improvised conversations. Use the props!

Song

The song *Wonderful tonight* appears in photocopiable format on TB p149. You will find the song after **T 11.10** on the Class Cassette/on CD2 Track 37. Students do a range of different activities on the song. The answers are on TB p171.

Don't forget!

Workbook Unit 11
Exercise 12 Vocabulary: parts of the body
Exercise 13 Listening practice on buying clothes
Exercise 14 Translation

Grammar Reference
Look at the exercises on SB p145 as a class, or set for homework. The answers are on TB p176.

Word list
Remind your students of the Word list for this unit on SB p157. They could translate the words, learn them at home, or transfer some of the words to their vocabulary notebook.

Pronunciation Book Unit 11

Video/DVD Episode 5 Change of a dress

12

going to future
Infinitive of purpose
The weather • Making suggestions

Life's an adventure!

Introduction to the unit

The theme of this unit is planning the future. We focus on the *going to* future for plans and intentions. We do not at the same time introduce and contrast the Future Simple with *will* (this rather complex distinction is for a later stage of learning), but in the *Everyday English* section we do focus on *shall* for suggestions and revise *will* for spontaneous decisions. The second presentation in the unit is the infinitive of purpose, which is relatively simple to operate in English but is often realized differently in other languages. The skills work includes a jigsaw reading about two relatively new adventure sports – free-diving and free-running. This continues the theme of adventure and provides opportunities to revise the grammar not only of this unit but also of previous units (Present Simple and Past Simple).

Language aims

Grammar – *going to* The *going to* future is made easier by the fact that students already know the present forms of the verb *to be*, both on its own and as part of the Present Continuous, which they met in Unit 11. These are, of course, intrinsic parts of this structure. Also, as this is the first future they have encountered (apart from the Present Continuous with future meaning touched on briefly in Unit 11), the problem of when to use it in relation to other future forms (always an area of difficulty for students) is deferred for the time being, and they can simply concentrate on this form. The two uses of *going to* are introduced in the unit: plans and intentions, such as *I'm going to be a photographer*; and making predictions based on present evidence, such as *It's going to rain./He's going to fall.*

> **POSSIBLE PROBLEMS**
>
> 1 With the verbs *go* and *come* we often avoid using the full *going to* future form, and just use the Present Continuous.
>
> *She's going to go to Rome next week.* → *She's going to Rome next week.*
>
> 2 The Present Continuous can be used for future arrangements and is often interchangeable with the *going to* future.
>
> *I'm going to see the doctor tomorrow./I'm seeing the doctor tomorrow.*

The infinitive of purpose The infinitive of purpose answers the question *why* replacing *because I wanted to*, e.g. *Why did you go to the shops? Because I wanted to buy a newspaper./To buy a newspaper.*

There is often a problem for learners when they attempt to translate this item from their own language and insert *for* which is wrong in English.

Common mistakes
*I went to the shops for to buy a newspaper.
*I went to the shops for buy a newspaper.
*I went to the shops for buying a newspaper.

Vocabulary Vocabulary to do with weather is introduced, such as *It's sunny/ windy/rainy*. The question for description *What … like?* is presented and practised in dialogues, but only in connection with weather: *What's the weather like?*

Everyday English Two of the most common functional exponents for asking for and making suggestions are introduced:
What shall we do?
Let's go to the cinema.

Writing The syllabus continues with a focus on writing a postcard and so recycles the vocabulary of the unit as it includes information about the weather. It also provides an opportunity to bring together *going to* with other tenses.

Workbook There are exercises to consolidate the uses of *going to* and the infinitive of purpose. All of the auxiliary verbs covered so far – *am/is/are* and *do/does/did* – are brought together and practised.

The *Vocabulary* section focuses on word stress, phonetic transcription, and matching sounds.

There is also an exercise on the prepositions *from, like, than*.

Notes on the unit

STARTER (SB p90)

1 Focus attention on *I'm going to Brazil* and *I went to Brazil*. Establish what time they refer to by asking *Past, present, or future?* about each sentence. Students should recognize *went* as the past of *go* but make sure that they realize *going to* refers to the future. (Do not go into a full presentation of the tense at this stage.)

Pre-teach/check the meaning of *retire*. Students work in pairs and make sentences using the time references in the second box. Check the answers with the whole class.

> **Answers**
> I'm going to Brazil soon/next month/in a year's time/ when I retire.
> I went to Brazil when I was a student/two years ago.

2 Demonstrate the activity by giving similar sentences about yourself, e.g. *I'm going to (London) soon. I went to (South America) when I was a student*, etc. Drill the sentences in the Student's Book and then get students to continue the activity in pairs.

Elicit any interesting or surprising examples in a short feedback session with the whole class.

FUTURE PLANS (SB p90)

going to

1 The context for the presentation of *going to* is the future plans not only of a young boy, but also of an older man who is about to retire.

Ask your students to look at the photographs of Jack and his sports teacher Danny Carrick. Elicit a few suggestions about what their future plans might be, but don't insist that students use the *going to* form at this stage.

Pre-teach/check the meaning of *grow up*, *train* (v), and *scuba-dive*.

> **POSSIBLE PROBLEM**
> The *when* clauses with *grow up* and *retire* require the Present Simple. Sometimes students find it strange that the Present Simple is used to talk about future events; they might want to say *When I will grow up …* . However, try not to go into this at this stage.

Make it clear that students are going to read about Jack's and Danny's future plans, and so they are looking at a future tense. Focus attention on the example and then put students into pairs to discuss the sentences and write J or D according to who they think is speaking. Tell them that sometimes Jack and Danny both have the same plan, so they must write J and D next to the sentence. (The sentences have been selected so that there are some surprises!)

T 12.1 [CD 2: Track 38] Play the recording of both Jack and Danny right through, asking students to listen carefully and check if they are right. At the end ask *Were all your answers right? Were there any surprises?*

> **Answers and tapescript**
> | J | 1 | I'm going to be a footballer. |
> | J, D | 2 | I'm going to travel all over the world. |
> | J, D | 3 | I'm going to train very hard. |
> | D | 4 | I'm going to try new things. |
> | J | 5 | I'm going to play for Manchester United. |
> | J | 6 | I'm not going to marry until I'm very old. |
> | D | 7 | I'm not going to stay at home and watch TV. |
> | D | 8 | I'm going to learn to scuba-dive. |
> | D | 9 | I'm going to write a book. |
> | J | 10 | I'm going to be famous. |
>
> **T 12.1**
> **Jack**
> When I grow up I'm going to be a footballer – a really good one. I'm in the school team and I play three times a week. But I'm going to train very hard, every day, so I can be really, really good. First I'm going to play for Manchester United, then Inter Milan, and then Real Madrid. Those are my favourite teams. I'm going to travel all over the world and I'm going to be famous. I'm not going to marry until I'm very old – about 25. Then I want to have two sons. I'm going to play football until I'm 35 – that's a very long time. And I'm going to teach my sons to play. I want them to be famous footballers, too!
> **Danny Carrick**
> When I retire next year … I'm going to retire early … I'm not going to stay at home and watch TV. I'm going to try lots of new things. First I want to go mountain-climbing. In fact, I want to climb Mount Everest, so I'm going to train very hard for that. I'm going to learn to scuba-dive, too, because I want to go scuba-diving in Australia. There are so many things I want to do! I'm going to travel all over the world, then I'm going to write a book about my adventures. I want to call it 'Life begins at 60!' In my book, I'm going to tell other retired people to try new things, too. You are only as old as you feel!

2 This exercise moves from first person to third person, still practising positive and negative sentences only. First ask individuals to give you some of Jack's and Danny's plans. Focus on the pronunciation of *going to*: /ˈɡəʊɪŋtə/ or /ˈɡəʊɪŋtʊ/. Practise it in isolation first, and then as part of a full sentence, drilling the examples in the book.

Now put your students into pairs, one to tell the other about Jack's plans, and the other about Danny's.

Students then focus on the plans they have in common, using *They're both going to ...* . Monitor and check for correct use and pronunciation of *going to*.

> **Answers**
>
> **Jack**
> Jack's going to be a footballer.
> He's going to play for Manchester United.
> He isn't going to marry until he's very old.
> He's going to be famous.
>
> **Danny**
> Danny's going to try new things.
> He isn't going to stay at home and watch TV.
> He's going to learn to scuba-dive.
> He's going to write a book.
>
> **The two plans that are the same**
> They're both going to travel all over the world.
> They're both going to train very hard.

3 **T 12.2** [CD 2: Track 39] Now we focus on the formation and pronunciation of the question, which should not cause your students too much difficulty because they are already familiar with the Present Continuous.

Play the recording and ask students to repeat the questions and answers. Encourage them to use falling intonation for *wh-* questions and to follow the highlighted stress patterns.

GRAMMAR SPOT

Demonstrate that the form of *going to* builds on what students already know by getting the class to chorus first the positive and then the negative forms of the verb *to be*. (Conjugating verbs may be deemed old-fashioned in these communicative days, but it is an effective way of consolidating grammatical forms!)

1 Read the notes with the whole class and then get students to complete the table using contracted forms. Check the answers with the whole class.

> **Answers**
>
> | I | 'm | |
> |---|---|---|
> | You | 're | |
> | He/She | 's | going to leave tomorrow. |
> | We | 're | |
> | They | 're | |

Get students to work out the question and negative forms in pairs, and then write the answers on the board or refer students to the Grammar Reference on p146.

> **Answers**
>
> **Questions**
>
> | Am | I | |
> |---|---|---|
> | Are | you | |
> | Is | he/she | going to leave tomorrow? |
> | Are | we | |
> | Are | they | |
>
> **Negatives**
>
> | I | 'm not | |
> |---|---|---|
> | You | aren't | |
> | He/She | isn't | going to leave tomorrow. |
> | We | aren't | |
> | They | aren't | |

2 Focus attention on the uses of the Present Continuous for the future and *going to*. Establish that there is little difference between the two sentences.

Read Grammar Reference 12.1 on p146 together in class, and/or ask students to read it at home. Encourage them to ask you questions about it.

PRACTICE (SB p91)

Questions about Jack

1 Elicit question 1 and the relevant answer as an example. Students work in pairs to form the questions about Jack and then match the answers.

> **Answers and tapescript**
> 1 e Why is he going to train very hard? Because he wants to be a footballer.
> 2 a How long is he going to play football? Until he's 35.
> 3 d When is he going to marry? Not until he's very old – about 25!
> 4 b How many children is he going to have? Two.
> 5 c Who is he going to teach to play? His sons.

2 **T 12.3** [CD 2: Track 40] Play the recording and get students to check their answers. Then ask them to practise saying the questions and answers in pairs. Go round and help and check as they do this. If students have problems with the falling intonation of the *wh-* questions, get them to listen and repeat the questions from the recording and then continue asking and answering in pairs.

Questions about you

3 Now we move away from Jack and Danny and get students to talk about themselves. Drill the example in the Student's Book individually and chorally following

the highlighted stress patterns. Get one or two students to demonstrate question 2 in open pairs. Then get students to work in closed pairs, asking and answering the rest of the questions. Go round and monitor as they do this, checking for correct use of the *Yes/No* questions. Pay attention to all aspects of pronunciation – sounds, stress, and intonation.

4 Focus attention on the example. Ask students to tell the class about themselves and their partner, thereby practising third person singular and first person singular and plural.

I'm going to sneeze!

Here we introduce the second use of *going to*, when we can see now that something is sure to happen in the future. Read the *Caution Box* with the whole class. If possible and necessary, use L1 to explain.

5 Ask students to look at the pictures and elicit the answer for picture 1. Students then write a sentence for each picture using *going to* with *it, you, I*, etc. If students have access to dictionaries, get them to look up new words, or they can ask you. Students can work in pairs so that they can help each other with vocabulary.

Check through the answers with the class as a whole. Ask individuals to read a sentence aloud.

Answers
1 It's going to rain.
2 I'm going to sneeze.
3 She's going to win the race.
4 He's going to jump.
5 You're going to be late.
6 They're going to kiss.
7 They're going to have a baby.
8 He's going to fall.

6 Pre-teach/check *due next month* to refer to a baby. Students work on their own or in pairs to fill the gaps, using sentences from exercise 5.

T 12.4 [CD 2: Track 41] Play the recording and get students to check their answers. There are some useful little expressions included in the sentences: *Look at the time! Oh dear. Bless you!* Illustrate the meaning of these when you go through the exercise and get the class to repeat them. It can also be interesting and fun to discuss what is said in the students' own language(s) when someone sneezes.

Students can then practise saying the sentences with a partner and have fun practising the stress and intonation in the expressions.

Answers and tapescript
1 Take an umbrella. **It's going to rain.**
2 Look at the time! **You're going to be late** for the meeting.
3 Anna's running very fast. **She's going to win the race.**
4 Look! Jack's on the wall! **He's going to fall.**
5 Look at that man! **He's going to jump.**
6 **They're going to have a baby.** It's due next month.
7 There's my sister and her boyfriend! **They're going to kiss.**
8 **A** Oh dear. **I'm going to sneeze.** Aaattishooo!
   B Bless you!

ADDITIONAL MATERIAL

Workbook Unit 12
Exercises 1–5 All aspects of *going to* future

I WANT TO SEE THE WORLD! (SB p92)

Infinitive of purpose

1 The aim of this activity is to set the scene and check the vocabulary needed for the presentation dialogue in exercise 2.

First ask your students to look at the photos and ask them which places they recognize. The photos will also help to check some of the vocabulary needed for the matching exercise. Briefly check the pronunciation of the names of the places, focusing on *Nepal* /nɪˈpɔːl/, *Hawaii* /həˈwaɪjiː/, and *China* /ˈtʃaɪnə/ in particular.

Students work in pairs to match a place with a photo, and then with an activity. Then check quickly through the exercise with the whole class. Point out the silent letters in *climb* /klaɪm/ and *whale* /weɪl/ and check students' pronunciation.

Answers
Nepal – climb Mount Everest (photo h)
Brazil – visit the rainforest (photo d)
The Great Barrier Reef – go scuba-diving (photo f)
China – walk along the Great Wall (photo c)
Hawaii – go surfing (photo g)
Alaska – watch whales (photo b)
the USA – fly over the Grand Canyon (photo a)
Kenya – take photographs of the lions (photo e)

2 In this activity, students meet Danny again. Ask students what they remember about him (he's going to retire soon and he's going to travel around the world). He is now planning all the places he is going to visit on his travels.

SUGGESTION
Danny's dialogue with his friend, Harold, incorporates revision of *going to* but some additional information is introduced: the fact that with the verb *go* we do not usually say *going to go*, but simply use the Present Continuous. The notes in the *Grammar Spot* spell this

out in more detail. You could read this with your students either after they first read the dialogue, or after they have listened to check the answer.

Go through the dialogue with the whole class. Ask one student to read Danny's lines and another Harold's. See if they can complete Danny's final line.

T 12.5 [CD 2: Track 42] Play the recording for your students, not only to check the line, but also to familiarize them with the stress and intonation patterns in the dialogue. Students practice the conversation in pairs.

Answers and tapescript
D = Danny, H = Harold
D First I'm going to Nepal.
H Why?
D To climb Mount Everest!
H Oh my goodness! Where are you going after that?
D Well, then I'm going to Kenya to **take photographs of the lions.**

---

3 Ask students if they would like to try any of the activities and/or elicit any other adventures students would like to go on.

GRAMMAR SPOT

1 Read through the notes with the class (if you have not done so earlier) and point out the use of *going/coming* rather than *going to go/going to come*.

2 Focus attention on the sentences and get students to decide if they mean the same.

> **Answer**
> Yes, the sentences do mean the same.

Explain, in L1 if possible, that the infinitive can be used in answer to a *Why ... ?* question and focus on the example in the Student's Book.

Read Grammar Reference 12.2 on p146 together in class, and/or ask students to read it at home. Encourage them to ask you questions about it.

PRACTICE (SB p93)

Roleplay

1 This is a controlled practice roleplay, where students work in pairs and take the roles of Danny and Harold, and ask and answer questions about the places on p92. Do the example in the book in open pairs across the class to illustrate the activity. Encourage students to sound surprised when delivering the line *Oh my goodness!* Then put your students into closed pairs to complete the activity.

2 This is an extension of the previous activity, so you could move on to the next activity if you are short of time.

Put students into groups of four so that the activity can be completed quite quickly. Ask them to take turns to tell part of Danny's planned journey. Remind them to use the adverbs *first, then, next, after that, finally*.

Sample answer
Student 1: First he's going to Nepal to climb Mount Everest. Then he's going to Brazil to visit the rainforest.
Student 2: Next he's going to The Great Barrier Reef to go scuba-diving, then to China to walk along the Great Wall, and after that to Hawaii to go surfing.
Student 3: After that he's going to Alaska to watch whales, and then to the USA to fly over the Grand Canyon.
Student 4: Finally, he's going to Kenya to take photographs of the lions.

Why ...? and When ...?

3 This activity personalizes the infinitive of purpose. It also moves away from practising the structure with *going to*, and revises the Past Simple. Encourage students to follow the highlighted stress patterns in the examples. Model the pattern for them if necessary.

You could introduce the activity by just going through the examples in the Student's Book, but it is much more interesting if you say some names of places you visited in the past and then get students to ask you why you went there and when, for example:

Teacher I went to Mi*lan*.
Student(s) *Why* did you go to Mi*lan*?
Teacher To *visit* a *friend* and to *practise* my *Italian*.
Student(s) *When* did you go?
Teacher *Eighteen months ago*.

Ask students to write down the names of some places they visited in the past – countries, cities, villages, or any places of interest. Then put them into pairs to ask each other questions about the places. Let this go on for as long as students are interested if you have time.

Round the activity off by asking one or two individuals to give feedback to the class about their partner.

4 This activity follows the same procedure as exercise 3, but focuses on the future. Remind students of the expressions of future time that they can use, e.g. *soon, next week/month/year, in a few weeks' time*, etc. Again, you can use the examples in the Student's Book or give examples about places you are going to visit.

Students work in pairs and ask each other questions about the places. Ask one or two individuals to give feedback to the class about their partner.

Check it

5 This exercise brings together the key structures from this unit. Ask your students to do it on their own as quickly as possible, then check their answers with a partner before you conduct feedback with the whole class.

> **Answers**
> 1 It's going to rain.
> 2 Are you going to wash your hair this evening?
> 3 She's going to have a baby.
> 4 I'm going to the post office to buy some stamps.
> 5 I'm going home early this evening.
> 6 I opened the window to get some fresh air.

ADDITIONAL MATERIAL

Workbook Unit 12
Exercises 6 and 7 Infinitive of purpose

READING AND SPEAKING (SB p94)

Born free

The reading section continues the theme of adventure with a jigsaw reading on two people who do an unusual sport/activity.

1 First, ask your students to work on their own and number the list according to which sports they think are the most dangerous. Make it clear that 1 is the most dangerous. Obviously, there are no right or wrong answers to this.

Students compare their ideas with a partner. Encourage them to give reasons for their choices.

Get students to compare their ideas with the whole class. Again, encourage them to justify their answers. Some freer speaking might result if there is disagreement across the group!

2 This activity pre-teaches some of the collocations that appear in the texts. Get students to work in pairs and match the verbs with the nouns or phrases. Check the answers with the whole class.

> **Answers**
> jump over a wall   swim underwater
> join a class   break a record
> win a medal   breathe oxygen

> **SUGGESTION**
> With weaker classes or if you are short of time, you could pre-teach/check the new vocabulary from the text before students read:
> **Free-diving:** *dive* (v), *seashells, discover, breath, calm, peace and quiet, pain, conservation*
> **Free-running:** *freedom, roofs, move* (n/v), *art, philosophy, human* (n)

3 Focus attention on the photos of Tanya and David and on the names of their respective sports. Elicit students' own ideas as to what the sports might be, but do not go into the details given in the texts as this would lessen students' reason for reading.

Divide the class into two groups. Tell Group A to read about Tanya and Group B to read about David and then answer the questions about their person. Each group has the same questions to work on. If they have access to dictionaries, allow students to look up new words. Otherwise, they can ask you for help or ask other students in their group.

Students check their answers with others from the same group. Then check the answers with Group A students and Group B students separately. (You do not need to insist on full answers – the information in brackets in the *Answers* below is optional.)

> **Answers**
> **Tanya Streeter**
> 1 (She grew up) in the Cayman Islands in the Caribbean.
> 2 (She liked) diving.
> 3 She joined a free-diving class in 1997.
> 4 (She feels) calm, but coming up again is painful.
> 5 (It's) very dangerous.
> 6 No, she doesn't at the moment.
> 7 She broke the world free-diving record.
> 8 She's going to teach free-diving and continue working for sea-life conservation.
>
> **David Belle**
> 1 (He grew up) in the countryside.
> 2 (He liked) running, jumping, and climbing trees in the woods.
> 3 He invented the sport in 1989.
> 4 (He feels) free.
> 5 (It's) often dangerous.
> 6 No, he doesn't at the moment.
> 7 He appeared on television for the first time.
> 8 He's going to take his art to the world and show people how to move.

4 Tell each student to find a partner from the other group and to compare Tanya and David, using their answers from exercise 4. Encourage them to exchange information in a meaningful way, rather than just read their answers, e.g.
> **A** *Tanya grew up near the sea. What about David?*
> **B** *He grew up in the countryside. What did Tanya like doing?*
> **A** *She liked diving. And David?*
> **B** *He liked running, jumping, and climbing trees in the woods.*

Speaking

5 Put students back into the A and B groups they were in for the reading task. Tell students that the As are Tanya and the Bs are David. Ask the As to get together in small groups to prepare the questions they are going to ask about David, and the Bs to get together in small groups to prepare the questions they are going to ask about Tanya. Make sure students understand they have to use a range of tenses in the questions.

Check the answers with Group A and B students separately.

Answers
Group A
1 Why do/did you like the countryside?
2 What did you like doing at school?
3 What sport did you invent?
4 What did you do in Lisses?
5 What are you going to do next?

Group B
1 What did you like doing as a child?
2 When did you join a diving class?
3 How long can you swim underwater?
4 What record did you break?
5 What are you going to do next?

6 Demonstrate the activity by getting two students to ask and answer question 1 from each set. Students work with a partner from the other group and interview each other. Make sure they work with a different partner from the reading stage and that they answer as either Tanya or David. Monitor and help where necessary.

Finally, ask a couple of pairs to act out their interview to the whole class. It would be a great idea to record some of the roleplays if possible and play them back to the whole class for them to comment on and correct. Students often find this very productive and satisfying.

ADDITIONAL MATERIAL

Exercises 8 and 9 Auxiliary verbs in tenses covered so far

VOCABULARY AND SPEAKING (SB p96)

The weather

1 Ask your students to look at the weather symbols. Elicit words for symbols students already know and then get them to continue working in pairs to match the remaining symbols and words. If students have access to dictionaries, get them to look up words they don't know.
Go through the answers with the class.

Answers
1 foggy   2 snowy   3 windy   4 rainy   5 sunny   6 cloudy

The next part of this exercise is to practise which pairs of adjectives commonly go together to describe weather. This will vary in different countries according to the climate, for example it can be warm and windy in many climates but is only rarely so in Britain.

Ask your class to give you their ideas about British weather. (Everyone always has something to say about British weather!)

CULTURAL NOTES
1 Despite London's reputation, the last big fog/smog (smoke + fog) was in 1957 when the Clean Air Act was passed!
2 There are lots of jokes about British weather. Can your students understand this one?
If you don't like English weather, wait ten minutes!

You could have a mini-discussion comparing which pairs they think will often go together in Britain and which for the climate of their own country.

Sample answers (for Britain)
cool and cloudy	cold and windy
cool and rainy	warm and sunny
cool and windy	hot and sunny
cold and cloudy	cold and foggy
dry and cloudy	cold and rainy
wet and windy	cold and snowy

Also you often hear the pairs *warm and dry, cold and wet* together.

2 **T 12.6** [CD 2: Track 43] Get students to look out of the window at the weather conditions. Either play the recording or model the questions yourself.

POSSIBLE PROBLEM
What … like? for descriptions always creates some difficulty because of the different use of *like*. You need to make two things very clear to your students:
1 It has nothing to do with the verb *like*. The *Caution Box* will help you do this.
2 The answer does not contain the word *like*.
What's the weather like?   It's sunny.
NOT **It's like sunny.*

Ask your students to listen and write in the weather for today, yesterday, and tomorrow. Check their answers.

Answers and tapescript
A What's the weather like today?
B It's **snowy** and it's very **cold**.
A What was it like yesterday?
B Oh, it was **cold** and **cloudy**.
A What's it going to be like tomorrow?
B I think it's going to be **warmer**.

Read through the *Caution Box* with the students (see *Possible problem* above).

Practise the questions and answers about where you are in open pairs. Drill the pronunciation as necessary, encouraging falling intonation in the *wh-* questions.

3 This is an information-gap activity. Ask your students to work in pairs. Tell Student A to look at the World Weather information on p96 of the Student's Book and Student B at the World Weather information on p151.

Briefly check the pronunciation of the cities, focusing in particular on *Edinburgh* /ˈedɪnbrə/ and *Los Angeles* /lɒsˈændʒəlɪz/. Illustrate the activity by doing the first question and answer about Athens across the class. This is a good time to feed in the modifier *quite*, if you feel your students can cope with it. (Make sure they realize that this is yesterday's weather and therefore they need to use *was* in the questions and answers.)

Get students to continue the activity in closed pairs. Monitor and check as they do it.

Check the answers with the whole class. Get students to read out their answers as complete sentences, e.g. *It was sunny and (quite) warm in Athens yesterday. 18 degrees.*

Answers
World weather: noon yesterday

		°C	It was:
Athens	S	18	sunny and warm
Berlin	R	7	wet/rainy and cold
Bombay	R	31	wet/rainy and hot
Edinburgh	C	5	cloudy and cold
Geneva	C	12	cloudy and cool
Hong Kong	S	29	sunny and hot
Lisbon	C	19	cloudy and warm
London	R	10	wet/rainy and cool
Los Angeles	Fg	21	foggy and warm
Luxor	S	40	sunny and very hot
Milan	Fg	19	foggy and warm
Moscow	Sn	−1	snowy and very cold
Oslo	Sn	2	snowy and cold

S = sunny	**C = cloudy**	**Fg = foggy**
R = rainy	**Sn = snowy**	

4 Get students to answer the questions about the weather report in pairs before checking with the whole class.

Answers
Luxor was the hottest. (Ask your students if they know where this is. It's in Egypt.)
Moscow was the coldest.
The month is in fact March. (Encourage a bit of discussion about this – it could be other months, but clearly, in Europe anyway, the season is either winter or early spring.)

ADDITIONAL MATERIAL

Workbook
Exercise 10–12 Vocabulary and pronunciation

EVERYDAY ENGLISH (SB p97)

Making suggestions

> **NOTES**
> In order not to overload students, we have restricted the exponents in this section to: *shall* to ask for suggestions and make suggestions, and *Let's* to make a suggestion for everyone.
> We also revise *will* for spontaneous decisions, which was introduced in the previous unit.

1 Focus attention on the two examples and then elicit a few more activities for good weather (*go for a walk, play tennis, do gardening,* etc.) and some for bad weather (*read a book, do a jigsaw, play chess,* etc.) Students continue the two lists on their own and then compare their lists with a partner. Ask for some feedback from the whole class and tell students that they will need their lists later.

2 **T 12.7** [CD 2: Track 44] Tell students that they are going to hear the beginnings of two conversations, one for good weather and one for bad. Ask them to read and listen at the same time and complete the suggestions.

Answers and tapescript
1 **A** It's a lovely day! What shall we do?
   B Let's **play tennis**!
2 **A** It's raining again! What shall we do?
   B Let's **stay at home** and **watch a DVD**.

Then get students to listen and repeat in chorus. First focus on the question, and then practise the answer. Encourage good stress and intonation.

What shall we do?   /wɒt ʃəl wi duː/
Let's play tennis.   /lets pleɪ tenɪs/

Ask students to practise the conversations in pairs.

Read through the *Caution Box* with the whole class. In a monolingual class, you could ask students to translate the sentences.

3 Ask your students to work in pairs. Ask them first to find the 'good weather' lines and then the 'bad weather' lines. Then ask them to put each set in order to complete the conversations from exercise 2, marking 1 or 2 in the first column to show which conversation the lines come from.

T 12.8 [CD 2: Track 45] Play the recording and get students to listen and check their answers.

Answers and tapescript
1b Well, let's go swimming.
2c OK. Which film do you want to see?
1a Oh no! It's too hot to play tennis.
2a Oh no! We watched a DVD last night.
1c OK. I'll get my swimming costume.
2b Well, let's go to the cinema.

T 12.8
1 **A** It's a lovely day! What shall we do?
  B Let's play tennis!
  A Oh no! It's too hot to play tennis.
  B Well, let's go swimming.
  A OK. I'll get my swimming costume.
2 **A** It's raining again! What shall we do?
  B Let's stay at home and watch a DVD.
  A Oh no! We watched a DVD last night.
  B Well, let's go to the cinema.
  A OK. Which film do you want to see?

MUSIC OF ENGLISH

T 12.8 [CD 2: Track 45] Read through the *Music of English* box as a class. Play the recording again. Students listen again, paying particular attention to the intonation and stress highlighting.

Play the recording again and get students to repeat, following the highlighted stress pattern in the Student's Book. Get students to practise the conversations in closed pairs.

4 Students continue to work in pairs. Ask them to look at the lists they made in exercise 1. Demonstrate the activity by asking for examples of a good weather and a bad weather activity and building the dialogues with the whole class. Get students to continue in pairs, using the activities in their lists. Monitor and check.

To round off the activity, you could either ask a couple of pairs to do their dialogues for the whole class, or record a few dialogues and play them for the class to correct any mistakes in the language and the pronunciation.

WRITING (SB p123)

Writing a postcard

This unit of the writing syllabus gives students the opportunity to write a holiday postcard. It is an ideal way to consolidate the weather vocabulary covered in the unit and also gives further practice in a range of tenses.

1 As a lead-in to the writing section, ask what information people typically include in a postcard (*weather, accommodation, food, activities, places to visit*). Divide the class into pairs and get them to discuss the questions

giving examples where possible. Elicit any interesting examples in a short feedback session. You could ask students to feed back on their partner's examples.

2 Get students to read the postcard quickly and ask *Who is on holiday?* (Lara and Mick from Unit 2 *Patrick's family*), *Where are they?* (in Corsica), *Who is the postcard to?* (their parents in Ireland). Students then read the postcard again and underline the words for good and bad weather. Check the answers with the class.

Answers
Good weather: glorious, changeable, warm and sunny, hot
Bad weather: not very good, changeable, cold and cloudy, foggy

3 Point out that there are two possible descriptions of the holiday in the postcard, one good and one bad. Divide the class into two groups and get Group A to write out the description of the good holiday and Group B the bad holiday. (If you are short of time, you can just get students to underline the key language for their description, or build the two descriptions on the board as a whole-class activity.) Allow pairs of students in each main group to work collaboratively to write the description. Check the answers.

Answers
Good holiday
We're having a wonderful time here in Corsica, and fortunately the weather is glorious. They say they the weather here in April is often quite changeable so we're very lucky. It is warm and sunny nearly every day so most of the time we go to the beach and swim and sunbathe. Yesterday it was so hot that we couldn't lie in the sun. Tomorrow we're not going to the beach, we're going to drive round the island and go sightseeing.

Bad holiday
We're having quite a good time here in Corsica, but unfortunately the weather is not very good. They say they the weather here in April is often quite changeable so we're just unlucky. It is cold and cloudy nearly every day so most of the time we stay in the hotel and play cards. Yesterday it was so foggy that we couldn't see the sea. Tomorrow we're not going to stay in the hotel, we're going to drive round the island and go sightseeing.

4 Focus attention on the writing plan and elicit possible ideas for each point. Check students use the correct tense for things they do often/most of the time (Present Simple), things they did yesterday (Past Simple), and things they are going to do tomorrow (*going to*). Give students time to decide if they are going to write about a good or bad holiday. Encourage them to base their ideas on a real holiday if appropriate.

If possible, bring in real postcards for students to write on to add authenticity. Give students time to write their postcard in class or set it for homework. If possible, display the postcards on the classroom wall or noticeboard to allow students to read each other's work. If appropriate, you could get students to vote for the best/worst holiday described in the postcards. When you check the students' work, point out errors but allow students to correct them themselves and try to limit correction to major problems to avoid demoralizing.

Don't forget!

Workbook Unit 12
Exercises 13 Prepositions: *from*, *like*, and *than*
Exercise 14 Translation
Exercise 15 Listening practice on making suggestions

Grammar Reference
Look at the exercises on SB p146 as a class, or set for homework. The answers are on TB p176.

Word list
Remind your students of the Word list for this unit on SB p157. They could translate the words, or learn them at home, or transfer some of the words to their vocabulary notebook.

Pronunciation Book Unit 12

Video/DVD Episode 5 Change of a dress

PHOTOCOPIABLE MATERIAL: EXTRA IDEAS UNITS 9–12
Reading TB p148

The reading exercise is about a dream house in the country and revises Units 9–12. It could be done for homework.

Activities to exploit the reading are provided and the answers are on p171.

13

Question forms • Adjectives and adverbs
Describing feelings • At the chemist's

Introduction to the unit

Question forms are the main target language of this unit. This is not a particularly new language area, as question forms have been introduced and practised throughout the book, but focusing on question forms allows a lot of language areas, especially tenses, to be pulled together and revised. This unit also gives a thorough review of the intonation of questions, which students have practised throughout the course.

The theme of the unit is stories. In the reading and listening section, students read a simplified story taken from the *Oxford Bookworms* series of readers. If you haven't already encouraged your students to read outside the coursebook, now is the time to start! Reading is one of the easiest, cheapest, and most pleasurable ways of learning a foreign language and there is a big range of simplified stories available in series of readers such as the *Oxford Bookworms*.

Language aims

Grammar – question forms All the *wh-* questions (*when, where, who, what, why, which, whose*), and questions with *how* + adjective (e.g. *How old … ?*) are revised. *What* + noun (*What nationality … ?/What kind … ?*) is also practised.

We 'drop in' two subject questions *What happens … ?* and *Who created … ?* in the quiz in the first presentation. We suggest that you do not embark on a detailed presentation of the difference between subject and object question forms. If students wonder (very sensibly) why *do/does/did* is not used in these questions, try to satisfy them with a quick explanation. Put on the board the sentences *Joe likes Betty. Betty likes Tim.* Ask these questions: *Who likes Betty?* (Joe does.) *Who does Betty like?* (She likes Tim.) to show them that the first question refers to the subject of the sentence, while the second one asks about the object of the sentence. Then tell them not to worry about it at this stage! In our experience, it would not be useful for students to go too deeply into it at this level, or at all, unless they ask about it.

Adjectives and adverbs In this unit, the difference between adjectives and adverbs, and regular and irregular adverbs are presented and practised.

Vocabulary The vocabulary section focuses on describing feelings and presents/reviews adjectives with both *-ed* and *-ing* endings. Students often find these confusing and so choose the wrong form.
Common mistakes
**I'm interesting in sport.*
**I was very boring.* (when the student meant to say *I was very bored*!)
**The problem is very worried.*

Everyday English The language for buying things in a chemist's is practised.

Writing Adjectives and adverbs are further practised in the context of a story, and students are invited to write a fairy story of their own.

Workbook Question words are further consolidated and the question *Which one … ?* is introduced and practised. *What sort … ?* is also introduced to supplement *What kind … ?*
There is further practice on adverbs and adjectives.
Noun and adjective suffixes are introduced, and *-ed* and *-ing* adjectives (*interested/interesting*) are further practised.

Notes on the unit

STARTER (SB p98)

This activity provides a quick review of the question words students have already met, without making them form complete questions. It also acts as a preview to the focus on stories later in the unit.

1 Demonstrate the activity with the whole class by asking students to match *When ... ?* and *Where ... ?* with the appropriate answer (*When ... ?* – 1991, *Where ... ?* – *Paris*). Students work in pairs and continue the activity. Check the answers with the whole class.

> **Answers**
>
> When ... ? – 1991.   Which ... ? – The red ones.
> Where ... ? – Paris.   How ... ? – By plane.
> What ... ? – Some roses.   How much ... ? – €50.
> Who ... ? – John.   How many ... ? – Six.
> Why ... ? – Because I love him.

2 Students look at the answers again and say what type of story they think it is (a love story). You could encourage students to make up a short story.

> **Answers**
>
> **Sample story:** In 1991 Mary went to Paris by plane with John. He bought her six red roses because he loved her. The roses cost £50.

A QUIZ (SB p98)

Question words

1 Tell students they are going to do a quiz on famous stories and characters. Focus attention on the pictures and ask students which stories they know. Get them to predict some of the names of the stories and characters in the questions.

2 Students work in groups to answer the Storytime quiz. Encourage discussion if/when students disagree about the answers. Elicit a range of answers to the quiz questions but do not confirm or reject students' ideas at this stage.

3 **T 13.1** [CD 2: Track 46] Students listen and check their answers.

> **Answers and tapescript**
> **Storytime Quiz**
> 1 When did Shakespeare die? b In the 17th century (1616).
> 2 What happens at the end of *Romeo and Juliet*?
>   They both die. They kill themselves.
> 3 How many dwarfs are there in *Snow White*? b 7
> 4 How much money do Hansel and Gretel's parents have?
>   c none
> 5 How long does Sleeping Beauty sleep? 100 years
> 6 Who does Cinderella marry? a the handsome Prince
> 7 Who created Mickey Mouse? Walt Disney
> 8 Where did Hans Christian Andersen come from?
>   b Denmark
> 9 What nationality are Don Quixote and Sancho Panza?
>   Spanish
> 10 Whose lamp is magic? a Aladdin's
> 11 Why does Pinocchio's nose grow long? Because he tells lies.
> 12 What kind of animal is Walt Disney's Dumbo?
>   a an elephant

> 13 Which city does Sherlock Holmes live in? b London
> 14 How old is Harry Potter in the first story *Harry Potter and the Philosopher's Stone*? b 11

Play some of the questions again and ask students to focus on the intonation. Ask them whether the voice rises or falls at the end (the voice falls because these are all questions with a question word).

When did *Shakespeare die?*

What happens at the end of *Romeo* and *Juliet?*

Drill the questions chorally and individually.

4 Lead in to the discussion by giving examples of your own favourite stories. Tell the class briefly the names of the stories you read as a child. Divide the class into groups and get them to discuss the questions. Elicit the most popular stories and the names of the most famous stories in the students' own country/culture.

GRAMMAR SPOT

This Grammar Spot extends the focus on question formation to include *Yes/No* questions. Students contrast the different intonations in *wh-* questions and *Yes/No* questions, and then go on to review short answers.

1 Ask students to underline the question words in the quiz. Remind them that some question words consist of two words. Check the answers.

> **Answers**
> 1 When ... ?   8 Where ... ?
> 2 What ... ?   9 What ... ?
> 3 How many ... ?   10 Whose ... ?
> 4 How much ... ?   11 Why ... ?
> 5 How long ... ?   12 What kind ... ?
> 6 Who ... ?   13 Which ... ?
> 7 Who ... ?   14 How old ... ?

Pronunciation

2 Focus students' attention on the two questions. Elicit the two differences between them (the first question has a *question word*, the second is a *Yes/No* question; the first question has falling intonation, the second has rising).

T 13.2 [CD 2: Track 47] Play the recording. Students listen and repeat closely following the intonation and stress patterns. Students then practise in open/closed pairs.

3 Do the first item as a class. Elicit the two different questions similar to those in Pronunciation above. Tell students to use contracted forms where possible. (*What's she wearing? Is she wearing jeans?*).

Then elicit the short answers for the two types of question (*Jeans. Yes, she is. No, she isn't*). Students work in pairs to continue writing the answers giving both a positive and negative answer to the *Yes/No* questions.

4 **T 13.3** [CD 2: Track 48] Play the recording. Students listen and check.

Answers and tapescript

1 **A** What's she wearing?
   B Jeans.
   A Is she wearing jeans?
   B Yes, she is.
   C No, she isn't.
2 **A** Where does she work?
   B In a bank.
   A Does she work in a bank?
   B Yes, she does.
   C No, she doesn't.
3 **A** When's he leaving?
   B Tomorrow.
   A Is he leaving tomorrow?
   B Yes, he is.
   C No, he isn't.
4 **A** Who did you visit?
   B My aunt.
   A Did you visit your aunt?
   B Yes, I did.
   C No, I didn't.
5 **A** How did you come?
   B By taxi.
   A Did you come by taxi?
   B Yes, we did.
   C No, we didn't.
6 **A** Why are they going to have a party?
   B Because it's her birthday.
   A Are they going to have a party?
   B Yes, they are.
   C No, they aren't.

Read Grammar Reference 13.1 on p146 together in class, and/or ask students to read it at home. Encourage them to ask you questions about it.

SUGGESTION

If there is time, and you feel your students will benefit from further discussion and/or question formation practice, put them into small groups to write some more storytime questions. Brainstorm possible stories with the whole class first, allowing adequate time for students to write their questions. Monitor and help with vocabulary, checking that students have formed their questions correctly.

When they have a reasonable number of questions, ask the groups to put the questions to the rest of the class. You could even make this a team game and allocate points.

PRACTICE (SB p99)

Questions and answers

1 Focus attention on the example. Explain that students will have to use some of the questions in B more than once. Students continue the activity, working in pairs.

Ask students for their answers before playing the recording for them to listen and check. This will allow you to see where students are going wrong.

T 13.4 [CD 2: Track 49] Play the recording. Students listen and check.

Answers and tapescript

Where did you go? To the shops.
When did you go? This morning.
Who did you go with? A friend from work.
How did you go? We drove.
Whose car did you go in? Joe's.
Why did you go? To buy some new clothes.
What did you buy? A new jacket.
Which one did you buy? The black leather one.
How much did you pay? £180.99.
How many did you buy? Only one.

If students have made a lot of mistakes, go back over the question words and how they relate to the answers. Then drill the questions and answers in open pairs, getting students to repeat in closed pairs if necessary.

POSSIBLE PROBLEM

If students get confused by the use of *one* in *Which one … ?*, *The black leather one* and *Only one*, explain that we say *Which one … ?* and *The black leather one* to avoid repeating the word *jacket*, and that *Only one* refers to the number one. This point is further practised in exercise 4 in the Workbook.

Listening and pronunciation

2 **T 13.5** [CD 2: Track 50] Play the first sentence and elicit the answer as an example. Students listen to the rest of the recording and tick the sentences they hear. Let students check in pairs before you give the answers.

> **Answers and tapescript**
> 1 Why do you want to go?
> 2 Who is she?
> 3 Where's he staying?
> 4 Why didn't they come?
> 5 How old was she?
> 6 Does he play the guitar?
> 7 Where did you go at the weekend?

Asking about you

3 Demonstrate the activity by getting students to put the words in question 1 in the correct order (*Do you like learning English?*). Students continue the activity in pairs.

Check the answers with the whole class.

> **Answers**
> 1 Do you like learning English?
> 2 What did you do last night?
> 3 How many languages does your mother speak?
> 4 When did you last go shopping?
> 5 Which football team do you support?
> 6 Did you come to school by car today?
> 7 How much homework do you have?
> 8 Who do you usually sit next to in class?
> 9 Why do you want to learn English?

4 Drill the questions around the class. Make sure that students use the correct intonation – falling on the *Wh-* questions and rising on the *Yes/No* questions as practised in the Grammar Spot on SB p99.

In pairs, students ask and answer the questions about themselves. Remind them that they can use short answers where appropriate. Monitor and check for correct intonation and for acceptable short answers.

> **Sample answers**
> 1 Yes, I do.   6 No, I came by bus.
> 2 I played tennis.   7 About six hours a week.
> 3 Two (French and Italian).   8 Laura.
> 4 A week ago.   9 Because I need it for my job.
> 5 Lazio.

ADDITIONAL MATERIAL

Workbook Unit 13
Exercises 1–5 Question forms including *What (sort)?*, *How (old)?*, *Which one?*

DO IT CAREFULLY! (SB p100)

Adjectives and adverbs

1 Focus on the first pair of sentences as an example. Elicit the answers (*bad* – adjective, *badly* – adverb). Students then work in pairs. Check the answers with the whole class. If students have problems with number 5 – the irregular form *hard* – go straight on to the *Grammar Spot*, where students focus on this point.

> **Answers**
> 1 *bad* – adjective *badly* – adverb
> 2 *carefully* – adverb *careful* – adjective
> 3 *easy* – adjective *easily* – adverb
> 4 *well* – adverb (*well* is the irregular adverb of *good*)
>   *good* – adjective
> 5 *hard* – adjective
>   *hard* – adverb (*hard* is irregular)

> ### GRAMMAR SPOT
>
> **1** Read the sentences and the explanation about adjectives and adverbs as a class.
>
> **2** If necessary, put some adjectives that have regular adverbs on the board, e.g. *quick, bad, careful*. Include an example of an adjective ending in -*y*, e.g. *easy*. Elicit the adverbs and get students to tell you the rule.
>
> > **Answers**
> > We make regular adverbs by adding -*ly* to the adjective. If the adjective ends in -*y*, it changes to -*ily*.
>
> **3** Ask students to look back at exercise 1 and find the irregular adverbs. Check the answers.
>
> > **Answers**
> > *well* and *hard* are irregular.
>
> Read Grammar Reference 13.2 on p146 together in class, and/or ask students to read it at home. Encourage them to ask you questions about it.

2 This activity focuses on adverbs that collocate with common verbs and phrases. Elicit adverbs that can go with *get up* as an example (*get up slowly/quietly/carefully/early/fast/quickly*).

Students work in pairs and continue the activity. Remind them to decide which adverbs in the box are irregular. Check the answers with the whole class.

PRACTICE (SB p100)

Order of adjectives/adverbs

1   Elicit the correct answer to number 1 as an example.
    Students put the word in brackets in the correct place in
    the sentences, changing the adjective to an adverb if
    necessary. Tell them that sometimes more than one
    answer is possible. Students can work in pairs, or alone
    and then check with a partner.

> **POSSIBLE PROBLEM**
> We do not overtly give the rules for the order of
> adverbs (front position, mid-position, end position),
> because the rules are rather complicated. We do not
> suggest that you try to go into them at this stage. You
> could perhaps point out that adverbs usually follow the
> verb and object if there is one, whereas adjectives go
> before the noun (unlike many other languages).
> Otherwise let students see how they get on without
> rules, and simply correct any mistakes.

Answers
1   We had a holiday in Spain, but unfortunately we had
    terrible weather.
2   Maria dances **well**.
3   When I saw the accident, I phoned the police **immediately**
    (or I **immediately** phoned . . .).
4   Don't worry. Justin is a **careful** driver.
5   Jean-Pierre is a **typical** Frenchman. He loves food, wine,
    and rugby.
6   Please speak **slowly**. I can't understand you.
7   We had an **easy** test today.
8   We all passed **easily**.
9   You speak **good** English./You speak English **well**.

Telling a story

2   Point out that adverbs are often used in storytelling to
    make the actions sound more vivid. Focus on sentence 1 as
    an example with the whole class. Elicit a range of endings

that will fit with the adverb *fortunately*, e.g. *… I had a
umbrella./… we were inside./… the rain didn't last long.*
Students continue working in pairs. Monitor and check
if their answers fit with the adverbs given. Where
possible, elicit a range of answers for each sentence that
highlight the meaning of the adverb.

Possible answers
1   Fortunately, I had an umbrella./we were inside./the rain
    didn't last long.
2   Unfortunately, I couldn't go./I was ill./I was on holiday.
3   . . . the phone rang./I heard a loud noise./the dog started
    to bark.
4   . . . I called the police./I told a police officer.

If you want to double-check that students have
understood the adverbs, explain or translate them. You
could get them to look up the definitions in dictionaries.

3   **T 13.6** [CD 2: Track 51] Students listen to the story and
    number the adverbs in the correct order. Check the
    answers.

Answers and tapescript

8	quickly	3	carefully
4	quietly	1	suddenly
2	slowly	7	fortunately
5	immediately	6	really

Noises in the night

T 13.6
It was about two o'clock in the morning, and ... suddenly I woke
up. I heard a noise. I got out of bed and went slowly downstairs.
There was a light on in the living room. I listened carefully. I
could hear two men speaking very quietly. 'Burglars!' I thought.
'Two burglars!' Immediately I ran back upstairs and phoned the
police. I was really frightened. Fortunately the police arrived
quickly. They opened the front door and went into the living
room. Then they came upstairs to find me. 'It's all right now, sir,'
they explained. 'We turned the television off for you!'

4   In pairs, students retell the story either one sentence at a
    time each, or one student first, then the other. Remind
    them to use the order of adverbs to help them. With
    weaker classes, you could write up key words on the
    board as prompts.

Check it

5   This exercise focuses on common mistakes in question
    formation and the use of adverbs. Elicit the correct
    answer to question 1 as an example. Students work in
    pairs to correct the mistakes.

ADDITIONAL MATERIAL

Workbook Unit 13
Exercises 6 and 7 Adverbs

VOCABULARY (SB p101)

Describing feelings

1   Focus attention on the stress highlighting and drill the pronunciation, making sure that students pronounce *bored* and *tired* as one syllable – /bɔːd/, /taɪəd/. Demonstrate the activity by getting students to find the correct picture for *bored* (photo d). Students match the rest of the feelings to the pictures.

Check the answers with the whole class.

2   Demonstrate the activity by getting students to find the correct reason for *bored* (*I am bored because I have nothing to do.*). Students continue the activity in pairs. Then check the answers with the whole class.

Focus attention on the *Caution Box*. Read the notes with the whole class. Using L1 if possible, explain that adjectives ending in -*ed* often describe a person's feeling or reactions, and that adjectives ending in -*ing* often describe the person or thing that provokes those feelings or reactions.

3   Focus on the pair of sentences in number 1 as an example (*Life in New York is very* **exciting**. *The football fans were very* **excited**.) Students complete the rest of the exercise.

Check the answers with the whole class.

4   Drill the pronunciation of the pairs of adjectives in exercise 3, making sure students can clearly distinguish the -*ing* and -*ed* forms. Drill the example in the Student's Book chorally and individually following the highlighted stress patterns.

Continue the activity by asking the questions below and getting students to respond with a suitable adjective in the correct form (sample answers are given in brackets). Elicit a range of answers by asking several students the same question.
Did you enjoy the last film you saw? (Yes, it was interesting.)
Why don't you run six kilometres every morning? (Because it's tiring.)
How do you feel after the lesson? (A bit tired.)
How do you feel before an exam? (Very worried.)
How do you feel if your friend is late? (A bit annoyed.)
Do you like football? (No, it's very boring.)
Do you like learning English? (Yes, it's interesting, but a bit tiring.)

ADDITIONAL MATERIAL

Workbook Unit 13
Exercises 8 and 9 Adjective suffixes, and -*ed*/-*ing* adjectives

READING AND LISTENING (SB p102)

A short story

> **NOTE**
> Notice that in many of the exercises in this section, a lot of the questions are in the Present Simple, not the Past Simple. This use of the Present Simple is called the Historic Present, and it is common when talking about stories, films, etc. We do not suggest that you point this out to students, and don't worry too much if students want to reply using the Past Simple.

1   Pre-teach/check *presents*. Demonstrate the activity by telling the class about your Christmases and best and worst presents. Then get the students to talk about themselves in pairs or small groups.

2 Focus attention on the pictures on pp102–4. Ask students the questions (*The story takes place in New York in the late 18th or early 19th century. The people are a married couple who are poor.*) Pre-teach/check *combs* and *watch chain*.

> **SUGGESTION**
> We suggest that students read and listen at the same time to discourage them from worrying too much about unknown vocabulary. However, if you think that your students will be put off by coming across words they don't recognize, you could pre-teach/check the following items from the three parts of the story: *dollar, cent, count* (v), *save, cry* (v), *lucky, put your arms around someone, cut off, belong, grow, it doesn't matter.*
>
> As an alternative approach, you could ask students to read in silence, deal with any vocabulary queries they have, and then play the recording afterwards.

3 **T 13.7** [CD 2: Track 52] Students read and listen to part one of the story.

4 Students answer the questions in pairs or small groups. (Question 7 revises *-ed/-ing* adjectives, so with weaker classes you may want to review these briefly before students do the exercise.) Check the answers with the whole class.

> **Answers**
> 1 She lives in New York.
> 2 Yes, she is.
> 3 She doesn't have/hasn't got a job.
> 4 It's Christmas/winter.
> 5 She wants to buy him a present (to show how much she loves him).
> 6 Students' own answers.
> 7 *Careful* because she counted the money twice and tried to find the cheapest food; *tired* because she walked for hours around the shops; *sad* because she couldn't buy a present for Jim; *happy* when Jim came home; *excited* when she went into town.

5 **T 13.8** [CD 2: Track 53] Elicit a range of ideas as to why Della goes into town. Students read and listen to part two and compare their ideas with what actually happens.

6 Students answer the questions about part two, working in pairs. Check the answers.

> **Answers**
> 1 She went to a woman who buys hair. She sold her hair.
> 2 She has twenty dollars for Jim's present.
> 3 She buys a gold watch chain, because his watch didn't have one.
> 4 She thinks she looks like a schoolboy (and she is worried what Jim is going to think).

5 He felt sad about Della's hair. (Elicit a range of possible answers as to what the problem is.)

6 *Happy* because she was at the shops with money for a present for Jim; *excited* when she arrived home with Jim's present; *worried* when she looked at her hair and when Jim saw her hair.

7 Divide the class into pairs and get students to discuss how the story is going to end. Elicit a range of ideas before students read part three and check.

8 **T 13.9** [CD 2: Track 54] Play the recording of part three and get students to read and listen.

9 Check students understand the meaning of *moral* (important message or lesson) in question 4. Students work in pairs and answer the questions.

> **Answers**
> 1 He wasn't worried about it./He said it didn't matter. He was unhappy because he bought Della some beautiful combs for her hair. (Elicit how many students guessed correctly.)
> 2 Yes, she does, but she feels a bit sad because she doesn't have her hair.
> 3 Jim sold his watch to buy the combs for Della.
> 4 The best present of all is love.

Language work

This section revises adjectives and adverbs, and question words. If you are short of time, it could be done quickly in class or set for homework.

10 Remind students that adjectives can be in comparative or superlative forms and elicit examples of adjectives and adverbs from paragraph 1 of the story (adjectives – *cheapest, tiring, next, little*; adverbs – *carefully, quietly*). Students continue in pairs to find adjectives and adverbs from the story. (If time is short, you could get students to work in groups and focus on just one paragraph of the story, before exchanging answers with the rest of the class.)

> **Answers**
> **Part 1**
> **Paragraph 1**
> *Adjectives:* cheapest, tiring, next, little
> *Adverbs:* carefully, quietly
> **Paragraph 2**
> *Adjectives:* poor, little, lucky, good, bad
> *Adverbs:* immediately
> **Paragraph 3**
> *Adjectives:* good, beautiful, long, old, brown
> *Adverbs:* suddenly, quickly
>
> **Part two**
> **Paragraph 1**
> *Adjectives:* small, fat
> *Adverbs:* slowly (*Quick!* is also used informally as an adverb; the standard form would be *Quickly!*)

Paragraph 2
Adjectives: next, happy, perfect, special, beautiful, gold, right
Adverbs: quickly, immediately

Paragraph 3
Adjectives: short, angry, surprised, strange
Adverbs: excitedly, quietly, sadly, fast

Part three
Adjectives: long, short, unhappy, little, beautiful, lovely, expensive, new
Adverbs: suddenly, excitedly

11 Focus attention on the examples and the highlighted stress pattern. Students write questions using the question words in the box. Check that students have formed the questions correctly.

Sample questions
How much did Della get for her hair?
What did Della buy for Jim?
Why did Jim sell his watch?
Where did Della go to sell her hair?
How did the story end?

Students ask and answer questions across the class.

WRITING (SB p124)

Writing a story

Using adjectives and adverbs

The Writing section in this unit builds on the focus on adjectives and adverbs, and story-telling with a story-writing task. Students complete a gapped version of the classic fairy story, *The Emperor's New Clothes*, before going on to write a shortened version of a fairy story that they know.

1 Focus attention on the picture and on the title of the story. Divide the class into pairs/small groups and get them to discuss what they know about the story. Then elicit the basic plot with the whole class. If your students are unfamiliar with the story, get them to read the gapped version through once.

2 Pre-teach/check the following vocabulary: *tailor, palace, magic, cloth, clever, minister, clap, cheer*. Briefly review the adjectives and adverbs in the box and focus attention on the example answer. Students continue the exercise, working in pairs. Check the answers with the class.

Answers

2	beautiful	10	new
3	wonderful	11	loudly
4	immediately	12	suddenly
5	worried	13	naked
6	unhappily	14	embarrassed
7	pleased	15	quickly
8	Unfortunately	16	angrily
9	Naturally		

3 Check students understand that *Once upon a time …* and *… they lived happily ever after* are the classic ways to start and end a fairy story. Elicit the key characteristics of fairy stories (magical characters/events, overcoming an ordeal, love winning out over evil, the story ending happily, etc.). Brainstorm a range of fairy stories students are familiar with and write up relevant vocabulary on the board. Elicit from students which are their favourite stories.

4 Get students to choose the story they want to write and brainstorm the vocabulary they will need. If appropriate, let them use dictionaries and/or be prepared to feed in vocabulary as necessary.

Give students time to write their story in class or set it for homework. If possible, display the stories on the classroom wall or noticeboard to allow students to read each other's work. If appropriate, you could get students to vote for the best story. When you check the students' work, mark errors but allow students to correct them themselves and try to limit correction to major problems to avoid demoralizing.

EVERYDAY ENGLISH (SB p105)

At the chemist's

> **NOTE**
> You may need to check that students understand what you can buy at the average chemist's in Britain. They all sell basic healthcare items such as painkillers, cough medicines, and stomach remedies along with a large range of toiletries. Many also have a pharmacist who is qualified to provide drugs and remedies prescribed by a doctor or dentist. Larger chemist's often also sell gifts and cosmetics such as perfumes and make-up.

1 Focus attention on the photos and elicit the names of the items that students recognize. Students match the words in the box with the photos. Check the answers.

Answers

i	a comb	g	deodorant	j	conditioner
f	suncream	d	plasters	c	soap
a	aspirin	h	a toothbrush	b	toothpaste
e	shampoo				

Elicit an example for each of the categories in the table and then give students time to complete the exercise, working in pairs. Check the answers.

Answers			
hair	**teeth**	**skin**	**health**
a comb	a toothbrush	suncream	aspirin
shampoo	toothpaste	deodorant	
conditioner		soap	
		plasters	

Check students' pronunciation, highlighting in particular the silent letter in *comb* /kəʊm/, the stress on *aspirin*, the stress on the first syllable in the compound nouns below:

toothbrush   *toothpaste*   *suncream*

Drill the words chorally and individually as necessary.

2 **T 13.10** [CD 2: Track 55] Play the recording and get students to complete the conversation. With weaker students, give them time to read the conversation through first and to guess some of the missing words before playing the recording.

Give students time to check their answers in pairs before checking with the whole class.

Answers and tapescript
A Hello. Can I help you?
B Yes, please. I'm not **feeling** very well. I'm **looking** for some aspirin. **Where** can I find them?
A Right here. What **size** do you want? Small or **large**?
B Large, please. And **I'd like** some shampoo, as well.
A What **kind** of shampoo? For dry hair? Normal hair?
B Um … for dry hair, please.
A There's Sunsilk or Palmolive. **Which** one do you want?
B Sunsilk's fine, thanks.
A **Anything** else?
B No, that's all. **How much** is that?
A Four pounds twenty.
B **There** you are.
A Ten pounds. Thank you. And here's five pounds eighty **change**.
B Thanks. Bye.
A Bye-bye. Thank you very much.

MUSIC OF ENGLISH

T 13.10 [CD 2: Track 55] Read through the *Music of English* box as a class. Play the recording again pausing where relevant to drill key expressions. Encourage students to follow the stress and intonation in the recording. Students practise the conversation in pairs.

3 Students use the words in exercise 1 to make up different conversations with their partner. With weaker classes, elicit an example conversation first with the whole class,

getting individual students to say one or two lines each. If your students are keen on roleplay and if you have time, you could get them to act out their conversations for the whole class.

SUGGESTION
You can give further practice in the language of buying things at a chemist's by using the photocopiable activity on TB p150. Photocopy enough sheets for each pair of students and divide them along the cut line.

1 Divide the class into pairs. Give each students the relevant half of the sheet and elicit an example for both Students A and B. Students continue reordering the words in brackets. Remind them to add capital letters where relevant. Check the answers.

Answers
Student A
1 Can I help you?
2 What size do you want?
3 What kind of conditioner?
4 Five euros eighty.
5 Here's four euros twenty change.

Student B
1 I'm looking for some plasters.
2 And I'd like some conditioner as well.
3 For normal hair, please.
4 How much is that?
5 Thank you very much.

2 Students practise the conversations in pairs paying attention to stress and intonation.

Don't forget!

Workbook Unit 13
Exercise 10 Translation
Exercise 11 Listening practice on the language of shopping

Grammar Reference
Look at the exercises on SB p147 as a class, or set for homework. The answers are on TB p157.

Word list
Remind your students of the Word list for this unit on SB p157. They could translate the words, learn them at home, or transfer some of the words to their vocabulary notebook.

Pronunciation Book Unit 13

Video/DVD Episode 6 A long weekend

14

Present Perfect + *ever, never, yet,* and *just*
At the airport

Have you ever?

Introduction to the unit

This unit introduces one of the most difficult tenses for students of English to learn. The Present Perfect is one of the most commonly used tenses in English, especially spoken English, but its presentation has been deferred until Unit 14. This is because until students have understood the concept that the Past Simple refers to the definite past, they will not be able to grasp the idea that the Present Perfect refers to the indefinite past.

The theme of this unit is 'in my life', and various people's experiences in life are explored. There is a jigsaw reading activity where students read about two people who have never learnt to drive. This gives further exposure to, and practice in, the Present Perfect contrasted with the Past Simple, and also provides a springboard for discussing travel. There is also a *Listening and vocabulary* section with the song *All around the world* and the *Everyday English* section *At the airport,* which further develop the travel theme.

Language aims

Grammar – Present Perfect In this unit, we introduce one of the main uses of the Present Perfect, that is, to refer to an experience some time in one's life. We also focus on another use (to refer to the present result of a past action) with the adverbs *yet* and *just.* We do not introduce at all the third main use of the Present Perfect, which is to refer to unfinished past (*I have been a teacher for ten years*), nor do we teach the Present Perfect Continuous.

The aim of this unit is to provide an introduction to the Present Perfect, but do not expect your students to master the area quickly! It takes a long time (and a lot of mistakes, correction, and reteaching) before students feel confident with this tense.

POSSIBLE PROBLEMS

The Present Perfect tense presents students with problems mainly because a similar form of auxiliary verb *have* + past participle exists in many European languages, but it is used in a very different way. In English, the Present Perfect expresses the concept of an action happening at an indefinite time before now, and so it cannot be used when a definite time is given. The following sentences are examples of incorrect usage.

Common mistakes
*I have seen him last week.
*When have you been to the States?
*Did you ever try Chinese food?
*In my life I went to most countries in Europe, but I never went to Greece.

Note that American English can use the Past Simple with *just* and *yet.*
Did you do your homework yet? I just did it.

Vocabulary There is no self-standing vocabulary section in this unit, but a lot of general vocabulary is recycled and extended through the structural input.

Everyday English Language useful in situations at an airport is introduced and practised.

Writing The writing syllabus concludes with a focus on writing a thank-you email. The context reintroduces a character from Unit 2 of the Student's Book, Danka, who is writing a thank-you email to her host family. Students are then invited to write a thank-you email to someone who has looked after them.

Workbook The Present Perfect is further practised in contrast with the Past Simple. The time expressions *ever* and *never, ago* and *last week, yet* and *just,* and *ever* or *ago* are consolidated with the appropriate tense. The difference between *been* and *gone* is presented.

In the *Vocabulary* section, phrasal verbs are revised or introduced.

Notes on the unit

STARTER (SB p106)

This section is a fun way of getting students into the topic of places people have visited.

1 Focus attention on the first two flags and elicit the names of the corresponding countries. Students continue matching the countries and flags.

Check the answers with the whole class. If students have problems with the pronunciation of the countries, drill them chorally and individually.

Answers

1	Germany	5	Brazil	8	the USA
2	Italy	6	Japan	9	Australia
3	Spain	7	Great Britain	10	Canada
4	France				

2 Tell students the countries you have been to. Students then tick (✓) the countries they have visited.

IN MY LIFE (SB p106)

Present Perfect + *ever* and *never*

POSSIBLE PROBLEMS

1 Students find the difference between *I've gone to Paris.* and *I've been to Paris.* quite confusing. This is dealt with in exercise 9 of the Workbook. We do not suggest that you attempt to sort this out at this stage of the presentation.

2 Students have already seen a Present Perfect form with the structure *have got*, but we do not suggest that you mention this at all. It would be very confusing for students, as *have got* expresses an essentially present-time concept.

1 **T 14.1** [CD 2: Track 56] Focus attention on the photo and elicit what students can see (Steve and Ryan looking at travel brochures). Play the conversation between Steve and Ryan and elicit the answers.

Answers and tapescript
They are talking about Ryan and Tara's honeymoon and places they could go.
Tara is Ryan's fiancée/girlfriend.

T 14.1
S=Steve, R=Ryan
S Ryan, where are you and Tara going for your honeymoon?
R Somewhere in Europe, we think. France, maybe, or Spain. I've been to Paris, but I haven't been to Barcelona.
S Yes, Paris is beautiful. But what about Venice? It's very romantic.
R Mmm, that's an idea. I've been to Italy, but I've never been to Venice.

S What about Tara? Where does she want to go?
R Oh, Tara doesn't mind where we go. She's been to Mexico and Brazil, but she hasn't been anywhere in Europe!

2 **T 14.2** [CD 2: Track 57] Students read and listen to the sentences. Remember that they will probably never have seen the Present Perfect tense before, and *been* will be unfamiliar. Using L1 if possible, explain that *been* is the past participle of the verb *to be*, and sometimes *to go*, and that *have been* is an example of the Present Perfect tense. Don't try to do a full presentation at this stage, but just explain that the sentences refer to the idea of 'some time in your life'.

Ask students to repeat the sentences on the recording (whether they are true for them or not). Do this chorally and individually, be sure to remind students to follow the highlighted stress patterns. Correct mistakes carefully.

Demonstrate the activity yourself with true information about the countries you have visited. Then ask students to make similar sentences, saying which countries they have/haven't been to. Elicit examples from the whole class, so you can check students' accuracy in the use and pronunciation of the structure. Students continue the activity in groups. Monitor and check.

3 **T 14.3** [CD 2: Track 58] This activity introduces the question form and addresses the 'experience' use of the Present Perfect in contrast to the Past Simple. Students read and listen to the conversation focusing attention on the stress highlighting as they listen. They can practise saying each sentence, either after the recording or with you modelling each one. Draw students' attention to the question form of the Present Perfect, then to *When did you go?* and *Did you like it?* and ask what tense this is (Past Simple). Just name the tenses at this stage and do not try to explain the different uses. (These are given in the *Grammar Spot* on p107.)

Get students to ask you questions about countries you have been to, following the model in exercise 3. Encourage them to ask *When did you go?* and *Did you like it?* and give appropriate answers.

Students continue in open pairs asking and answering about countries they have been to, when, and if they liked them. This might sound repetitive and laborious, but remember you are introducing students to a very new concept with the Present Perfect tense and they need practice with forming questions, answers, and negatives.

4 Students write down the names of four cities, and in pairs make similar conversations. Go round and check as they do this. Monitor for accuracy in the use and pronunciation of the two tenses.

5 This practises the third person singular for the first time, so students will need to make the change from *have* to *has*. Focus attention on the examples and on the contracted form *'s = has*. Drill the examples chorally and individually. Ask three or four students to talk about their partner.

1   Read the notes with the whole class. Point out the use of *ever* with the Present Perfect in the question form to mean 'at any time in your life'. Stress that we do not use *ever* in the answer.

2   Read the notes with the whole class. Focus attention on the use of the Past Simple to say exactly when something happened. Elicit other past time references that can be used with the Past Simple, e.g. *last month*, *a long time ago*, *yesterday*, etc.

3   Read the notes with the whole class and get students to complete the table. Check the answers.

Answers

	Positive	Negative	
I You We They	have	haven't	been to Paris.
He/She/It	has	hasn't	

4   Students complete the sentences with *ever* or *never*. Check the answers.

Answers
Has he **ever** been to Barcelona?
He's **never** been to Barcelona.

If your students have a similar tense form in their language, and if you can use L1, you might like to make a brief comparison between the way L1 and English use the auxiliary verb *have* + past participle. Be careful, however! Keep it short, and as simple as possible, because it would be very easy to overload students with too much information at this early stage of their exposure to the Present Perfect.

Read Grammar Reference 14.1 on p147 together in class, and/or ask students to read it at home. Encourage them to ask you questions about it.

PRACTICE (SB p107)

Past participles

1   Remind students of the terms *past participle* and *infinitive* and focus attention on the example *eaten – eat*. Tell students that they will often be able to guess which infinitive a past participle comes from.

Students write in the infinitives for the rest of the verbs. Many of the verbs are used in exercises that come later in this unit and they are very common verbs when talking about experiences. Get students to check in pairs before checking with the whole class.

Answers

eaten	**eat**	made	**make**	given	**give**
seen	**see**	taken	**take**	won	**win**
met	**meet**	ridden	**ride**	had	**have**
drunk	**drink**	cooked	**cook**	stayed	**stay**
flown	**fly**	bought	**buy**	done	**do**

2   Ask students to look at the selection of verbs and decide which two are regular. Check the answers.

Answers
The two regular verbs are *cook* and *stay*.

3   Elicit the Past Simple forms of *eat* (*ate*) and *see* (*saw*) and get students to continue the list in pairs.

4   Refer students to the list of irregular verbs on SB p158 and get them to check their answers.

What has Ryan done?

1   Remind students of Ryan who appeared at the beginning of the unit and elicit some basic information about him. Pre-teach/check the vocabulary in the list, especially: *foreign*, *company*, *jumbo jet*, *play* (n), *motorbike*, *competition*.

Also check the following items from the recording: *politician*, *fall off*, *lottery*.

T 14.4 [CD 2: Track 59] Focus attention on the list. Students listen and tick the things Ryan has done. Ask students to check in pairs before they give you the answers.

Answers and tapescript

lived in a foreign country	✓
worked for a big company	✓
stayed in an expensive hotel	✗
flown in a jumbo jet	✓
cooked a meal for a lot of people	✗
met a famous person	✗
seen a play by Shakespeare	✓
ridden a motorbike	✓
been to hospital	✗
won a competition	✗

T 14.4
What has Ryan done?
Yes, I've lived in a foreign country. In Japan, actually. I lived in Osaka for a year. I enjoyed it very much. I loved the food. And, yes, I have worked for a big company. I worked for Nissan, the car company, that's why I was in Japan. That was three years ago, then I got a job back in London.
Have I stayed in an expensive hotel? No, never – only cheap hotels for me, I'm afraid, but I have flown in a jumbo jet – lots of times, actually. Oh, I've never cooked a meal for a lot of people. I love food but I don't like cooking much. Sometimes I cook for me and my girlfriend Tara, but she likes it better if

we go out for a meal! And I've never met a famous person –
oh, just a minute, well not met, but I've seen ... er... I saw a
famous politician at the airport once – oh, who was it? I can't
remember his name, um ... I've only seen one Shakespeare
play, when I was at school, we saw *Romeo and Juliet*. It was
OK. I've ridden a motorbike though. My brother's got one. It's
very fast. Fortunately, I've never been to hospital. My brother
has – he fell off his motorbike! Unfortunately, I've never won
a competition. I do the lottery every week, but I've never,
ever won a thing!

2   First ask students to go through the questionnaire to
produce some sentences about Ryan. This is to further
practise the third person singular. Get some positive
sentences first, then some negative ones. Drill them
around the class, correcting carefully.

Read the instructions for this exercise. Ask for the
positive sentences in the Present Perfect again. This time,
where possible, ask follow-up questions in the Past
Simple, which students will answer in the Past Simple.
(You might want to play the recording again before you
do this to remind students of the information about
Ryan.) Although these questions and answers practise
the Past Simple, you are also indirectly helping students
with the Present Perfect, because you are showing them
when the Present Perfect isn't applicable.

Follow-up questions (and the students' answers)
(Note that not all the Present Perfect sentences which
students might produce from the questionnaire have a
possible follow-up question in the Past Simple.)

Which city did he live in? (Osaka.)
Did he enjoy it? (Yes, he did.)
Did he like the food? (Yes, he did.)
What sort of company did he work for? (A car company.)
When did he work there? (Three years ago.)
Who did he see at the airport? (A famous politician.)
What play did he see? (*Romeo and Juliet*.)
When did he see *Romeo and Juliet*? (When he was at school.)
Whose motorbike did he ride? (His brother's.)
Why did his brother go to hospital? (He fell off his
motorbike.)

3   This activity gives further practice in the question forms.
Drill the example questions in the Student's Book
focusing attention on the highlighted stress patterns.
Make sure students use rising intonation on the *Yes/No*
questions
in the Present Perfect and falling intonation on the *wh-*
questions in the Past Simple. Students ask you the rest of
the questions. Make sure they remember to include *ever*
in the Present Perfect questions. Answer their questions.

4   Students then ask a partner the same questions as in
exercise 1. Monitor and check for correct pronunciation
and formation of the questions.

Students tell the class about their partner. Encourage
them to give follow-up information in the Past Simple
where appropriate, e.g. *Anna has flown in a jumbo jet. She
flew from London to New York five years ago.*

SUGGESTION
You can give further practice in the Present Perfect with
ever and the Past Simple by using the photocopiable
activity on TB p151. If you have ten students or fewer,
make just one photocopy of the sheet and divide it
along the cut lines. If you have a larger group, you can
divide up two sheets to create two parallel mingling
activities.

Hand out a question card to each student. If you have
fewer than ten students, give the stronger students
more than one card. Check students understand the
questions on their card and that they understand they
will need to ask a question of their own to get more
information. Briefly review the use of the Present
Perfect with *ever* to mean 'at some time in your life' and
the use of the Past Simple to ask about a specific time
in the past with *When*.

Demonstrate the activity by getting two students to ask
and answer sample questions in open pairs. Point out
that if someone answers *No, I haven't* to the first
question, the student asking the question should just
say *OK, thank you* and move on to the next person. Get
the students to stand up and do the mingling activity,
encouraging them to ask their question to as many
other students as possible and to modify their follow-
up questions as appropriate.

Elicit any interesting information from the class in a
short feedback. Remind students to use the Past Simple
if they say exactly when someone did something.

ADDITIONAL MATERIAL

Workbook Unit 14
Exercises 1 and 2 Present Perfect and Past Simple
Exercise 3 and 4 Time expressions: *ever* and *never*; *ago* and
last week

A HONEYMOON IN VENICE (SB p108)

Present Perfect + *yet* and *just*

SUGGESTIONS
1   The concepts expressed by *yet* and *just* are very
subtle and they are realized by different structures in
different languages. We do not ask any questions in
the *Grammar Spot* that test concept (only form),
because the language required would be more
complex than the target item itself. Students should
be able to get the meaning through context and use,

but you can check comprehension of the two adverbs by translating into L1 and/or getting students to look up the adverbs in dictionaries.

2 It might be a good idea to do exercise 9 in the Workbook on *been* versus *gone* before you do the presentation of Present Perfect + *yet* and *just*. This clarifies the difference of meaning between *been* and *gone* as the two past participles of *to go*.

1 Read the introduction and the list as a class. Check that students understand *honeymoon* (a holiday after two people get married). Ask students what they know about places and activities in the list. Refer them to the photo and use the background information below if necessary.

BACKGROUND INFORMATION ON VENICE

St Mark's Square The square at the heart of Venice which is home to some of the city's most famous buildings, including St Mark's Cathedral. The square was originally designed as the administrative centre of Venice as well as a symbol of its wealth and power. Today it is one of the city's most famous landmarks. Both local people and tourists meet to relax in pavement cafés or simply to enjoy the beauty of the surroundings.

The Bell Tower The tower is 99 metres high and was built in the ninth century as a lighthouse. It has been modified over the centuries and famously collapsed in 1902, but the one bell survived. It was rebuilt *dov'era com'era* (where it was and how it was) and opened ten years later. The tower is the tallest structure in Venice, and the entire city, and even the Dolomites, can be seen from the top.

The Doge's Palace The Palazzo Ducale dates from 1309 and has been rebuilt several times. It was once the seat of government, the Palace of Justice, and the home of the Doge of the Republic of Venice. The Bridge of Sighs connects the Doge's Palace to the New Prisons, and visitors can walk through the bridge and view some of the prison cells!

The Gondola/Grand Canal The *canalazzo* is Venice's High Street! It divides the city into half and is almost four kilometres long, between thirty and seventy metres wide, but only five metres deep. Now, Venetians and tourists travel along it on a *vaporetto*, a water-bus, or a gondola.

The Rialto Bridge The first bridge to be built over the Grand Canal was from the Rialto, the commercial heart of Venice. Today the area is famous for its lively fruit and vegetable market and the bridge itself is full of stalls selling tourist souvenirs.

Murano Island The island of Murano became self-governed in 1276. By the early sixteenth century

---

Murano had thirty thousand inhabitants, including the Mocenigo family and the Cornaro family, and it continued to grow. Murano is famous for its glass-blowing industry, and has numerous showrooms and shops selling glass ornaments, as well as the Murano glass museum.

The Lido The 'Marriage to the Sea' ceremony originated here; this commemorated the Doge's journey to the Dalmatian coast in 1000, and later, in 1177, Pope Alexander III is said to have given the first gold ring that wedded Venice with the Adriatic Sea. At the end of the eighteenth century it became a popular bathing resort and is now popular with tourists for sunbathing!

2 **T 14.5** [CD 2: Track 60] Read the instructions as a class. Play the recording as far as *had a coffee* and elicit the answer to the first item in the list as an example. Students listen to the rest of the recording and put a tick next to the things Tara and Ryan have done.

Answers and tapescript

have a coffee in St Mark's Square	✓
climb up the Bell Tower	✗
see the paintings in the Doge's Palace	✗
go on a gondola	✓
have a boat ride along the Grand Canal	✓
walk across the Rialto Bridge	✗
visit the glass factories on Murano Island	✓
go to the beach at the Lido	✗

T 14.5
A honeymoon in Venice
T=Tara, A=Amy

T We're having a great time!

A Tell me about it! What have you done so far?

T Well, we've been to St Mark's Square. That was the first thing we did. It's right in the centre of Venice. We sat outside in the sun and had a coffee. We've seen the paintings in the Doge's Palace. It was wonderful. But we haven't climbed up St Mark's Bell Tower yet. It was too busy. We're going early tomorrow morning.

A Have you been in a gondola yet?

T Oh yes, we have! We had a gondola trip yesterday evening. It was so romantic! And we've just had a fantastic boat ride along the Grand Canal and we went under the Rialto Bridge! But we haven't walked across it yet. I wanna do that.

A Wow! You're busy! Have you visited the Murano glass factories yet? Don't forget – I want a glass horse!

T I haven't forgotten. In fact, we took a boat to Murano island yesterday, and I got your horse. OK?

A Oh, thank you, thank you! So what else are you going to do?

T Well, I'd like to go to the beach, you know – at the Lido. It's so hot here! But we haven't really decided what else to do yet. There's so much to see.

A Oh, you're so lucky! Have a lovely time. Give my love to Ryan!

T Yeah. Bye, Amy. See you next week at the airport!

GRAMMAR SPOT

POSSIBLE PROBLEMS

1 Remember that these questions focus on the form of *yet* and *just*, not the concept, because any questions that tested students' understanding of these items would be more complex than the items themselves. You need to make sure, probably via translation if possible, that students have understood them. Explain that *(not) yet* means '(not) before now' whereas *just* means 'a short time before now', using examples from the text or putting examples on the board.

2 Be prepared to prompt and help with the questions in the *Grammar Spot*, as students may find them hard.

Look at the questions in the *Grammar Spot* as a class.

1 Get students to think about which words they need to complete the gapped sentences. If necessary, refer them back to the 'things to do list' for the correct information and for the infinitives that will provide the past participles. Check the answers.

> **Answers**
> 1 Have you **been** on a gondola yet?
> 2 We **haven't** climbed up the Bell Tower yet.
> 3 We've just **had** a boat ride along the Grand Canal.

Focus on the use of *yet* and *just* in the sentences and check comprehension (see *Possible problems* above).

2 Elicit the answers to the questions about the position of *yet* and *just*.

> **Answers**
> *yet* comes at the end of a sentence.
> *just* comes before the past participle.

3 Allow students time to work out the rules for the use of *yet*. Check the answer.

> **Answer**
> We can use *yet* only in questions and negative sentences, not in positive sentences.

Read Grammar Reference 14.2 on p147 together in class, and/or ask students to read it at home. Encourage them to ask you questions about it.

3 Refer students back to the 'things to do' list. Elicit the past participle of each of the verbs in the list, making sure students give *been* as the participle of *go*. Remind students that the ticks refer to things that Tara and Ryan have done. Drill the examples in the Student's Book and elicit one or two more examples.

Students continue working in pairs, saying what Tara and Ryan have and haven't done. Monitor and check for the correct form of the Present Perfect and the correct position of *yet*.

T 14.5 [CD 2: Track 60] Play the recording again so that students can check their answers. Then check the answers with the whole class.

> **Answers**
> They've had a coffee in St Mark's Square.
> They've seen the paintings in the Doge's Palace.
> They haven't climbed up the Bell Tower yet.
> They've been on a gondola.
> They've had a boat ride along the Grand Canal.
> They haven't walked across the Rialto Bridge yet.
> They've visited the glass factories on Murano Island.
> They haven't been to the beach at the Lido.

PRACTICE (SB p109)

I've just done it

1 Students haven't practised Present Perfect questions with *yet* or answers with *just*, so now's the time to do it! Drill the question and answer in the Student's Book, making sure students imitate the rising intonation on the question and the falling intonation on the answer, and stress patterns as highlighted. Students give one or two more examples in open pairs. Remind students that they will need to use different pronouns in their answers (*it/him/her*) and point out that some questions can have more than one answer.

Students continue working in closed pairs. Then check the answers with the whole class.

> **Answers**
> 2 Have you done the shopping yet?
>   Yes, I've just done it.
> 3 Have you washed your hair yet?
>   Yes, I've just done/washed it.
> 4 Have you cleaned the car yet?
>   Yes, I've just done/cleaned it.
> 5 Have you made the dinner yet?
>   Yes, I've just done/made it.
> 6 Have you met the new student yet?
>   Yes, I've just met him/her.
> 7 Have you checked your email yet?
>   Yes, I've just done/checked it.
> 8 Have you given your homework to the teacher yet?
>   Yes, I've just given it to her/him.
> 9 Have you finished the exercise yet?
>   Yes, I've just finished it.

Check it

2 This exercise revises the grammar just covered in the unit. Students work in pairs to choose the correct sentence. Then check the answers with the whole class.

> **Answers**
> 1 I saw Ryan yesterday.
> 2 Have you ever eaten Chinese food? (Note: This is the 'correct' version for British English but *Did you ever eat ...* is common in American English.)
> 3 Tara won £5,000 last month.
> 4 I've never drunk champagne.
> 5 Steve has never been to America.
> 6 Has your sister had the baby yet?
> 7 I haven't done my homework yet.
> 8 Has she just bought a new car?

ADDITIONAL MATERIAL

Workbook Unit 14
Exercise 5 *yet*
Exercise 6 Adverbs: *ago/ever/last year/yet/never/just/yesterday*
Exercise 7 *yet* and *just*
Exercise 8 Translation
Exercise 9 *been* or *gone?*

READING AND SPEAKING (SB p110)

We've never learnt to drive!

1 This activity acts as a lead-in to the topic of transport and introduces the different modes of transport that are described in the texts whilst reviewing the Present Perfect. Divide the class into pairs and get students to ask and answer the questions giving as much extra information as possible. Elicit feedback from students on their partners, encouraging them to share any additional details. Establish which are the most and least popular modes of transport.

2 This exercise pre-teaches some of the important vocabulary in the texts. If students have access to dictionaries, they can look up the new words. Alternatively, in a monolingual class, get students to work in pairs or small groups to help each other with the translations.

Check comprehension of the nouns, eliciting simple paraphrases or using mime where appropriate.

3 Focus attention on the heading and on the photos and elicit what Tudor and Josie have never learnt to do (*drive*). Ask the class how they travel. (*He hitch-hikes. She rides a bicycle.*)

4 Divide the class into pairs and get the A students to read about Tudor and the B students to read about Josie.

5 Get students to read through the questions and check they understand them. Students read the text again and work in pairs/small groups (A students together and B students together) to answer the questions. If they have access to dictionaries, they can check any unknown vocabulary or they can ask you.

Check the answers with the A and B groups separately before students compare the two travellers.

> **Answers**
> **Tudor Bowen-Jones**
> 1 No, he doesn't. He's retired.
> 2 He started travelling 60 years ago.
> 3 He went abroad for the first time in 1947.
> 4 Yes, he does.
> 5 He's been to 40 countries.
> 6 Yes, he has.
> 7 Yes, he has.
> 8 Yes, he has. The driver of the car took out a gun, but he cleaned it and put it back again.
> 9 Possible answers: He has hitch-hiked with a horse and cart in Hungary. He has ridden a motorbike across Spain. He sat In the back of a hearse in France. He enjoyed the comfort of a Rolls-Royce in Germany.
> 10 He's going to spend his [90th] birthday in Vienna.
>
> **Josie Dew**
> 1 No, she doesn't, but she writes book about her journeys.
> 2 She started travelling in 1985.
> 3 She went abroad for the first time in 1985.
> 4 No, she doesn't.
> 5 She's been to 40 countries.
> 6 No, she hasn't.
> 7 Yes, she has.
> 8 Yes, she has. A man attacked her in Bulgaria.
> 9 Possible answers: She has cycled through the Himalayan mountain in Nepal, then down into India. She has cycled through millions of locusts in the Moroccan desert. She has travelled through tornadoes in the USA. She was in Romania when President Ceauçescu was executed.
> 10 She's going to cycle around New Zealand.

6 Run through the pronunciation of the proper names in the texts that students might have problems with (*Tudor* /ˈtjuːdə/, *Josie* /ˈdʒəʊsiː/, *Nepal* /nɪˈpɔːl/, *Romania* /ruːˈmeɪnɪə/, *Ceauçescu* /tʃaʊˈtʃesku/, *Iraq* /ɪˈrɑːk/, *Kuwait* /kʊˈweɪt/, *Bulgaria* /bʌlˈɡeərɪə/. Tell students they are going to work with a student from the other group and find out about another traveller. Show them how they can do this in a meaningful way, rather than just read off their answers in order, e.g.

A *Tudor doesn't have a job because he's retired. What about Josie?*
B *She doesn't have a job but she writes books about her journeys.*

Remind students that they will need to use the Present Perfect, Past Simple, and Present Simple tenses, and *going to* in their answers. Students compare the two travellers in pairs. Monitor and check how students manage with the different tenses, but don't expect them to get everything right. You can note down and give feedback on common errors, but bear in mind that the main focus is the information exchange through reading and speaking, not grammar accuracy.

What do you think?

Discuss the questions as a class. Encourage students to give reasons for their answers. If you have time, elicit any appropriate anecdotes on a time when students went hitch-hiking or cycling.

LISTENING AND VOCABULARY (SB p112)

All around the world

1   Ask students to mask the words of the song and to look at the picture. Get them to predict what the song might be about and accept any suggestions at this stage.

   T 14.6 [CD 2: Track 61] Ask students to close their books and listen to the song. Play the recording through once and then establish the general topic and answer the questions in exercise 1 (the singer's partner/boyfriend has left her and she wants to find him, her 'baby' is her partner/boyfriend; *gonna* means 'going to'). Get students to check if their predictions were correct.

2   Students open their books. Focus attention on exercise 2 and elicit the meaning of the first word in bold. Students continue matching the words with their meanings, using a dictionary if appropriate. Check the answers.

   Answers
   We had a quarrel. – We disagreed/fought.
   He gave a reason. – He explained it.
   He was so mad. – He was really angry.
   I lied to him. – I didn't tell him the truth.
   I wasted time. – I did nothing with my time.

3   **T 14.6** [CD 2: Track 61] Students read through the gapped version of the song to check the overall content. Check/pre-teach *gone away, scared, cry* (v), *open-hearted, weak, do someone wrong*. Check students understand that *I let myself go* in line 7 means 'I said some awful things'. Explain that this is the meaning within the context of the song and that *let go* can have a range of meanings. Point out that *gonna* is originally informal American English, but that it often appears in songs as it has fewer syllables than *going to* and so helps the number of syllables fit the line.

   Elicit the answers for the first two gaps. Students then work in pairs to complete as many lines as they can.

Remind them to look at the context, rhyme, and also to think about grammar! Play the recording again and get students to complete/check their answers. Focus attention on the last but one line and elicit what's missing before *been around the world* (*I've*).

If students want to hear the song again, play the recording and encourage them to sing along.

Answers and tapescript
All around the world
Chorus
I've **been** around the world and I
I can't **find** my baby
I don't know when, I don't know **why**
Why he's **gone** away
And I don't know **where** he can be, my baby
But I'm gonna find **him**

We had a quarrel and I let myself go
I said so **many** things, things he didn't know
And I was oh so **bad**
And I don't think he's **coming** back
He gave the reason, the reasons he should **go**
And he said so many things he's never said **before**
And he was oh so mad
And I don't **think** he's coming, coming back
I did too much lying, wasted too **much** time
Now I'm **here** crying.
Chorus
So open-hearted, he never did me **wrong**
I was the one, the weakest one of **all**
And now I'm oh so **sad**
And I don't **think** he's coming back, coming back
I did too much lying, wasted too much time
Now I'm **here** crying.
Chorus
I've **been** around the world **looking** for my baby
Been around the world and I'm gonna
I'm gonna find **him**

What do you think?

Give a few examples of your favourite English songs. Give students time to write their list and then compare with a partner. Elicit some examples in class feedback and try to establish the most popular songs/styles of music.

EVERYDAY ENGLISH (SB p113)

At the airport

1   Get students to read through the sentences and check any new vocabulary. Students then put them in the correct order, working in pairs or small groups.
   Check the answers with the whole class.

Answers

5 You wait in the departure lounge.
7 You board the plane.
2 You get a trolley for your luggage.
1 You arrive at the airport.
3 You check in your luggage and get a boarding pass.
4 You go through passport control.
6 You check the departures board for your gate number.

2 **T 14.7** [CD 2: Track 62] Focus attention on the chart and the examples, and check students understand the headings. Tell students to listen carefully and complete the chart with the missing information. Play the recording and get students to check in pairs. If necessary, play the recording again to let students complete their answers.

Check the answers with the whole class.

Answers and tapescript

Flight	Destination	Gate	Remark
BA 516	Geneva	4	LAST CALL
SK 832	Frankfurt	–	DELAYED **1 hour**
AF 472	Amsterdam	17	NOW BOARDING
LH 309	Miami	32	NOW BOARDING
VS 876	New York	–	WAIT IN LOUNGE

T 14.7

British Airways flight BA516 to Geneva boarding at gate 4, last call. Flight BA516 to Geneva, last call.
Scandinavian Airlines flight SK 832 to Frankfurt is delayed one hour. Flight SK 832 to Frankfurt, delayed one hour.
Air France flight 472 to Amsterdam is now boarding at gate 17. Flight AF 472 to Amsterdam, now boarding, gate 17.
Lufthansa flight 309 to Miami is now boarding at gate 32. Flight LH 309 to Miami, now boarding, gate 32.
Virgin Airlines flight to New York, VS 876 to New York. Please wait in the departure lounge until a further announcement. Thank you.
Passengers are reminded to keep their hand luggage with them at all times.

3 **T 14.8** [CD 2: Track 63] Get students to cover the gapped conversations in exercise 4. Play the first conversation and elicit the answers to the questions as an example. Play the rest of the conversations. Get students to check their answers in pairs before checking with the whole class.

Answers and tapescript

1 two passengers waiting in the departure lounge
2 check-in assistant and passenger checking in luggage
3 Tara and Ryan meeting Tara's sister, Amy, in the arrival hall
4 a couple saying goodbye

T 14.8

1 **A** Listen! ... BA 516 to Geneva. That's our flight.

B Did the announcement say gate 4 or 14?
A I couldn't hear. I think it said 4.
B Look! There it is on the departure board. It *is* gate 4.
A OK. Come on! Let's go.
2 **A** Can I have your ticket, please?
B Yes, of course.
A Thank you. How many suitcases have you got?
B Just one.
A And have you got much hand luggage?
B Just this bag.
A That's fine.
B Oh ... can I have a seat next to the window?
A Yes, that's OK. Here's your boarding pass. Have a nice flight!
3 **A** Ryan! Tara! Over here!
B Hi! Amy! Great to see you!
A It's great to see you too. You look terrific! Did you have a good honeymoon?
B Fantastic. Everything was fantastic.
A Well, you haven't missed anything here. Nothing much has happened at all!
4 **A** There's my flight. It's time to go.
B Oh no! It's been a wonderful two weeks. I can't believe it's over.
A I know. When can we see each other again?
B Soon, I hope. I'll email every day.
A I'll phone too. Goodbye, my darling. Give my love to your family.
B Goodbye, Lukas.

4 Students complete the conversations with the correct question. Get students to check in pairs.

Play the recording again and get students to check their answers.

Answers

1 Did the announcement say gate 4 or 14?
2 have you got much hand luggage?
3 Did you have a good honeymoon?
4 When can we see each other again?

MUSIC OF ENGLISH

Read through the *Music of English* box as a class. Students choose a conversation to practise with a partner. Get them to rehearse the conversation. Go round monitoring and helping. Model key sentences for individual students as necessary. Students act out their conversation to the class.

Writing an email

Saying thank you

The final unit in the writing syllabus focuses on a thank-you email. Email has become more and more popular and is now routinely used for communication that used to be handwritten and sent by post. Saying 'thank you' is a good example of this and students may well find themselves in the position of needing to email and thank someone at some stage in the future.

1 Discuss the questions briefly as a class. Allow students time to continue their discussions in pairs or small groups. Get class feedback.

2 Remind students of Danka from Unit 2 of the Student's Book and elicit what they can remember about her. Get students to read the gapped email through quickly to find the answers to the questions in exercise 1. You can set a time limit of two minutes to encourage students to look for the information they need and not to focus on the details. Check the answers.

> **Answers**
> - She's in Poland.
> - Becky and family are in Britain.
> - Jacek is Danka's brother.
> - She's writing to Becky and her family.
> - She's writing to say thank you.

3 Get students to read the first sentence of the email again and elicit the answers to the first two gaps as examples. Students continue completing the email, working individually. Give students time to check their answers with a partner before a whole-class check.

> **Answers**
>
> | | | |
> |---|---|---|
> | 1 just | 5 going | 9 quickly |
> | 2 but | 6 has | 10 going |
> | 3 had | 7 lot | 11 like |
> | 4 much | 8 couldn't | 12 visit |

4 Get students to brainstorm possible ideas for a thank you email, e.g. being looked after during a trip or visit, when you were ill, at a party or dinner, etc. Give students time to make notes on what they want to say in their email, working from the following framework:
- say where you are now
- say thank you for what the person did
- say how the person helped you
- offer to do something for them in the future

Elicit the appropriate greeting and closing expressions (*Dear* (name) and *Lots of love/Love to you all/With love/With best wishes*). Point out useful language from Danka's email, e.g. *miss someone, have a wonderful time,*

it was very kind of you, enjoy yourself, I'll never forget + -ing, I hope that one day … , I would love to … .

Give students time to write their email in class or set it for homework. If possible, display the emails on the classroom wall or noticeboard to allow students to read each other's work. When you check the students' work, point out errors but allow students to correct them themselves and try to limit correction to major problems to avoid demoralizing.

Song

The song *Summertime* appears in photocopiable format on TB p153. You will find the song after Unit 14 **T 14.8** on the Class Cassette/on CD2 Track 64. Students decide what is missing from several words which end in *-in'*, then listen and complete the song with the words they hear. The answers are on p172.

Don't forget!

Workbook Unit 14

Exercise 10 Vocabulary practice of phrasal verbs

Exercise 11 Listening practice on the language of saying goodbye

Grammar Reference

Look at the exercises on SB p147 as a class, or set for homework. The answers are on TB p176.

Word list

Remind your students of the Word list for this unit on SB p157. They could translate the words, learn them at home, or transfer some of the words to their vocabulary notebook.

Pronunciation Book Unit 14

Video/DVD Episode 6 A long weekend

PHOTOCOPIABLE MATERIAL: EXTRA IDEAS UNITS 13–14

Reading TB p152

The reading exercise is about Johnny Depp and revises Units 13–14. It could be done for homework.

Activities to exploit the reading are provided and the answers are on p171.

Photocopiable material

Unit 1

Hello and goodbye (TB p10)

1 Read the conversations. Put the lines in the correct order.

2 Where are the people in each conversation: on the phone or in the street?

3 Practise the conversations with a partner. Use your own names and phone numbers.

1

| **A** Hello, 778214. | **B** Hi, Tony! It's me, Rachel. How are you? | **A** Very well, thanks. And you? | **B** I'm OK, thanks. And the family? | **A** They're all fine, thanks. |

2

| **A** Have a nice day, Helen! | **B** Thanks, Dave, and you! See you later at the restaurant! | **A** Yes, at 8.00. | **B** Great! Bye, Dave. | **A** Bye, Helen. |

1 Read the conversations. Put the lines in the correct order.

2 Where are the people in each conversation: on the phone or in the street?

3 Practise the conversations with a partner. Use your own names and phone numbers.

1

| **A** Hello, 778214. | **B** Hi, Tony! It's me, Rachel. How are you? | **A** Very well, thanks. And you? | **B** I'm OK, thanks. And the family? | **A** They're all fine, thanks. |

2

| **A** Have a nice day, Helen! | **B** Thanks, Dave, and you! See you later at the restaurant! | **A** Yes, at 8.00. | **B** Great! Bye, Dave. | **A** Bye, Helen. |

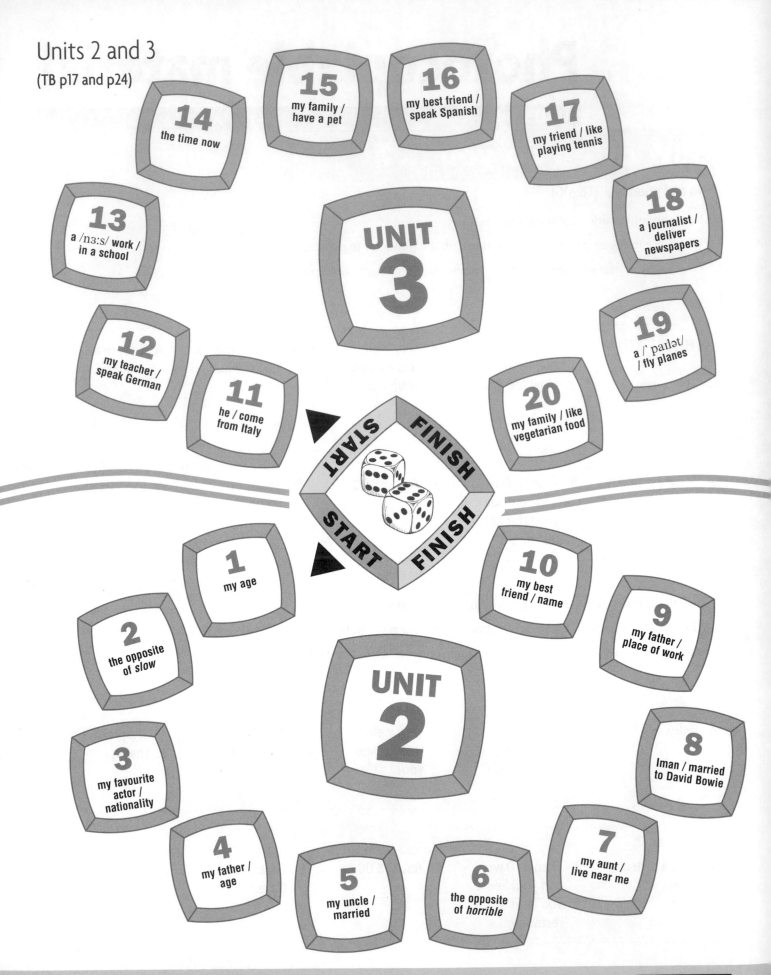

Units 2 and 3
(TB p17 and p24)

14 the time now

15 my family / have a pet

16 my best friend / speak Spanish

17 my friend / like playing tennis

13 a /nɜːs/ work / in a school

UNIT 3

18 a journalist / deliver newspapers

12 my teacher / speak German

11 he / come from Italy

19 a /ˈpaɪlət/ / fly planes

20 my family / like vegetarian food

START FINISH
START FINISH

1 my age

10 my best friend / name

2 the opposite of slow

9 my father / place of work

UNIT 2

3 my favourite actor / nationality

8 Iman / married to David Bowie

4 my father / age

5 my uncle / married

6 the opposite of horrible

7 my aunt / live near me

© Oxford University Press   **Photocopiable**

Unit 4

Leisure activities (TB p30)

1 Complete the questions. For questions 9 and 10 use your own ideas.

How often do you ...?	Answers
1 play computer games _How often do you play computer games?_	_Every evening._
2 go to the cinema	
3 go running	
4 listen to music	
5 watch TV	
6 cook	
7 go swimming	
8 sunbathe	
9 ?	
10 ?	

2 Work in pairs. Ask and answer the questions.

3 Work in groups of four. Discuss your answers and find ...:

- an activity your group does every day
- an activity your group never does

Extra ideas Units 1–4 Revision

Reading

1 A magazine called *Weekend* interviewed a businesswoman, Angela Franklin. Read about her.

Meet ...

Angela Franklin

Me and my family

I'm from York, in the north of England, and I'm thirty-eight years old. I'm married, and my husband's name is Mike. He's a teacher in a business school. We have two children – a boy and a girl. I have two brothers, but they don't live in York.

Me and my work

I'm the director of a food company. I work in York for part of the week, but I also travel a lot to Europe and the United States. I love my job, because I meet a lot of people and it is very interesting. I work about forty or fifty hours a week.

Me and my home

We have a flat in Paris, but my home is in York, and we have a large house there. There are about ten rooms, and the house is like a hotel. So many people come and go! We have a garden where we grow fruit and vegetables.

Me and my free time

Well, I have very little free time, but when I can, I like having friends for dinner. We sit, eat, drink, and talk for hours! I also enjoy going to the theatre and to the cinema. I like all kinds of music but especially classical music.

2 Complete the questions or answers from the interview with Angela Franklin.

1 A What's your name?
   B **Angela Franklin.**

2 A _____ ?
   B F – R – A – N – K – L – I – N.

3 A Where are you from?
   B _____ .

4 A _____ ?
   B I'm thirty-eight.

5 A Are you married?
   B _____ .

6 A _____ ?
   B Mike.

7 A What does your husband do?
   B _____ .

8 A Do you have any children?
   B _____ .

9 A _____ ?
   B Yes. I have two brothers.

10 A Do you enjoy your job?
   B _____ .

11 A _____ ?
   B Because I meet a lot of people.

12 A Where do you live?
   B _____ .

13 A Do you have a garden?
   B _____ .

14 A _____
     in your free time?
   B Having friends for dinner, going to the theatre and cinema, and listening to music.

3 With a partner, practise the interview. Pay attention to stress and intonation.

Song

1 Listen to the song and cross out the wrong words in italics.

Colours

Donovan Leitch

(1) *Yellow / ~~Orange~~* **is the colour of my true love's hair**	1
In the (2) *morning / evening* **when we rise**	2
In the (3) *morning / evening* **when we rise3**	3
That's the time, that's the time I love the best	4
(4) *Grey / Green* **is the colour of the sparklin' corn**	5
In the morning when we rise	6
In the morning when we rise	7
That's the time, that's the time I love the best	8
Mellow is the feelin' that I (5) *have / get*	9
When I see her mm-hmm	10
When I see her uh-huh	11
That's the time, that's the time I love the best	12
Freedom is a word I (6) *rarely / never* **use**	13
Without (7) *talkin' / thinkin'* **mm-hmm**	14
Without (8) *talkin' / thinkin'* **mm-hmm**	15
Of the time when I've been loved.	16

2 Choose the correct definition for these words from the song.

1 *true love*   best friend / girlfriend or wife
2 *rise*   get up / go to bed
3 *sparklin'*   shiny / old
4 *mellow*   relaxed / sad

3 Who does *her* refer to in lines *10* and *11*?

Song

1 Listen to the song and cross out the wrong words in italics.

Colours

Donovan Leitch

(1) *Yellow / ~~Orange~~* **is the colour of my true love's hair**	1
In the (2) *morning / evening* **when we rise**	2
In the (3) *morning / evening* **when we rise**	3
That's the time, that's the time I love the best	4
(4) *Grey / Green* **is the colour of the sparklin' corn**	5
In the morning when we rise	6
In the morning when we rise	7
That's the time, that's the time I love the best	8
Mellow is the feelin' that I (5) *have / get*	9
When I see her mm-hmm	10
When I see her uh-huh	11
That's the time, that's the time I love the best	12
Freedom is a word I (6) *rarely / never* **use**	13
Without (7) *talkin' / thinkin'* **mm-hmm**	14
Without (8) *talkin' / thinkin'* **mm-hmm**	15
Of the time when I've been loved.	16

2 Choose the correct definition for these words from the song.

1 *true love*   best friend / girlfriend or wife
2 *rise*   get up / go to bed
3 *sparklin'*   shiny / old
4 *mellow*   relaxed / sad

3 Who does *her* refer to in lines *10* and *11*?

Unit 5

Suggestion (TB p40)

1 Annie Mason is 30. She's single, so she doesn't need a very big place to live. She's a painter, so she needs one room for a studio. She wants to live near the city centre, because she doesn't have a car.

a A large ground-floor flat in a lovely, quiet area. It has three bedrooms and a big garden. The flat is ideal for a young family or for students. It has excellent transport links to motorways, the university, and the airport.

2 Helen and Paul Clarke are married with two young children. Paul stays at home to look after them, but Helen travels with her job, so they want to live near the airport. They need a garden for the children.

b A beautiful five-bedroomed house near Kington-on-Sea. It has a small garden, but is only five minutes from the beach. The local towns offer excellent watersports.

3 Simon Fisher is a young businessman. He has a lot of money, but no free time. He wants to buy a beautiful flat with modern furniture. He only needs one bedroom, but he needs a garage for his sports car.

c A new, luxury block of flats. All rooms have designer furniture and a new fridge, cooker and washing machine in the kitchen. One-, two-, or three-bedroomed flats for sale, with space for two cars.

4 Laura, Keiko, Dave, and Karl are all students. They want to share a house or flat for next year. They don't have cars, so they need good transport to the university. They don't smoke and Dave has a cat.

d A small, but comfortable flat in the heart of the city. It only has one bedroom, but there's a large garage next to the flat – great as a workshop or home office.

5 Emily and Henry Davies are retired, but they are both very active. They like sailing and walking on the beach. They need a big house, because their grandchildren visit a lot. They don't want a flat and they prefer houses with gardens.

e A large flat with four lovely big bedrooms for rent for 12 months. Space for two cars and good bus and rail links to the city centre and university. No smokers, please, but pets are welcome.

Unit 6

Reading and speaking 6 (SB p48)
Alternative to roleplay

| **A** = Interviewer | **B** = Joss or Christopher |

A Hello, _____ ! Can I (1) _____ you a few questions?

B Yes, of course.

A First of all, how old (2) _____ you?

B I'm _____ .

A And do you (3) _____ to school?

B _____ .

A And (4) _____ do you live with?

B I live in _____ with _____ .

A Where (5) _____ you born?

B I _____ in _____ .

A I see. And what could you do when you (6) _____ very young?

B Well, _____ .

A I can't believe it! Tell me, (7) _____ do your parents think about your talent?

B They _____ .

A Oh! And do you (8) _____ to different places?

B Yes, last month I _____ in _____ .

A Really? Why?

B I was there _____ .

A Fantastic! That's all the time we have. Thank you very much and good luck in the future!

| **A** = Interviewer | **B** = Joss or Christopher |

A Hello, _____ ! Can I (1) _____ you a few questions?

B Yes, of course.

A First of all, how old (2) _____ you?

B I'm _____ .

A And do you (3) _____ to school?

B _____ .

A And (4) _____ do you live with?

B I live in _____ with _____ .

A Where (5) _____ you born?

B I _____ in _____ .

A I see. And what could you do when you (6) _____ very young?

B Well, _____ .

A I can't believe it! Tell me, (7) _____ do your parents think about your talent?

B They _____ .

A Oh! And do you (8) _____ to different places?

B Yes, last month I _____ in _____ .

A Really? Why?

B I was there _____ .

A Fantastic! That's all the time we have. Thank you very much and good luck in the future!

Unit 7

Suggestion (TB p58)

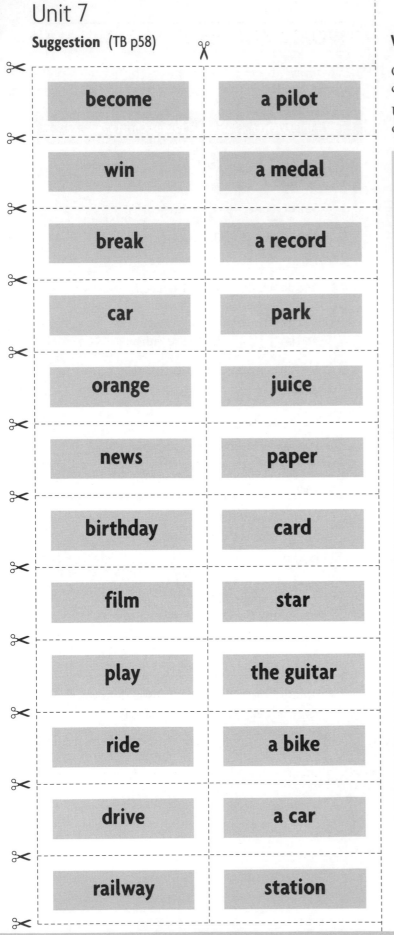

become	**a pilot**
win	**a medal**
break	**a record**
car	**park**
orange	**juice**
news	**paper**
birthday	**card**
film	**star**
play	**the guitar**
ride	**a bike**
drive	**a car**
railway	**station**

Words that go together

Complete the sentences with verbs and nouns or with compound nouns.

Use the correct form of the verb and check the spelling of the compound nouns (one or two words).

1   **A**   Why ___did___ you ___become a pilot___ ?
      B   I love very fast planes.

2   I'm late for my train. Can you drive me to the _____ ?

3   **A**   Can you _____ ?
      B   Yes, and I have a new sports car.

4   **A**   Would you like an _____ ?
      B   No thanks. I'm not thirsty.'

5   Mum is 40 on Saturday. Don't forget to buy her a _____ .

6   **A**   Can you _____ ?
      B   No, but I'm quite good at the piano.

7   You have to train very hard to _____ at the world championships.

8   **A**   Who's your favourite _____ ?
      B   Johnny Depp, I think.

9   **A**   _____ Carl Lewis _____ in the Olympics?
      B   Yes, he won four golds.

10   **A**   When did you learn to _____ ?
      B   When I was about six – I fell off all the time!

11   We can't leave the motorbikes in front of the cinema. We need to find a _____ .

12   I want to read about yesterday's match. Can I borrow your _____ ?

Extra ideas Units 5–8 Revision

Reading and speaking

1 Work in groups. How good is your memory? Answer the questions.

  1 When is your best friend's birthday?
  2 What did you have to eat last night?
  3 Where were you ten days ago? What did you do?
  4 Where were the Olympic Games in 2004?
  5 When was your mother born?
  6 How many phone numbers can you remember?

2 Read the newspaper article about Dominic O'Leary. Then answer the questions.

  1 What are some of the things he can remember?
  2 How did he become world champion?
  3 Was he good at school? Why not?
  4 What did his teachers say about him?
  5 When did he start to improve his memory? What did he see?
  6 Why isn't he popular with casino managers?
  7 How many clubs did he visit with the interviewers?
  8 How many clubs did he play in? Why?
  9 What do you think of his suggestions for a good memory?

Try his ideas to remember some words in English!

3 Here are the answers to some questions. Write the questions. Read the article again to help!

1 _____ ?

  Wednesday.

2 _____ ?

  Last October.

3 _____ ?

  Eight hundred pounds a day.

4 _____ ?

  She's a clothes designer.

5 _____ ?

  Seven hundred and fifty pounds.

6 _____ ?

  He loves number games, crosswords, writing music, and playing the piano.

4 What do these numbers from the article refer to?

  1 1876   **April 21, 1876 was a Wednesday.**

  2 35   4 £1,000   6 £1,250
  3 34   5 7   7 5

WORLD CHAMPION MEMORY MAN

Dominic O'Leary is the man with the best memory in the world. He can tell you the day of any date in any year. What day was April 21, 1876? 'Wednesday,' says Dominic. He can remember the teams and the scores of every football match in every World Cup. And he became world champion memory man when he remembered the order of thirty-five packs of playing cards!

At school, Dominic was a pupil who couldn't remember his lessons. 'My maths and English teachers said I was stupid because I could never remember what they taught me.' But four years ago he saw a programme on television which showed people how to improve their memory, and last October he became world champion. 'I remembered the order of thirty-five packs of cards,' said Dominic. 'It was quite easy.'

Dominic, 34, can earn £800 a day on European TV programmes. He lives with his wife, Alison, a clothes designer, in a small village near Bath, and he is the manager of an office cleaning company.

Winning

Casino managers don't want Dominic to visit their casinos, because he can remember every card. 'I played as a professional gambler for a few months, and I won £1,000 a night, but then the managers asked me to leave.'

We went with Dominic to seven clubs in London and Brighton. He started with £500, and four hours later, he had £1,250 in his pocket. He won £750.

He played in just three clubs for four hours. The other four clubs knew his face and didn't want him to play.

In his free time, Dominic loves number games and crosswords, writing music, and playing the piano. He says children can learn to improve their memory from the age of five. 'Then they can do anything,' he says.

How to improve your memory

Dominic says anyone can have a good memory. These are his suggestions:

1 When you go to bed, remember everything you did that day.
2 Remember things in pictures, not words. 'Words are difficult to remember, but pictures are easy.' For example, if you want to remember the name Kate, think of a cat. For the number 8814, think of two snowmen, a tree and a bird.
3 If you forget something, remember where you were when you *could* remember it.

Song

Choose the correct words to complete the song.
Listen and check.

STEVIE WONDER

I Just Called To Say I Love You

No New Year's (1)_____ to   *Day/Eve*
    celebrate,
No chocolate covered candy
    (2)_____ to give away,   *smiles/hearts*
No first of spring, no song to
    (3)_____ ,   *play/sing*
In fact here's just another
    ordinary (4)_____ .   *day/time*

No April rain, no (5)_____   *flowers/colours*
    bloom,
No (6)_____ Saturday   *wedding/birthday*
    within the month of June.
But what it is is something
    (7)_____ ,   *blue/true*
Made up of these three
    (8)_____ that I must say   *lines/words*
    to you

Chorus

I just called to say I love you
I just called to say how much
    I (9)_____   *care/know*
I just called to say I love you,
And I (10)_____ it from the   *mean/give*
    bottom of my heart.

No summers high, no
    (11)_____ July   *warm/hot*
No harvest (12)_____ to   *sun/moon*
    light one tender August night
No autumn breeze, no falling
    (13)_____   *leaf/leaves*
Not even time for birds to
    (14)_____ to southern   *fly/go*
    skies

No Libra sun, no hallowe'en
No giving (15)_____ to all   *thanks/presents*
    the Christmas joy you bring
But what it is, though old, so new
To fill your (16)_____ like   *heart/time*
    no three words could ever do.

Chorus

Song

Choose the correct words to complete the song.
Listen and check.

STEVIE WONDER

I Just Called To Say I Love You

No New Year's (1)_____ to   *Day/Eve*
    celebrate,
No chocolate covered candy
    (2)_____ to give away,   *smiles/hearts*
No first of spring, no song to
    (3)_____ ,   *play/sing*
In fact here's just another
    ordinary (4)_____ .   *day/time*

No April rain, no (5)_____   *flowers/colours*
    bloom,
No (6)_____ Saturday   *wedding/birthday*
    within the month of June.
But what it is is something
    (7)_____ ,   *blue/true*
Made up of these three
    (8)_____ that I must say   *lines/words*
    to you

Chorus

I just called to say I love you
I just called to say how much
    I (9)_____   *care/know*
I just called to say I love you,
And I (10)_____ it from the   *mean/give*
    bottom of my heart.

No summers high, no
    (11)_____ July   *warm/hot*
No harvest (12)_____ to   *sun/moon*
    light one tender August night
No autumn breeze, no falling
    (13)_____   *leaf/leaves*
Not even time for birds to
    (14)_____ to southern   *fly/go*
    skies

No Libra sun, no hallowe'en
No giving (15)_____ to all   *thanks/presents*
    the Christmas joy you bring
But what it is, though old, so new
To fill your (16)_____ like   *heart/time*
    no three words could ever do.

Chorus

Unit 9

Plan a party (TB p75)

1 Imagine you want to have an end-of-term party. Complete the lists. You can include three famous people in the guest list.

Food

Drink

Guests

2 Work in groups of three. Discuss your preferences. Decide on five things to eat, three things to drink and three famous guests.

> I'd like hamburgers and chips for the party.

> Oh, I don't like hamburgers and chips. I'd like pizza and pasta.

> I'd like to invite Robbie Williams to the party. He can sing really well.

3 Roleplay your party. Use some of these ideas.

Saying hello and goodbye

> Hello, how are you?

> Fine, thanks.

> Hi, Sorry I'm late.

> Don't worry.

> Hello, thanks for coming.

> Thank you for a great party. See you soon.

Making offers and requests

> Does anybody want more pizza?

> No, thanks.

> Could you pass me a sandwich?

> Yes, of course. Here you are.

> What would you like to drink?

> Can I have a cola, please?

Talking to famous guests

> Could you sing for us?

> Yes, of course. What's your favourite song?

> Could you tell us about your new film?

> Yes, of course. It's a love story.

> What would you like to do next?

> I'd like to play for the national team.

Unit 10

The biggest and best! (TB p83)

1   Complete the questions with the correct form of the adjectives. Then write the answers for your country. You cannot choose your own city / region!

Where's the best place to live?   Answers

1	Which city is <u>the most expensive</u> ? (*expensive*)	_____
2	Which city has _____ population? (**high**)	_____
3	Which region has _____ food? (**good**)	_____
4	Which airport is _____ ? (busy)	_____
5	Who are _____ people? (*friendly*)	_____
6	Which region has _____ architecture? (**modern**)	_____
7	Where are _____ resorts? (interesting)	_____
8	Which city is _____ ? (*dangerous*)	_____
9	Which region has _____ beaches? (bad)	_____
10	Where's _____ place? (*beautiful*)	_____

2   Work in groups and discuss your answers. Give reasons for your choices.

3   Work as a class. Which is the best / worst place to live in your country?

Unit 11

Suggestion (TB p94)

hair	wear	short	bought	red	said
eyes	size	green	mean	list	kissed
those	knows	near	beer	grey	pay

hair	wear	short	bought	red	said
eyes	size	green	mean	list	kissed
those	knows	near	beer	grey	pay

Extra ideas Units 9–12 Revision

Vocabulary

Match the words (1–8) to the definitions (a–h).

1 fall in love   a natural beauty you see in the country
2 hole   b the part of a house that covers the top
3 roof   c with nothing inside
4 mad   d someone who builds houses
5 scenery   e a space in something solid
6 empty   f make something that is broken good again
7 builder   g to start to love someone or something
8 repair   h crazy

A dream house in the *country*

Amy and Phil King had a modern house in London with three bedrooms, but with only a small garden. It was on a busy road, so it was very noisy and the air wasn't very clean. 'We wanted a quieter and more relaxing life in the country,' they explained. 'We looked at a lot of cottages, then one evening we saw an old house in a beautiful country village. We fell in love with it immediately – the only problem was that it didn't have any windows, electricity, or water, and there were some holes in the roof!'

They arrived back in London and described the house to their teenage children. Their son Daniel said, 'Are you mad? We can't live in a house without electricity or water!' and their daughter Vicky said, 'I'm not going to live in that house. I'm going to stay in London!' Amy then said, 'There is a lot of work to do on the house, but let's visit it together. We can go next weekend and you can see if you like it.'

The following Saturday the family drove to the village. The children looked at the scenery and they couldn't believe their eyes. There were green fields, a clean river, and a beautiful wood. The family had lunch in the local pub before they went to see the house. The people were all so friendly. They told the family about the history of the house. 'The local music teacher lived there all her life. She died ten years ago. It was a very happy house when she was there. She gave piano and guitar lessons, and the house was always full of people and music. It's so sad to see the house empty now.'

The family then drove to the house. The children saw the number of rooms – five downstairs and six upstairs – and the size of the garden. There was so much space! 'We can have a music room where I can play my guitar,' said Daniel, 'And I can have a big bedroom and a horse in the field next to the house,' said Vicky. One month later, the family sold their house in London and bought the one in the country. Local builders are repairing the old house and the family hope to move there in six months.

Reading

Read the text and answer the questions.

Who …
1 lived in London? **the King family**
2 liked the house the moment they saw it? _____
3 didn't want to live in the house? _____
4 told the family about its history? _____
5 lived in the house before? _____
6 wanted to have a music room? _____
7 wanted to have a horse? _____
8 is working on the house? _____

Language work

1   Here are some answers. Complete the questions.

1   Where **did the King family live**?
    They lived in a modern house in London.
2   What _____ ?
    It was very noisy and the air wasn't very clean.
3   Why _____ ?
    They wanted a quieter and more relaxing life in the country.
4   Where _____ ?
    In a beautiful country village.
5   Did _____ ?
    No, they didn't. They hated it.
6   What _____ like?
    The green fields, a clean river, and a beautiful wood.
7   What _____ ?
    She gave piano and guitar lessons
8   How many _____ ?
    Eleven – five downstairs and six upstairs.
9   When _____ ?
    One month later.
10 When _____ ?
    In six months.

2   Find and underline the following in the text…

1   the past of *have got*
2   a comparative sentence
3   three irregular past tenses
4   an example of *any*
5   an example of *some*
6   two examples of *going to*
7   a suggestion
8   a description of what is happening now

Song

Wonderful tonight

ERIC CLAPTON

VERSE 1
Complete the verse with the verbs in the box.

> asks   say   puts   wear   brushes

It's late in the evening

She's wondering what clothes to (1) _____ .

She (2) _____ on her make-up

Then (3) _____ her long blond hair

And then she (4) _____ me,

'Do I look all right?'

And I (5) _____ 'Yes,

You look wonderful tonight.'

VERSE 2
Underline the correct word in *italics*. Think about the rhyme to help you.

We go to a (1) *dinner / party*

And everyone turns to (2) *see / find*

This beautiful (3) *woman / lady*

That's walking around with me

And then she asks me,

Do you feel (4) *all right / OK?*

And I say 'Yes,

I feel wonderful tonight.'

VERSE 3
Complete this verse with the lines in the box.

> Because I see
> How much I love you
> And the wonder of it all

I feel wonderful

(1) _____

The lovelight in your eyes

(2) _____

Is that you just don't realize

(3) _____

VERSE 4
Number the lines of this verse in the correct order.

As I turn out the light   ☐

You were wonderful tonight.'   ☐

So I give her the car keys,   ☐

And I've got an aching head   ☐

It's time to go home now   1

She helps me to bed   ☐

And then I tell her   ☐

I say, 'My darling,   ☐

Listen to the song and check.

Unit 13

Suggestion (TB p112)

Student A

1 Write the words in the correct order. Add capital letters where necessary.

   A Hello.
   (1) _____
   (help / I / can / you / ?)

   B Yes, please. I'm looking for some plasters. Where can I find them?

   A Right here.
   (2) _____
   (you / size / want / what / do / ?) Small or large?

   B Large, please. And I'd like some conditioner, as well.

   A (3) _____
   (kind / conditioner / what / of / ?)
   For dry hair? Normal hair?

   B Er ... for normal hair, please.

   A Anything else?

   B No, that's all. How much is that?

   A (4) _____
   (eighty / euros / five)

   B There you are.

   A Ten euros. Thank you.
   (5) _____
   (euros / change / twenty / here's / four / .)

   B Thank you very much. Bye-bye.

   A Thanks. Bye.

2 Practise the conversation with a partner. Pay attention to stress and intonation.

Student B

1 Write the words in the correct order. Add capital letters where necessary.

   A Hello. Can I help you?

   B Yes, please.
   (1) _____
   (for / I'm / plasters / some / looking / .)Where can I find them?

   A Right here. What size do you want? Small or large?

   B Large, please.
   (2) _____
   (conditioner / like / and / some / as / I'd / well / .)

   A What kind of conditioner? For dry hair? Normal hair?

   B Er ... (3) _____
   (please / hair / for / , / normal / .)

   A Anything else?

   B No, that's all.
   (4) _____
   (that / much / is / how / ?)

   A Five euros eighty.

   B There you are.

   A Ten euros. Thank you. And here's four euros twenty change .

   B (5) _____
   (much / you / very / thank / .) Bye-bye.

   A Thanks. Bye.

2 Practise the conversation with a partner. Pay attention to stress and intonation.

© Oxford University Press **Photocopiable**

Unit 14

Suggestion (TB p117)

1

Have you ever eaten Greek food? Yes/No
What was it like?

_____

(your own question)

_____

2

Have you ever ridden a horse? Yes/No
Where did you ride a horse?

_____

(your own question)

_____

3

Have you ever watched a film in English? Yes/No
What was it?

_____

(your own question)

_____

4

Have you ever met a film star? Yes/No
Who was it?

_____

(your own question)

_____

5

Have you ever won a prize? Yes/No
What did you win?

_____

(your own question)

_____

6

Have you ever been abroad? Yes/No
Where did you go?

_____

(your own question)

_____

7

Have you ever drunk champagne? Yes/No
Why did you drink it?

_____

(your own question)

_____

8

Have you ever hitch-hiked? Yes/No
Why did you hitch-hike?

_____

(your own question)

_____

9

Have you ever had an accident? Yes/No
Where did it happen?

_____

(your own question)

_____

10

Have you ever flown in a helicopter? Yes/No
Where did you go?

_____

(your own question)

_____

Extra ideas Units 13–14 Revision

Speaking

Answer the questions.
- What films have you seen recently?
- What's your favourite film?
- Who are your favourite films stars?

Reading

1 Read the text about Johnny Depp and choose the correct words.

2 Answer the questions about Johnny Depp.
   1 When was he born?
   2 What happened when he was 12?
   3 Which actor helped him at the start of his career?
   4 Did he enjoy being popular with teenage girls?
   5 Does he like to play the same type of character in each of his films?
   6 Which was one of his most popular films?
   7 How many times has he been married?
   8 Who is the mother of his children?

Language work

1 Put the words in the right order to make a question.
   1 born where he was ?

   _____

   In Owensboro, Kentucky.
   2 he school why did leave ?

   _____

   To follow a career in music.
   3 money did he how earn ?

   _____

   He became a salesman.
   4 film his what was first ?

   _____

   A Nightmare on Elm Street.
   5 has he many how children got ?

   _____

   Two – a boy and a girl.
   6 music continued interest has he his in ?

   _____

   Yes, he plays in a music club.

2 Find and underline the following in the text…
   1 three verbs in the Past Simple in the first paragraph
   2 three verbs in the Present Perfect in the last paragraph

Meet Johnny DEPP

JOHNNY DEPP (1) *has/ (was)* born on June 9, 1963 in Owensboro, Kentucky. His parents (2) *has moved/moved* their four children to Florida when Johnny was young. At the age of 12, his mother bought him a guitar and music (3) *quick/quickly* became his love. Johnny decided to leave school at the age of 16 to follow a career in music. He played guitar for a band called 'The Kids' and moved with the band to Los Angeles. They didn't have (4) *immediate/immediately* success and so Johnny started a job as a salesman to earn some money.

He (5) *has got/got* married at the age of 20 to a make-up artist, Lori Allison. They got divorced quite soon, but Lori introduced Johnny to the actor Nicholas Cage. He saw a future for Johnny in films and persuaded him to try acting. Johnny (6) *made/has made* his first film *A Nightmare on Elm Street* in 1984. After a couple of other small parts in films, Johnny worked for three years in a TV series for teenagers called *21 Jump Street*. Teenage girls became big fans and Johnny appeared in popular magazines and on posters. He was (7) *annoyed/annoying* by this, because he wanted to be a serious actor.

Johnny has (8) *ever/never* appeared in just one type of film and he has always been (9) *interested/interesting* in playing different characters. In the early 1990s he played a series of eccentric characters including Edward Scissorhands in the film of the same name. Johnny has continued to act in a big range of films and has won the respect of Hollywood, critics and of film fans round the world. In 1996 he (10) *has taken/took* the time to write, direct and appear in *The Brave*, which appeared at the 1997 Cannes Film Festival. In 2003, *Pirates of the Caribbean* became one of his most popular films.

Johnny Depp has also had an (11) *interesting/interested* life outside films. He has had a series of famous girlfriends including American actress Winona Ryder and the British model Kate Moss. In 1988 Johnny began to go out with Vanessa Paradis, the French actress and singer. Their first child, a daughter, was born in May 1999 and their second, a son, in April 2002. And he (12) *didn't ever forget/hasn't ever forgotten* the world of music – he plays in a club in Los Angeles that he owns and he has also directed music videos for Vanessa.

Song

1 Look at the underlined words. What is missing?
2 Listen and complete the song.

Summertime and the <u>livin'</u> is
(1) _____

Fish <u>are jumpin'</u> and the cotton is
(2) _____

Oh your Daddy's (3) _____ and
your ma is <u>good-lookin'</u>

So hush little baby, don't you
(4) _____ .

One of these (5) _____
you<u>'re goin'</u> to rise up singing

Then you'll spread your wings and
you'll take to the (6) _____

But till that morning there's a <u>nothin'</u>
can harm you

With daddy and mammy <u>standin'</u> by.

Song

1 Look at the underlined words. What is missing?
2 Listen and complete the song.

Summertime and the <u>livin'</u> is
(1) _____

Fish <u>are jumpin'</u> and the cotton is
(2) _____

Oh your Daddy's (3) _____ and
your ma is <u>good-lookin'</u>

So hush little baby, don't you
(4) _____ .

One of these (5) _____
you<u>'re goin'</u> to rise up singing

Then you'll spread your wings and
you'll take to the (6) _____

But till that morning there's a <u>nothin'</u>
can harm you

With daddy and mammy <u>standin'</u> by.

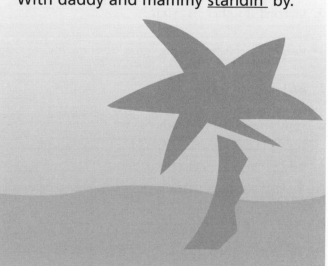

Stop and check 1

Correct the mistakes

Each sentence has a mistake. Find it and correct it.

1 Paola is ~~Italiana~~. **Paola is Italian.**
2 New York is a city very big.
3 My mother works in a restaurant. Is a chef.
4 My father watch football on TV.
5 He's like playing tennis.
6 On Sundays we go the cinema.
7 Mark is pilot.
8 You family is very nice.
9 I like go to the gym.
10 Our school have a lot of students.
11 The childrens go to school near here.
12 We go to the bed at 11.00.
13 Spring and summer are my favourites seasons.
14 My sister no have a car.
15 Do you want a ice-cream?
16 Is near here, my school.

15

Word order

Put the words in the correct order.

1 Bristol Daniel from comes
Daniel comes from Bristol.
2 journalist from is Peter a New York

3 married brother is your ?

4 mountains sister skiing goes the in my

5 isn't big my very town

6 your what name teacher's is ?

7 surname how spell do your you ?

8 often weekends go I at sailing

7

Choose the correct sentence

One sentence is correct. Which one?

1 Where she from?   ✗
  Where does she from?   ✗
  Where is she from?   ✓
2 a Diane is a nice girl, and I like.
  b Diane is a nice girl, and I like her.
  c Diane is a nice girl, and I like him.
3 a He has 19 years old.
  b He's 19 years.
  c He's 19.
4 a Pietro works with his father.
  b Pietro works with he's father.
  c Pietro works with him father.
5 a Ana and Juan live in Madrid. They're flat is lovely.
  b Ana and Juan live in Madrid. Their flat is lovely.
  c Ana and Juan live in Madrid. There flat is lovely.
6 a She lives in a house or a flat?
  b Does she lives in a house or a flat?
  c Does she live in a house or a flat?
7 a I don't like going running.
  b I don't like go running.
  c I no like going running.
8 a How many languages you speak?
  b How many languages do you speak?
  c How many languages does you speak?
9 a My brother work in a hospital.
  b My brother he works in a hospital.
  c My brother works in a hospital.

8

Questions

1 Match a line in **A** with a line in **B** to make questions.

A	B
Where	do you do at weekends?
What	do you go to bed?
Who	do you usually sit next to?
What time	is a cup of coffee and a sandwich?
How much	languages do you speak?
How many	do you go on holiday?

5

2 Here are the answers to some questions. Write the questions. Use the words in brackets.

1 **What do you do?**
   (you/do) I'm an architect.
2 _____ ?
   (Helen/start work)   At 8.00.
3 _____ ?
   (Nicole and Jean/come)   From France.
4 _____ ?
   (your wife's)   Sally.
5 _____ ?
   (you/have)   Three. Two boys and a girl.
6 _____ ?
   (you/like/taking photographs)
   Yes, I do. I have a very good camera.

| | 5 |

Prepositions

Complete the text with the prepositions from the box.

| at | in | about | after | for | with | by | to | on |

Linda lives (1)____**in**____ a small flat (2)_____ Oxford. She lives (3)_____ two other girls who are students (4)_____ Oxford University. They work hard during the week, but (5)_____ weekends they invite a lot of friends to their house. They cook a meal (6)_____ their friends, and then they go out (7)_____ the pub (8)_____ a drink, or they stay (9)_____ home and listen (10)_____ music.
Linda has two jobs. (11)_____ Mondays, Tuesdays, and Wednesdays she works (12)_____ a hospital, where she helps to look (13)_____ children who are ill. She goes to the hospital (14)_____ bus. She starts (15)_____ ten o'clock and works until quarter (16)_____ five. On Thursdays and Fridays she works (17)_____ home. She has a computer (18)_____ her bedroom and she writes stories. (19)_____ the evening, one of the girls cooks a meal. (20)_____ dinner they look in the newspaper to see what's on TV, or they talk (21)_____ their day. They usually go to bed at about midnight.

| | 20 |

Vocabulary

Put the words in the correct column.

| egg menu nurse lovely tuna model collect |
| sailing cake sunbathing want deliver dictionary |
| fast expensive chicken journalist postcard |
| sell friendly lawyer magazine chips running |
| cooking actor dancing newspaper young listen |

Things to read	Jobs	Things to eat	Activities	Verbs	Adjectives

| | 30 |

am/ is/ do/ does (not)

Complete the sentences with the verbs in the box.

| am/'m not is/isn't are/aren't does/doesn't do/don't |

1 I _'m not_____ English.
2 Where _____ you from?
3 What time _____ the shop open?
4 My sister _____ eat meat because she _____ a vegetarian.
5 I _____ hungry. How much _____ a chicken salad?
6 Where _____ you usually go on holiday?
7 Daddy, we _____ want to go to bed. We _____ tired.
8 Learning English _____ boring! It's interesting!

| | 10 |

| TOTAL | 100 |

TRANSLATE

Translate the sentences. Translate the *ideas*, not word by word.

1 I am a student.
   _____
2 My sister is a lawyer.
   _____
3 She isn't at home. She's at work.
   _____
4 I live in a flat.
   _____
5 My mother works in a school.
   _____
6 I don't smoke.
   _____
7 My father doesn't like watching TV.
   _____
8 What do you do at weekends?
   _____

Stop and check 2

Correct the mistakes

Each sentence has a mistake. Find it and correct it.

1 ~~Where you live?~~ **Where do you live?**
2 There no is a bank near here.
3 Look at this photos.
4 Is a post box near here?
5 I arrive at the airport at ten o'clock last night.
6 She could to speak three languages when she was eight.
7 Where did you went last weekend?
8 The sofa is in front the window.
9 I don't can go out because I have a lot of homework.
10 In the kitchen is a table.
11 I was to the theatre last weekend.
12 Who are these people over there?
13 I buyed a new DVD player.
14 Did you watch the football on TV last evening?
15 Spanish people is very friendly.
16 I like cities because I can to go to good restaurants.

| 15 |

Past Simple

Complete the text with the Past Simple form of the verbs in brackets. There are regular and irregular verbs.

> Leonardo da Vinci (1)____**lived**____ (live) in Italy in the fifteenth and sixteenth centuries. He was a student in Florence, where he
> (2)_____ (study) painting, sculpture, and design. He
> (3)_____ (begin) a lot of paintings, but he (4)_____
> (not finish) many of them. His picture of the Mona Lisa is the most famous portrait in the world.
> Leonardo (5)_____ (be) interested in many things. He
> (6)_____ (want) to know about everything he saw. He examined the human body. He (7)_____ (think) that the sun
> (8)_____ (not go) round the earth. He (9)_____ (write) music. He designed a flying machine 400 years before the first one flew. Many people (10)_____ (not understand) his ideas. It is difficult to think that one man (11)_____ (can) do so much.

| 20 |

Irregular verbs

Write the Past Simple form of these irregular verbs.

1	sing	_____	6	make	_____
2	come	_____	7	break	_____
3	sell	_____	8	see	_____
4	get	_____	9	win	_____
5	leave	_____	10	take	_____

| 10 |

can/ could/ was/ were (not)

Complete the sentences with the verbs in the box.

| can   can't   was   wasn't   were   weren't   could   couldn't |

1 I ___**can't**___ drive. I'm only 14 years old.
2 Our teacher _____ at school last week because she _____ ill.
3 Leonardo _____ a student in Florence. He _____ draw, write music, and design buildings.
4 People _____ see the Mona Lisa in the Louvre in Paris.
5 'Where _____ you last night? You _____ at home. I phoned you, but there _____ no answer.'
6 'I _____ get into my flat because I lost my keys. I _____ at a friend's house.'

| 10 |

some/ any/ a/ an

Complete the sentences with some, any, a, or an.

1 Heathrow is ___**an**___ international airport.
2 Did Amelia Earhart have _____ children?
3 I bought _____ book and _____ magazines.
4 Jane lives in _____ old house in Cornwall.
5 There are _____ trees in my garden, but there aren't _____ flowers.
6 Do you have _____ books by Christopher Paolini?
7 There are _____ letters for you on the table.

| 8 |

Questions and negatives

Write the statements as questions and negatives.

1 He can swim. _Can he swim? He can't swim._
2 There's a good café in this town. _____
3 There are some eggs in the fridge. _____
4 You can speak Spanish. _____
5 He was born in 1983. _____
6 She could play the violin when she was three. _____
7 They were on holiday last week. _____
8 Your parents studied English at school. _____
9 The students went to the cinema last night. _____

16

Vocabulary – noun + noun

Match a noun in **A** with a noun in **B**. Use each word once only.

A	B
birthday	pool
chocolate	friend
orange	park
swimming	bag
car	star
news	station
boy	card
film	machine
hand	cake
railway	room
living	juice
washing	paper

11

Vocabulary – verb + noun

Match a verb in **A** with a noun in **B**.

A	B
watch	the guitar
speak	a pilot
drink	a sandwich
win	a record
earn	a meal
cook	a cup of coffee
ride	German
break	a medal
play	TV
become	a lot of money
eat	a bike

 10

TOTAL 100

TRANSLATE

Translate the sentences. Translate the *ideas*, not word by word.

1 Is there a chemist's near here?
_____

2 There are two books on the table.
_____

3 There are some flowers in the garden.
_____

4 Are there any glasses in the cupboard?
_____

5 I can ski, but I can't swim.
_____

6 I couldn't go to the party last night.
_____

7 I was ill.
_____

8 Where were you born?
_____

9 I was born in Mexico.
_____

10 She started work when she was twelve.
_____

11 He didn't like his first job.
_____

12 Where did you go on holiday last year?
_____

Stop and check 3

Correct the mistakes

There is a mistake in each sentence. Find it and correct it.

1 ~~Where you live?~~ **Where do you live?**
2 It's very hot today – do you like something to drink?
3 Peter has got a lot of books, because he'd like reading.
4 How many brothers and sisters do you got?
5 How many money has he got?
6 Who's is that new car?
7 I'm go home now, because it's late.
8 Last night I went to the pub for to meet my friends.
9 We're going have a test next week.
10 I'm wear my old clothes because I'm going to clean the car.
11 Juan is Spanish, he's coming from Madrid.
12 What you doing this evening?
13 My brother is more old than me.
14 I think is going to rain.
15 Your flat is bigger than my.
16 Who is the most rich person in the world?

☐ 15

Questions and answers

Match a question in **A** with an answer in **B**.

A	B
Where does your sister work?	Yes, of course. What can I do for you?
Whose is this mobile phone?	Yes. I think he's very nice.
How many dogs have you got?	To buy some fruit.
How much did your bike cost?	To Mexico.
Could you help me, please?	In an office.
Would you like some more to eat?	I stayed at home.
Do you like Henry?	Two.
Where are you going on holiday?	It's Sally's.
Why are you going to the market?	£295.
What did you do last night?	Her name's Mrs Taylor.
Who's the new teacher?	No, thanks. I'm full.

☐ 10

Comparatives and superlatives

Complete the chart.

Adjective	Comparative	Superlative
big	_____	_____
_____	more intelligent	_____
	_____	worst
popular	_____	_____
noisy	_____	_____

☐ 10

Comparing hotels

1 Look at the information about the two hotels. Write five sentences about the hotels using the comparative forms of the adjectives in the box.

good	big	expensive	near	far	modern

	The Strand	The Ritz
Number of stars	★★★	★★★★
Number of rooms	102	55
Price	£80–£100	£120–£140
How many minutes to the sea?	10 minutes	15 minutes
How many minutes to the town centre?	20 minutes	8 minutes
Old or new?	New–1990	Old–1870

1 __The Ritz is a better hotel than The Strand.__
2 _____
3 _____
4 _____
5 _____
6 _____

☐ 10

2 Look at the information about The Star hotel. Write five more sentences, comparing the three hotels. Use the superlative form of the adjectives above.

	The Star
Number of stars	★★★★★
Number of rooms	45
Price	£150–£175
How many minutes to the sea?	1 minute
How many minutes to the town centre?	15 minutes
Old or new?	Old – 1920

1 The Star is the best.
2 _____
3 _____
4 _____
5 _____
6 _____

☐ 10

some/any/a

Complete the sentences with *some*, *any*, or *a*.

1 I don't have ___any___ brothers or sisters.
2 Would you like _____ glass of wine?
3 You have _____ lovely pictures on the walls!
4 Is there _____ petrol in the car?
5 Can I have _____ strawberries, please?
6 I'd like _____ hamburger and _____ chips, please.
7 Do you want _____ sandwich?
8 The shop doesn't have _____ brown bread.
9 There are _____ eggs in the cupboard, but there isn't _____ sugar.

☐ 10

Present Simple and Present Continuous

Complete the sentences with the correct form of the verbs in brackets.

1 I often __watch__ (watch) TV in the evenings, but tonight __I'm going__ (go) to the cinema.
2 Pierre _____ (smoke) twenty cigarettes a day, but he _____ (not smoke) now because he's in class.
3 Alice and Peter _____ (look) for a new house. They _____ (not like) living in London.
4 I always _____ (wear) nice clothes for work. Today I _____ (wear) a blue jacket and skirt.
5 'Why _____ you _____ (go) to bed? It's only 10.00.' 'I always _____ (go) to bed early.'
6 Jane _____ (work) in a bank, but today she's at home. She _____ (write) emails.

☐ 10

going to

Complete the sentences with *going to*. Use a verb and a place or person from the boxes.

buy	send	see	borrow	have	do

my friend	Turkey	library	theatre	baker's	living room

1 I _'m going to do_ my homework in the __living room__ .
2 Peter _____ some bread at the _____ .
3 I _____ some books from the _____ .
4 We _____ a play at the _____ .
5 They _____ a holiday in _____ .
6 I _____ an email to _____ .

☐ 10

Vocabulary

Put the words in the correct column.

cake wine chips dress meat suit carrots milk shirt cheese jumper water juice jeans beer

Clothes shop	Food	Drinks

☐ 15

TOTAL **100**

TRANSLATE

Translate the sentences. Translate the *ideas*, not word by word.

1 I like coffee. I'd like a coffee.
_____

2 There is some bread on the table. There isn't any coffee.
_____

3 You're older than me, but Tim is the oldest in the class.
_____

4 My sister has got three children.
_____

5 I usually wear jeans, but today I'm wearing a suit.
_____

6 'Whose is this book?' 'It's mine.'
_____

7 We're going to have a party.
_____

8 I went into London to buy some books.
_____

Stop and check 4

Correct the mistakes

There is a mistake in each sentence. Find it and correct it.

1 We ~~was~~ in Paris last year. **We were in Paris last year.**
2 Why you want to learn Italian?
3 She hasn't never been to New York.
4 I've wrote to her three times and she hasn't answered yet.
5 I didn't enjoy the film. It was very bored.
6 How many times you been to Spain?
7 I'm very exciting about my holiday.
8 The students worked very hardly.
9 'Who's keys are these?' 'They're Linda's.'
10 What kind books do you like reading?
11 Did you ever been to Ireland?

$\boxed{10}$

Questions and tenses

Ask questions about the statements.

1 John went to New York.
When **did he go** _____?
2 I'm tired.
Why _____?
3 I don't go to work by bus.
How _____ you _____?
4 This mobile phone isn't mine.
Whose _____?
5 I met a famous film star.
Who _____ you _____?
6 Sarah's bought a new car.
What kind _____?
7 We saw Bill yesterday.
Where _____ you _____?
8 Sue's watching a film.
What _____?
9 They're going on holiday.
Where _____?
10 My brother left the party.
Why _____?
11 She spent a lot of money.
How much _____?

$\boxed{20}$

Past Simple and Present Perfect

1 Underline the correct tense.

1 I _saw_ / _have seen_ Jill yesterday.
2 I _met_ / _have met_ my boyfriend ten years ago.
3 My sister _did never go_ / _has never been_ to Italy.
4 I'm sorry. I _didn't finish_ / _haven't finished_ my work yet.
5 I _ate_ / _have eaten_ a lot of ice-cream when I was a child.
6 They _climbed_ / _have climbed_ Everest in 2002.

$\boxed{5}$

2 Put the verb in brackets in the correct form: the Present Simple or the Present Perfect.

1 I **travelled** (travel) by plane for the first time last year.
2 We _____ (go) to Thailand two years ago.
3 _____ you ever _____ (eat) Mexican food?
4 I _____ never _____ (be) to hospital.
5 Where _____ you _____ (live) when you were a child?
6 I can't give you your DVD back, because I _____ (not see) it yet.

$\boxed{10}$

Adverb or adjective?

Underline the correct form.

1 I'm driving _careful_ / _carefully_ because it is raining.
2 Our village is always very _quiet_ / _quietly_. Nothing happens.
3 Please speak more _slow_ / _slowly_. I can't understand you.
4 She's a very _good_ / _well_ driver.
5 He doesn't drive very _good_ / _well_.
6 It's important to have a _healthy_ / _healthily_ diet.

$\boxed{5}$

Word order

Put the words in the correct order.

1 letter you yet have written?
   Have you written the letter yet?

2 many got you how cousins have?
   _____

3 Rome they just have in arrived
   _____

4 well speak you very English
   _____

5 quickly road along man the walked the
   _____

6 by play a have Shakespeare seen ever you?
   _____

7 exam students the yesterday a did long
   _____

8 carefully work you did your check?
   _____

9 exercise this do please quickly
   _____

10 people going many invite party how are
    to to your you?
   _____

11 up is because she tired she got early
   _____

   [ ] 10

Auxiliaries

Complete the sentences with an auxiliary verb from the box.

am/is/are	do/does	did have/has

1 I ___ **am** ___ listening to music.
2 Look at those children – they _____ smoking cigarettes!
3 _____ your daughter speak French well?
4 _____ you learn German when you were at school?
5 _____ Ben ever been to China?
6 We _____ never hitch-hiked abroad.
7 I _____ going to learn to drive soon.
8 _____ Dave and Rachel live near you?
9 _____ Nick going to phone you tomorrow?
10 'What time _____ you start work?' 'Hours ago.'
11 _____ you finished your homework yet?

   [ ] 10

Vocabulary – word groups

Put the words in the correct column. Each column has a different number of words.

soap quiet walk annoying luggage departure lounge worried aspirin cycle suncream arrival hall hitch-hike tiring plasters flight toothpaste boarding pass gate ride surprised

Travel verbs	Travel by plane	Adjectives	Chemist's

   [ ] 20

Prepositions

Complete the sentences with the prepositions from the box.

about	in	out of	by	on	for	to	from

1 Pamela lives ___ **on** ___ the second floor.
2 I'm reading a story _____ life in China.
3 The *Harry Potter* books are _____ J K Rowling.
4 Is it far _____ your house to the airport?
5 Is Mexico City the biggest city _____ the world?
6 Jane's worried _____ her exam.
7 What's _____ television tonight?
8 Are you interested _____ politics?
9 She works _____ a big company.
10 Can I speak _____ you for a moment?
11 He drove _____ the garage and down the street.

   [ ] 10

   TOTAL **100**

TRANSLATE

Translate the sentences. Translate the *ideas*, not word by word.

1 Tim drives carefully. Tim's a careful driver.
   _____

2 Have you ever been to China? I went to China last year.
   _____

3 He hasn't finished his homework yet.
   _____

4 I've just finished my homework.
   _____

5 I want to go home.
   _____

6 I'm interested in literature.
   _____

Progress test 1

UNITS 1–5

Exercise 1 Asking about people

Surname	Clarke
First name	Karen
Country	Britain
Age	28
Address	33 East St, Brighton
Job	Teacher
Place of work	Language school in Brighton
Married	No
Free time	Sailing

Read about Karen Clarke. Write the questions.

1 **What's her first name?**

Her first name's Karen.

2 _____

Her surname is Clarke.

3 _____

She's from Britain.

4 _____

She's 28.

5 _____

33 East St, Brighton.

6 _____

She's a teacher.

7 _____

In a language school in Brighton.

8 _____

No, she isn't. She's single.

9 _____

She goes sailing.

8

Exercise 2 Word order

Put the words in the correct order.

1 you from are Where ?

   Where are you from?

2 do at What weekends you do ?

   _____

3 work she does Where ?

   _____

4 a shelf There photo is the on

   _____

5 near there bank a Is here ?

   _____

6 coffee please I a Can have ?

   _____

7 children How they do have many ?

   _____

8 English in Emily Brazil teaches

   _____

9 any Is milk the there fridge in ?

   _____

10 not work Rosy go by does to car

   _____

11 Sue going Dave and the cinema like to

   _____

10

Exercise 3 Questions

Match a line in A with a line in B to make a question.
Then find an answer in C.

A	B	C
Who	do you do on Sundays?	At seven o'clock.
How much	do you meet on Saturday evenings?	To the theatre.
What	do you go on Friday evenings?	My friends, Dave and Paul.
Where	do you get up?	I play tennis.
How	is a ham sandwich?	By bus.
What time	do you travel to work?	£2.50.

5

Exercise 4 *some, any, a,* and *an*

Complete the sentences with *some, any, a,* or *an.*

1 There are ___*some*___ flowers in the garden.
2 There are _____ magazines on the coffee table.
3 Can I have _____ ice-cream, please?
4 Are there _____ photos in the living room?
5 There aren't _____ good restaurants in our town.
6 There's _____ newsagent's opposite the post office.
7 John has _____ computer games in his living room.
8 Are there _____ Japanese students in your class?
9 There's _____ armchair in front of the window.
10 There aren't _____ photographs on the wall.
11 There are _____ plates next to the cooker.

$\boxed{10}$

Exercise 5 Present Simple

Complete the text with the correct form of the verb in brackets.

I (1)_____ (have) two brothers, Mark and Nick. They (2)_____ (live) in London. Mark (3)_____ (be) a pilot and Nick (4)_____ (work) in a garage. Mark (5)_____ (like) flying, but Nick (6)_____ _____ (not like) mending cars. At weekends I (7)_____ (go) to London and I (8)_____ (stay) with them. We (9)_____ (go) to the theatre or to the cinema on Saturday evening, and on Sunday we (10)_____ (walk) in Hyde Park.

$\boxed{10}$

Exercise 6 *be* and *do*

Complete the sentences with a verb from the box.

am / am not	does / doesn't	is / isn't
do / don't	are / aren't	

1 Peter ___*is*___ a teacher.
2 I _____ hungry. Can I have a sandwich?
3 Rome _____ in Spain. It _____ in Italy.
4 Mary and Sarah _____ like fast food.
5 _____ James have two jobs?
6 Ben _____ like travelling by bus.
7 We aren't from Spain – we _____ from Portugal.
8 '_____ you like coffee?' 'No, I _____ .'

$\boxed{9}$

Exercise 7 Plural forms

Write these sentences in the plural.

1 She's a doctor.
   They *'re doctors.*_____
2 I go swimming on Saturdays.
   _____
3 He watches TV every day.
   _____
4 The dictionary is over there.
   _____
5 This watch is expensive.
   _____
6 Look at that lovely flower.
   _____
7 Do you have a stamp?
   _____
8 She's our child.
   _____
9 He's an interesting person.
   _____
10 That man is American.
   _____
11 The school doesn't have a computer.
   _____

$\boxed{10}$

Exercise 8 Prepositions

Complete the sentences with the correct preposition.
Write one word on each line.

1 There are two chairs _____ the living room.

2 The sofa is _____ _____ the table.

3 There's a lamp _____ the sofa.

4 There's a picture _____ the wall.

5 The chairs are _____ the television.

6 There's a cat on the rug _____ _____
_____ the fireplace.

7 The telephone is _____ the table.

7

Exercise 9 Choose the correct sentence

Tick (✓) the correct sentence.

1 a Let's go to home.
  b Let's go home. ✓

2 a Jo and Liz are students in Oxford University.
  b Jo and Liz are students at Oxford University.

3 a Let's go out to the pub!
  b Let's go out at the pub!

4 a On Thursdays I get home at six o'clock.
  b In Thursdays I get home at six o'clock.

5 a Richard lives at London.
  b Richard lives in London.

6 a To weekends I go swimming.
  b At weekends I go swimming.

5

Exercise 10 Which one is different?

Underline the different word.

1 Cambridge	London	Oxford	Rome
2 magazine	pen	newspaper	book
3 milk	apple	ice-cream	ham
4 cup	spoon	cupboard	knife
5 actor	model	architect	teach
6 boring	interesting	like	funny
7 father	sister	mother	man
8 house	bathroom	kitchen	living room
9 often	near	next to	opposite
10 France	England	American	Japan
11 my	we	his	your

10

Exercise 11 Adjectives

Match the opposites.

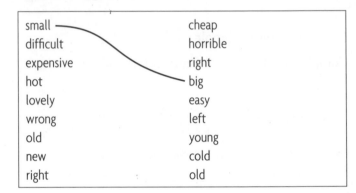

small	cheap
difficult	horrible
expensive	right
hot	big
lovely	easy
wrong	left
old	young
new	cold
right	old

8

Exercise 12 Words that go together

Match a verb in A with a line in B.

A	B
drive	football
play	a plane
go	tea
speak	television
drink	a car
travel	to music
fly	running
listen	by bus
watch	Italian

8

TOTAL 100

Progress test 2

Exercise 1 The past tense of the verb *to be*

What are the past tense forms of the verb *to be*?

		Positive	Negative
1	I	was	wasn't
2	You	_____	_____
3	He/She/It	_____	_____
4	We	_____	_____
5	They	_____	_____

8

Exercise 2 *can* and *can't*

Read the information, then complete the sentences with *can* or *can't* and a verb.

	swim	play tennis	speak German	speak Italian
Sylvia	✓	✗	✓	✓
Linda	✓	✓	✗	✓
Marianne	✗	✗	✓	✓

1 Linda ___can swim___ and she ___can play tennis___ .

2 Sylvia can swim, but she _____ .

3 Marianne _____ and she
_____ .

4 Linda _____ , but Sylvia and Marianne can.

5 Everybody _____ .

6 Only Linda _____ .

7 Sylvia and Linda _____ , but Marianne can't.

7

Exercise 3 Past Simple

Write the Past Simple of these verbs.

Regular		Irregular	
1 like	_____	6 have	_____
2 study	_____	7 become	_____
3 earn	_____	8 sing	_____
4 decide	_____	9 sell	_____
5 start	_____	10 make	_____

10

Exercise 4 Past Simple and Present Simple

Complete the text with the correct form of the verb in brackets: the Past Simple or the Present Simple.

My friend Jack is 40. He (1)_____ (leave) Britain when he was 20 and (2)_____ (go) to Italy. He (3)_____ (work) in Naples for ten years, then he (4)_____ (move) to Rome. There he (5)_____ (meet) Antonella. They (6)_____ (get) married in 1995 and now they (7)_____ (live) in Florence. Jack (8)_____ (teach) English in a language school. And what (9)_____ (do) Antonella do? She (10)_____ (sell) computer software.

10

Photocopiable

Exercise 5 Past Simple: negative

Make these positive sentences negative.

1 He bought a new shirt.
  He didn't buy a new shirt.
2 We enjoyed the film.
  _____
3 I took a photograph of my family.
  _____
4 Angela sent an email to her friend.
  _____
5 Yuri Gagarin became an astronaut in the 1970s.
  _____
6 England won the World Cup in 2000.
  _____
7 Her father died when she was 14.
  _____
8 I lost €20 last night.
  _____
9 People flew by plane 100 years ago.
  _____
10 That book was very interesting.
  _____
11 We arrived at school at eight o'clock.
  _____

[10]

Exercise 6 would like

Tick (✓) the correct sentence.

1 A Would you like | a drink? ✓
     Do you like | ✗
  B No, thanks, I'm not thirsty.
2 A Would you like | some fruit?
     Do you like |
  B Yes. An apple, please.
3 A Would you like | windsurfing?
     Do you like |
  B Yes, but I prefer swimming.
4 A What | do you like | for dinner this evening?
         | would you like |
  B Steak and salad.
5 A Would you like | your new boss?
     Do you like |
  B No. He isn't very nice.
6 A Can I help you?
  B Yes. | I like | a bottle of mineral water, please.
          | I'd like |

[5]

Exercise 7 Countable and uncountable

Write **C** next to the count nouns and **U** next to the uncount nouns.

1 book   _C_   6 dollar   ___
2 rice   _U_   7 biscuit ___
3 apple   ___   8 toast   ___
4 homework   ___   9 cheese   ___
5 money   ___

[7]

Exercise 8 some, any, or a

Write some, any, or a in the gaps.

1 Do you have ___any___ rice?
2 I've got _____ stamps in my bag.
3 Can I have _____ glass of water, please?
4 There isn't _____ sugar in this coffee.
5 Have you got _____ photographs of Jim?
6 I'd like _____ fruit, please.
7 Peter put _____ water and _____ glasses on the table.
8 There wasn't _____ petrol or oil in the car.

[8]

Exercise 9 How much and How many

Complete the questions with How much or How many.

1 _How many_ students are there in your class?
2 _____ bread is there in the cupboard?
3 _____ emails do you send every day?
4 _____ people were there at the party?
5 _____ cola is there in the fridge?
6 _____ money did you spend last month?

[5]

Exercise 10 Comparatives and superlatives 1

Read about the castles.

Abergoran Castle

Price: £200,000
Built: 1072
Rooms: 0

Footleby Castle

Price: £10 million
Built: 1835
Rooms: 160

Haywood Castle

Price: £2 million
Built: 1450
Rooms: 20

These sentences are false. Correct them.

1 Abergoran Castle is more modern than
Haywood Castle.
No, it isn't. It's older

2 Footleby Castle is cheaper than Haywood Castle.

_____

3 Abergoran Castle is bigger than Footleby Castle.

_____

4 Abergoran Castle is the biggest.

_____

5 Abergoran Castle is more expensive than Footleby
Castle.

_____

6 Footleby Castle is the cheapest.

_____

7 Footleby Castle is older than Haywood Castle.

_____

8 Abergoran Castle is the most modern.

_____

7

Exercise 11 Comparatives and superlatives 2

Complete the chart.

Adjective	Comparative	Superlative
_____	more exciting	_____
_____	_____	best
bad	_____	_____
interesting	_____	_____

8

Exercise 12 Ordinal numbers

Write the ordinal numbers in words.

1 6th   _sixth_
2 1st   _____
3 2nd   _____
4 3rd   _____
5 12th   _____
6 20th   _____

5

Exercise 13 Opposites

Choose a word from the box and write it next to its
opposite.

interesting	old	fast	relaxing	friendly
quiet	cheap	dirty	new	safe

1 big   _small_
2 boring   _____
3 unfriendly _____
4 clean   _____
5 slow   _____
6 dangerous   _____
7 noisy   _____
8 old   _____
9 modern   _____
10 expensive _____
11 busy   _____

10

TOTAL 100

Progress test 3

UNITS 11–14

Exercise 1 Present Continuous: -ing form

Write the correct -ing form.

1	walk	walking
2	smoke	smoking
3	drive	_____
4	stop	_____
5	work	_____
6	use	_____
7	look	_____
8	get	_____
9	buy	_____
10	think	_____
11	swim	_____
12	cry	_____

10

Exercise 2 Present Continuous

Complete the sentences with the Present Continuous form of the verb in brackets.

1 Julie **is wearing** a new dress. (wear)
2 I _____ on holiday tomorrow. (not go)
3 **A** Why _____ you _____? (smile)
  B Because Mr Black hasn't given us any homework.
4 **A** Where's Richard?
  B He _____ in the garden. (stand)
5 The students _____ at their desks. (not sit)
6 **A** What _____ Sue _____? (cook)
  B Chicken and rice.
7 **A** What _____ you _____ ? (do)
  B I _____ to my friend. (write)
8 We can't watch a film. The DVD player _____.
  (not work)

8

Exercise 3 Present Simple and Continuous

Complete the sentences with the Present Simple or the Present Continuous form of the verbs in brackets.

1 Be quiet! I **'m watching** (watch) this film!
2 We usually _____ (go) to town by bus, but today we _____ (go) by car.
3 **A** Where _____ you usually _____ (go) on Friday evenings?
  B To the cinema.
4 **A** It's 11.30. Why _____ you _____ (work) so late?
  B Because I _____ (have) a lot of homework.
5 **A** Where _____ your parents _____ ? (live)
  B In a small village near Oxford.
  A _____ they _____ (like) living in the country?
  B Yes, they do.
6 **A** What _____ you usually _____ (have) for breakfast?
  B Toast. But today I _____ (have) some fruit because there isn't any bread.
7 **A** The telephone _____ (ring). Can you answer it?
  B OK.

10

Exercise 4 Possessive pronouns

Write the sentences using a possessive pronoun.

1 It's my pen.   It's mine.
2 They're her keys.   They're hers.
3 It's your dictionary.   _____
4 They're his CDs.   _____
5 It's her mobile phone. _____
6 They're our DVDs.   _____
7 This is their flat.   _____

[5]

Exercise 5 *going to*

Make positive sentences, negative sentences, or questions using *going to*.

1 she / pilot
   She's going to be a pilot.

2 he / not / bus driver
   He isn't going to be a bus driver.

3 you / hairdresser?
   Are you going to be a hairdresser?

4 they / pilots
   _____

5 he / not / actor
   _____

6 you / architect?
   _____

7 I / not / lawyer
   _____

8 we / footballers
   _____

9 she / not / model
   _____

10 he / singer?
   _____

11 I / accountant
   _____

12 he / not / chef
   _____

13 you / music teacher?
   _____

[10]

Exercise 6 Infinitive of purpose

Rewrite these sentences using the infinitive of purpose.

1 I went to Alaska because I wanted to watch whales.
   I went to Alaska to watch whales.

2 I'm going to Moscow because I want to learn Russian.
   _____

3 Paul is going to London because he wants to buy some clothes.
   _____

4 Roger went to India because he wanted to visit the Taj Mahal.
   _____

5 Tracey goes to the gym because she wants to get fit.
   _____

6 Tim is going to the USA because he wants to see his family.
   _____

7 Mario is learning English because he wants to get a better job.
   _____

8 David is saving money because he wants to buy a car.
   _____

9 Henry went to Japan because he wanted to visit Kyoto.
   _____

10 Chris went to the chemist's because he wanted to buy some aspirins.
   _____

11 Brian and Jane are going to Venice because they want to see the Grand Canal.
   _____

[10]

Exercise 7 Adverbs

Write the adverbs next to the adjectives.

1 quick   _quickly_   6 hard   _____
2 slow   _____   7 sudden _____
3 early   _____   8 fast   _____
4 careful _____   9 bad   _____
5 good   _____

[8]

Exercise 8 Question words

Complete the questions with a word from the box.

Where	Which	Why	How	Who	What	When	Whose

1 A ___How___ tall is your sister?
   B 152 cm.

2 A _____ often do you go to the cinema?
   B About once a month.

3 A _____ time does the programme start?
   B At nine o'clock.

4 A _____ did you close the window?
   B Because I'm cold.

5 A _____ bag is this?
   B It's mine.

6 A _____ did you go to town with?
   B Jim and Lucy.

7 A _____ kind of books do you like?
   B I like crime novels.

8 A _____ is Dublin?
   B It's in Ireland.

9 A _____ are you going to clean your room?
   B When this film has finished.

10 A _____ is your favourite season?
    B I like summer best.

9

Exercise 9 Past Simple and Present Perfect

Write the Past Simple and the Past Participle of these verbs.

1 stay   _stayed_   _stayed_
2 sing   _sang_   _sung_
3 drink   _____   _____
4 win   _____   _____
5 live   _____   _____
6 have   _____   _____
7 do   _____   _____
8 play   _____   _____
9 go   _____   _____
10 write _____   _____

8

Exercise 10 Present Perfect and Past Simple

Tick (✓) the correct sentence.

1 a When have you been to the USA?
   b When did you go to the USA? ✓

2 a I went to Milan last week.
   b I have been to Milan last week.

3 a Have you ever been to India?
   b Did you ever go to India?

4 a Kate has finished work two hours ago.
   b Kate finished work two hours ago.

5 a Did he go on holiday last week or the week before?
   b Has he been on holiday last week or the week before?

6 a I haven't seen that film yet.
   b I didn't see that film yet.

7 a I've just bought my plane ticket to Paris – here it is!
   b I just bought my plane ticket to Paris – here it is!

8 a Jim and Cathy won £1,000 last month.
   b Jim and Cathy have won £1,000 last month.

7

Exercise 11 Word groups

Put the words in the correct column.

sad foggy happy jumper tie sunny bored cloudy T-shirt snowing angry suit skirt excited windy

Feelings	Clothes	Weather

15

TOTAL 100

Answer keys

Reading

2 **A** How do you spell it?
3 **B** York, in the north of England.
4 **A** How old are you?
5 **B** Yes, I am.
6 **A** What's your husband's name?
7 **B** He's a teacher (in a business school).
8 **B** Yes, I do. I have a boy and a girl.
9 **A** Do you have any brothers or sisters?
10 **B** Yes, I do.
11 **A** Why do you enjoy your job?
12 **B** In a large house in York.
13 **B** Yes, I/we do.
14 **A** What do you like doing in your free time?

Song – Colours

1 2, 3 morning   6 rarely
   4 Green   7 thinkin'
   5 get   8 thinkin'
2 1 girlfriend or wife
   2 get up
   3 shiny
   4 calm and relaxed
3 the singer's girlfriend or wife

Extra ideas Units 5–8

Reading

1 4 Athens
2 1 the day of any date in any year; the teams and the scores of every football match in every World Cup.
   2 He remembered the order of 35 packs of playing cards.
   3 No, he wasn't. He couldn't remember his lessons.
   4 They said he was stupid.
   5 Four years ago. He saw a programme on TV which showed people how to improve their memory.
   6 Because he can remember every card.
   7 Seven.
   8 Three. The other four clubs knew him and didn't want him to play.
3 1 What day was April 21, 1876?

2 When did he become world champion?
3 How much can he earn a day on European TV programmes?
4 What does his wife do?
5 How much did he win?
6 What does he like doing in his free time?
4 2 He remembered the order of 35 packs of cards.
3 Dominic is 34 years old.
4 He won £1,000 a night.
5 He went to 7 clubs (with the interviewers).
6 He had £1,250 in his pocket.
7 Children can learn to improve their memory from the age of five.

Song – I Just Called To Say I Love You

1 Day   9 care
2 hearts   10 mean
3 sing   11 warm
4 day   12 moon
5 flowers   13 leaves
6 wedding   14 fly
7 true   15 thanks
8 words   16 heart

Extra ideas Units 9–12

Reading

Vocabulary

1g 2e 3b 4h 5a 6c 7d 8f

Reading

2 Amy and Phil
3 Daniel and Vicky
4 the local people (in the pub)
5 the music teacher
6 Daniel
7 Vicky
8 local builders

Language work

1 2 What was the problem with the house in London?
   3 Why did the King family/Amy and Phil want to move?
   4 Where did they find a house?
   5 Did Daniel and Vicky like the description of the house?
   6 What was the scenery like?
   7 What did the music teacher do?

8 How many rooms did the house have?
9 When did the family sell their house?
10 When are they going to move in?
2 1 Amy and Phil King had a modern house in London. It didn't have any windows, electricity, or water.
   2 We wanted a quieter and more relaxing life in the country
   3 had, was/wasn't, saw, fall, were, said, drove, couldn't, went, told, gave, sold, bought
   4 It didn't have any windows, electricity, or water.
   5 there were some holes in the roof!
   6 'I'm not going to live in that house. I'm going to stay in London!'
   7 Let's visit it together.
   8 Local builders are repairing the old house.

Song – Wonderful tonight

Verse 1
1 wear   4 asks
2 puts   5 say
3 brushes
Verse 2
1 party   3 lady
2 see   4 all right
Verse 3
1 Because I see
2 And the wonder of it all
3 How much I love you
Verse 4
As I turn out the light   ⑥
You were wonderful tonight.'   ⑧
So I give her the car keys,   ③
And I've got an aching head   ②
It's time to go home now   ①
She helps me to bed   ④
And then I tell her   ⑤
I say, 'My darling,   ⑦

Extra ideas Units 13–14

Reading

1 1 was   7 annoyed
2 moved   8 never
3 quickly   9 interested
4 immediate   10 took
5 got   11 interesting
6 made   12 hasn't ever forgotten

2　1　June 9, 1963.
　　2　His mother bought him a guitar.
　　3　Nicholas Cage.
　　4　No, he didn't.
　　5　No, he doesn't.
　　6　Pirates of the Caribbean.
　　7　Once.
　　8　Vanessa Paradis.

Language work

1　1　Where was he born?
　　2　Why did he leave school?
　　3　How did he earn money?
　　4　What was his first film?
　　5　How many children has he got?
　　6　Has he continued his interest in music?
2　1　was, moved, bought, became, decided, played, didn't have, started
　　2　has had, hasn't forgotten, has directed

Song – Summertime

1　The letter *g* is missing.
2　1　easy　　　4　cry
　　2　high　　　5　mornings
　　3　rich　　　6　sky

Stop and check 1

Correct the mistakes

2　New York is a very big city.
3　My mother works in a restaurant. She is a chef. / My mother is a chef in a restaurant.
4　My father watches football on TV.
5　He likes playing tennis.
6　On Sundays we go to the cinema.
7　Mark is a pilot.
8　Your family is very nice.
9　I like going to the gym.
10　Our school has a lot of students.
11　The children go to school near here.
12　We go to bed at 11.00.
13　Spring and summer are my favourite seasons.
14　My sister doesn't have a car.
15　Do you want an ice-cream?
16　My school is near here.

Word order

2　Peter is a journalist from New York.
3　Is your brother married?
4　My sister goes skiing in the mountains.
5　My town isn't very big.
6　What is your teacher's name?
7　How do you spell your surname?
8　I often go sailing at weekends./I go sailing often at weekends.

Choose the correct sentence

2b　3c　4a　5b　6c　7a　8b　9c

Questions

1　What do you do at weekends?
　　Who do you usually sit next to?
　　What time do you go to bed?
　　How much is a cup of coffee and a sandwich?
　　How many languages do you speak?
2　2　What time does Helen start work?
　　3　Where do Nicole and Jean come from?
　　4　What's your wife's name?
　　5　How many children do you have?
　　6　Do you like taking photographs?

Prepositions

2	in	9	at	16	to
3	with	10	to	17	at
4	at	11	On	18	in
5	at	12	in	19	In
6	for	13	after	20	After
7	to	14	by	21	about
8	for	15	at		

Vocabulary

Things to read menu, dictionary, postcard, magazine, newspaper
Jobs nurse, model, journalist, lawyer, actor
Things to eat egg, tuna, cake, chicken, chips
Activities sailing, sunbathing, running, cooking, dancing
Verbs collect, want, deliver, sell, listen
Adjectives lovely, fast, expensive, friendly, young

am/is/do/does (not)

2	are	6	do
3	does/is	7	don't; aren't
4	doesn't; is	8	isn't
5	'm; is		

Translate

The idea behind this is that students begin to be aware of similarities and differences between English and L1. Emphasize that they must not translate word by word. Obviously it will only be possible to check their answers in a monolingual class, but a multilingual class can discuss their answers together in nationality groups.

Stop and check 2

Correct the mistakes

2　There isn't a bank near here.
3　Look at this photo/these photos.
4　Is there a post box near here?
5　I arrived at the airport at ten o'clock last night.
6　She could speak three languages when she was eight.
7　Where did you go last weekend?
8　The sofa is in front of the window.
9　I can't go out because I have a lot of homework.
10　There is a table in the kitchen.
11　I went to the theatre last weekend.
12　Who are those people over there?/these people over here?
13　I bought a new DVD player.
14　Did you watch the football on TV last night/yesterday evening?
15　Spanish people are very friendly.
16　I like cities because I can go to good restaurants.

Past Simple

2	studied	7	thought
3	began	8	didn't go
4	didn't finish	9	wrote
5	was	10	didn't understand
6	wanted	11	could

Irregular verbs

1	sang	6	made
2	came	7	broke
3	sold	8	saw
4	got	9	won
5	left	10	took

can/could/was/were (not)

2　wasn't; was　　5　were; weren't; was
3　was; could　　　6　couldn't; was
4　can

some/any/a/an

2	any	5	some; any
3	a; some	6	any
4	an	7	some

Questions and negatives

2　Is there a good café in this town?
　　There isn't a good café in this town.
3　Are there any eggs in the fridge?
　　There aren't any eggs in the fridge.
4　Can you speak Spanish?
　　You can't speak Spanish.
5　Was he born in 1983?
　　He wasn't born in 1983.
6　Could she play the violin when she was three?

She couldn't play the violin when she was three.

7 Were they on holiday last week?
They weren't on holiday last week.

8 Did your parents study English at school?
Your parents didn't study English at school.

9 Did the students go to the cinema last night?
The students didn't go to the cinema last night.

Vocabulary – noun + noun

chocolate cake	film star
orange juice	handbag
swimming pool	railway station
car park	living room
newspaper	washing machine
boyfriend	

Vocabulary – verb + noun

speak German
drink a cup of coffee
win a medal
earn a lot of money
cook a meal
ride a bike
break a record
play the guitar
become a pilot
eat a sandwich

Translate

See note about translation on p172.

Stop and check 3

Correct the mistakes

2 It's very hot today – would you like something to drink?
3 Peter's got a lot of books because he likes reading.
4 How many brothers and sisters have you got/do you have?
5 How much money has he got?
6 Whose is that new car?
7 I'm going home now, because it's late.
8 Last night I went to the pub to meet my friends.
9 We're going to have a test next week.
10 I'm wearing my old clothes because I'm going to clean the car.
11 Juan is Spanish, he comes from Madrid.
12 What are you doing this evening?
13 My brother is older than me.
14 I think it is going to rain.
15 Your flat is bigger than mine.

16 Who is the richest person in the world?

Questions and answers

Whose is this mobile phone? It's Sally's.
How many dogs have you got? Two.
How much did your bike cost? £295.
Could you help me, please? Yes, of course. What can I do for you?
Would you like some more to eat? No, thanks. I'm full.
Do you like Henry? Yes. I think he's very nice.
Where are you going on holiday? To Mexico.
Why are you going to the market? To buy some fruit.
What did you do last night? I stayed at home.
Who's the new teacher? Her name's Mrs Taylor.

Comparatives and superlatives

Adjective	Comparative	Superlative
big	**bigger**	**biggest**
intelligent	more intelligent	**most intelligent**
bad	**worse**	worst
popular	**more popular**	**most popular**
noisy	**noisier**	**noisiest**

Comparing hotels

1 2 The Strand is bigger than the Ritz.
3 The Ritz is more expensive than the Strand.
4 The Strand is nearer the sea than the Ritz.
5 The Strand is further from the town centre than the Ritz.
6 The Strand is more modern than the Ritz.

2 2 The Strand is the biggest.
3 The Star is the most expensive.
4 The Star is the nearest to the sea/The Ritz is the furthest from the sea.
5 The Strand is the furthest from the town centre/The Ritz is the nearest to the town centre.
6 The Strand is the most modern.

some/any/a

2	a	5	some	8	any
3	some	6	a; some	9	some; any
4	any	7	a		

Present Simple and Present Continuous

2 smokes; isn't smoking
3 are looking; don't like

4 wear; 'm wearing
5 are you going; go
6 works; 's writing

going to

2 Peter is going to buy some bread at the baker's.
3 I am going to borrow some books from the library.
4 We are going to see a play at the theatre.
5 They are going to have a holiday in Turkey.
6 I am going to send an email to my friend.

Vocabulary

Clothes shop	Food	Drinks
dress	cake	wine
suit	chips	milk
shirt	meat	water
jumper	carrots	juice
jeans	cheese	beer

Translate

See note about translation on p172.

Stop and check 4

Correct the mistakes

2 Why do you want to learn Italian?
3 She hasn't ever been to New York. / She has never been to New York.
4 I've written to her three times and she hasn't answered yet.
5 I didn't enjoy the film. It was very boring.
6 How many times have you been to Spain?
7 I'm very excited about my holiday.
8 The students worked very hard.
9 'Whose keys are these?'
'They're Linda's.'
10 What kind of books do you like reading?
11 Have you ever been to Ireland?

Questions and tenses

2 Why are you tired?
3 How do you go to work?
4 Whose is this mobile phone? / Whose mobile phone is this?
5 Who did you meet?
6 What kind of car did she buy?
7 Where did you see him?
8 What is she watching?
9 Where are they going?
10 Why did he leave?
11 How much (money) did she spend?

Past Simple and Present Perfect

1
2 met
3 has never been
4 haven't finished
5 ate
6 climbed

2
2 went
3 Have … eaten
4 have … been
5 did … live
6 haven't seen

Adverb or adjective?

2 quiet
3 slowly
4 good
5 well
6 healthy

Word order

2 How many cousins have you got?
3 They have just arrived in Rome.
4 You speak English very well.
5 The man walked quickly along the road.
6 Have you ever seen a play by Shakespeare?
7 The students did a long exam yesterday.
8 Did you check your work carefully?
9 Please do this exercise quickly.
10 How many people are you going to invite to your party?
11 She is tired because she got up early.

Auxiliaries

2 are
3 Does
4 Did
5 Has
6 have
7 am
8 Do
9 Is
10 did
11 Have

Vocabulary – word groups

Travel verbs walk, cycle, hitch-hike, ride

Travel by plane luggage, departure lounge, arrival hall, flight, boarding pass, gate

Adjectives quiet, annoying, worried, tiring, surprised

Chemist's soap, aspirin, suncream, plasters, toothpaste

Prepositions

2 about
3 by
4 from
5 in
6 about
7 on
8 in
9 for
10 to
11 out of

Translate

See note about translation on p172.

Exercise 1

2 What's her surname?
3 Where's she from?
4 How old is she?
5 Where does she live? / What's her address?
6 What does she do? / What's her job?
7 Where does she work / teach?
8 Is she married?
9 What does she do in her free time?

Exercise 2

2 What do you do at weekends?
3 Where does she work?
4 There is a photo on the shelf.
5 Is there a bank near here?
6 Can I have a coffee, please?
7 How many children do they have?
8 Emily teaches English in Brazil.
9 Is there any milk in the fridge?
10 Rosy does not go to work by car.
11 Sue and Dave like going to the cinema.

Exercise 3

How much is a ham sandwich?
£2.50.
What do you do on Sundays?
I play tennis.
Where do you go on Friday evenings?
To the theatre.
How do you travel to work?
By bus.
What time do you get up?
At seven o'clock.

Exercise 4

2 some
3 an/some
4 any
5 any
6 a
7 some
8 any
9 an
10 any
11 some

Exercise 5

1 have
2 live
3 is
4 works
5 likes
6 doesn't like
7 go
8 stay
9 go
10 walk

Exercise 6

2 am
3 isn't, is
4 don't
5 Does
6 doesn't
7 are
8 Do, don't

Exercise 7

2 We go swimming on Saturdays.
3 They watch TV every day.
4 The dictionaries are over there.
5 These watches are expensive.
6 Look at those lovely flowers.
7 Do you have any stamps?
8 They're our children.
9 They're interesting people.
10 Those men are American.
11 The schools don't have any computers.

Exercise 8

1 in
2 next to
3 behind
4 on
5 near
6 in front of
7 on

Exercise 9

2b 3a 4a 5b 6b

Exercise 10

2 pen (You can read the others.)
3 milk (You can drink milk.)
4 cupboard (The others are types of cutlery.)
5 teach (The others are professions.)
6 like (The others are adjectives.)
7 man (The others are names of family members.)
8 house (The others are rooms.)
9 often (The others describe position.)
10 American (American is an adjective.)
11 we (The others are possessive adjectives.)

Exercise 11

difficult – easy
expensive – cheap
hot – cold
lovely – horrible
wrong – right
old – young
new – old
right – left

Exercise 12

play football
go running
speak Italian
drink tea
travel by bus
fly a plane
listen to music
watch television

Exercise 1

2 were weren't
3 was wasn't
4 were weren't
5 were weren't

Exercise 2

2 can't play tennis
3 can speak German / can speak Italian can't swim / can't play tennis
4 can't speak German
5 can speak Italian
6 can play tennis
7 can swim

© Oxford University Press

Exercise 3

1 liked	5 started	9 sold
2 studied	6 had	10 made
3 earned	7 became	
4 decided	8 sang	

Exercise 4

1 left	5 met	9 does
2 went	6 got	10 sells
3 worked	7 live	
4 moved	8 teaches	

Exercise 5

2 We didn't enjoy the film.
3 I didn't take a photograph of my family.
4 Angela didn't send an email to her friend.
5 Yuri Gagarin didn't become an astronaut in the 1970s.
6 England didn't win the World Cup in 2000.
7 Her father didn't die when she was 14.
8 I didn't lose €20 last night.
9 People didn't fly by plane 100 years ago.
10 That book wasn't very interesting.
11 We didn't arrive at school at eight o'clock.

Exercise 6

2 Would you like …
3 Do you like …
4 would you like …
5 Do you like …
6 I'd like …

Exercise 7

3 C 4 U 5 U 6 C 7 C 8 U 9 U

Exercise 8

2 some	6 some
3 a	7 some; some
4 any	8 any
5 any	

Exercise 9

2 How much	5 How much
3 How many	6 How much
4 How many	

Exercise 10

2 No, it isn't. It's more expensive.
3 No, it isn't. It's smaller.
4 No, it isn't. It's the smallest.
5 No, it isn't. It's cheaper.
6 No, it isn't. It's the most expensive.
7 No, it isn't. It's more modern/newer.
8 No, it isn't. It's the oldest.

Exercise 11

Adjective	Comparative	Superlative
exciting	more exciting	**most exciting**
good	**better**	best
bad	**worse**	**worst**
interesting	**more interesting**	**most interesting**

Exercise 12

2 first	5 twelfth
3 second	6 twentieth
4 third	

Exercise 13

2 interesting	7 quiet
3 friendly	8 new
4 dirty	9 old
5 fast	10 cheap
6 safe	11 relaxing

Progress test 3

Exercise 1

3 driving	8 getting
4 stopping	9 buying
5 working	10 thinking
6 using	11 swimming
7 looking	12 crying

Exercise 2

2 am not going	6 is … cooking
3 are … smiling	7 are … doing
4 is standing	am writing
5 aren't sitting	8 isn't working

Exercise 3

2 go; are going
3 do … go
4 are … working; have
5 do … live; Do … like
6 do … have; am having
7 is ringing

Exercise 4

3 It's yours.	6 They're ours.
4 They're his.	7 It's theirs.
5 It's hers.	

Exercise 5

4 They're going to be pilots.
5 He isn't going to be an actor.
6 Are you going to be an architect?
7 I'm not going to be a lawyer.
8 We're going to be footballers.
9 She isn't going to be a model.
10 Is he going to be a singer?
11 I'm going to be an accountant.
12 He isn't going to be a chef.
13 Are you going to be a music teacher?

Exercise 6

2 I'm going to Moscow to learn Russian.
3 Paul is going to London to buy some clothes.
4 Roger went to India to visit the Taj Mahal.
5 Tracey goes to the gym to get fit.
6 Tim is going to the USA to see his family.
7 Mario is learning English to get a better job.
8 David is saving money to buy a car.
9 Henry went to Japan to visit Kyoto.
10 Chris went to the chemist's to buy some aspirins.
11 Brian and Jane are going to Venice to see the Grand Canal.

Exercise 7

2 slowly	6 hard
3 early	7 suddenly
4 carefully	8 fast
5 well	9 badly

Exercise 8

2 How	5 Whose	8 Where
3 What	6 Who	9 When
4 Why	7 What	10 Which

Exercise 9

3 drank drunk	7 did done
4 won won	8 played played
5 lived lived	9 went gone
6 had had	10 wrote written

Exercise 10

2a 3a 4b 5a 6a 7a 8a

Exercise 11

Feelings	Clothes	Weather
sad	jumper	foggy
happy	tie	sunny
bored	T-shirt	cloudy
angry	suit	snowing
excited	skirt	windy

Grammar Reference exercises

Unit 1

1 1 are 2 'm/am 3 is 4 are 5 are
2 1 My 2 your 3 My 4 Her 5 His
3 1 What 2 How 3 Where
4 1 a 2 a 3 an 4 a 5 an
5 1 dictionaries 4 children
  2 students 5 days
  3 oranges

Unit 2

1 1 How old 2 Where 3 How much
  4 What 5 Who
2 1 Are you cold?
  2 We don't speak English.
  3 Do they like cafés?
  4 I'm not from Italy.
  5 Does she play tennis?
3 2 my friend's bag
  3 my family's house
  4 John's son
  5 Andrea's brother
  6 his wife's name
4 1 e 2 c 3 d 4 a 5 b

Unit 3

1 1 does 2 watches 3 listens
  4 speaks 5 has 6 walks
2 1 Olivier doesn't come from Belgium.
  2 Sandra doesn't work in a school.
  3 Bill doesn't speak Japanese.
  4 My sister doesn't have two children.
  5 Lucy doesn't go to Greece every year.
  6 Peter doesn't study art at college.
3 1 Does Harry study German at school?
  2 Where does she live?
  3 Where does this stamp come from?
  4 What sports does she enjoy?
  5 Has Guy got a dog?
4 1 Does … live 4 has
  2 don't work 5 don't speak
  3 watch 6 Does … study

Unit 4

1 1 lives 2 speak 3 goes
  4 work 5 plays
2 1 Does he like swimming?
    No, he doesn't.
  2 Do you have a computer?
    Yes, I do.
  3 Do they live in Paris?
    Yes, they do.
  4 Does she start at 9.00?
    No, she doesn't.
  5 Do we speak English?
    Yes, we do.
3 1 George always walks to work.
  2 Sandra never watches TV.
  3 You don't often go running.
4 1 Vicky loves listening to the radio.
  4 David likes cooking.

Unit 5

1 1 c 2 d 3 a 4 b
2 1 Are 2 isn't 3 are
  4 Is 5 aren't 6 is
3 1 many 2 some 3 any
  4 some 5 many
4 1 this 2 those 3 These 4 that

Unit 6

1 1 Tanya can sing, but she can't dance.
  2 Mark could swim two years ago.
  3 Can you play tennis?
  4 What can I do today?
2 Student's own answers
3 1 I was in London.
  2 They were at a party.
  3 Where were you?
  4 You weren't at school.
  5 She was at home.
  6 Were they in the restaurant?
  7 Where was David?
  8 We weren't at work.

Unit 7

1 1 stopped 6 did … arrive
  2 worked 7 decided
  3 didn't see 8 had
  4 Did … go 9 did … finish
  5 lived 10 wanted
2 last night, year, week
  yesterday morning, afternoon, evening
3 1 walked 5 became 9 sang
  2 went 6 wrote 10 heard
  3 saw 7 studied
  4 ate 8 ran
4 Student's own answers

Unit 8

1 1 Sue went to the cinema yesterday.
  2 I met Nick two years ago.
  3 They didn't go out last night.
  4 Jack was born three weeks ago.
  5 We met last Friday.
2 1 I didn't watch TV last night.
  2 They didn't travel by train.
  3 Mary didn't sing in the concert last week.
  4 Pete didn't see three men outside the bank.
  5 We didn't go to New York in 2002.
3 1 fell 2 sent 3 found
  4 drank 5 bought
4 1 on 2 in 3 at 4 in 5 on

Unit 9

1 1 U 2 U 3 U 4 C 5 C 6 U
  7 U 8 U
2 1 'd like 3 Would … like
  2 Would … like 4 Would … like
3 1 some 2 any 3 some
  4 some 5 any
4 1 much 2 some 3 Is
  4 many 5 are 6 any

Unit 10

1 1 easier, the easiest
  2 more boring, the most boring
  3 further, the furthest

4 noisier, the noisiest
5 nicer, the nicest
2 1 My computer's bigger than yours.
  2 This is the noisiest city I know!
  3 It's the worst film in the world.
  4 Seville is hotter than London.
  5 Museums are more boring than parks.
3 1 I've got a brother.
  2 Have you got a pet?
  3 They haven't got a car.
  4 Have we got any money?
  5 He hasn't got a computer.
  6 It's got a cinema.

Unit 11

1 1 is studying 4 isn't enjoying
  2 'm not going 5 Are … seeing
  3 Are … working
2 1 writing 2 stopping 3 travelling
  4 going 5 dancing
3 1 Whose 2 Who's 3 Who's
  4 Whose 5 Whose
4 1 comes 4 wears
  2 'm meeting 5 Are … coming
  3 are … laughing

Unit 12

1 1 's going to 6 Are … going to
  2 Is … going to 7 's going to
  3 'm not going to 8 'm not going to
  4 're going to 9 Are … going to
  5 aren't going to
2 1 I'm going out to walk the dog.
  2 They're saving money to buy a flat.
  3 She's going to the bank to get some cash.
  4 Nick is running to get fit.
  5 You are studying to learn English.

Unit 13

1 1 How 2 Where 3 What
  4 When 5 How
2 1 Who did Sally marry?
  2 What happens at the start of the film?
  3 Which town do you live in?
  4 How far is it to the town hall?
  5 Why do you want to buy that CD?
3 1 well 4 fast
  2 hard 5 carefully
  3 immediately
4 1 boring 4 interesting
  2 amazed 5 frightened
  3 bored

Unit 14

1 1 I went to Finland last year.
  2 Have you ever met a famous person?
  3 Kate's not here. She's gone to Paris.
  4 You met him when you were six.
2 1 's travelled 4 've read
  2 Have … seen 5 Has … done
  3 haven't been 6 haven't sent
3 1 Have you finished the report yet?
  2 I've never been to Australia.
  3 Tom has just called.
  4 Has Tony ever lived in London?
4 Student's own answers